DISTURBING PR**A**CTICE

Higher Ed

Questions about the Purpose(s) of Colleges & Universities

Norm Denzin, Josef Progler, Joe L. Kincheloe, Shirley R. Steinberg
General Editors

Vol. 8

PETER LANG
New York • Washington, D.C./Baltimore • Bern
Frankfurt am Main • Berlin • Brussels • Vienna • Oxford

Avner Segall

DISTURBING PRACTICE

readingteachereducationastext

PETER LANG
New York • Washington, D.C./Baltimore • Bern
Frankfurt am Main • Berlin • Brussels • Vienna • Oxford

Library of Congress Cataloging-in-Publication Data

Segall, Avner.
Disturbing practice: reading teacher education as text / Avner Segall.
p. cm. — (Higher ed; vol. 8)
Includes bibliographical references and index.
1. Teachers—Training of—Canada—Case studies. I. Title. II. Series.
LB1719.C2 S44   370'.71'171—dc21   2001034687
ISBN 0-8204-5102-9
ISSN 1523-9551

Die Deutsche Bibliothek-CIP-Einheitsaufnahme

Segall, Avner:
Disturbing practice: reading teacher education as text / Avner Segall.
–New York; Washington, D.C./Baltimore; Bern;
Frankfurt am Main; Berlin; Brussels; Vienna; Oxford: Lang.
(Higher ed; Vol. 8)
ISBN 0-8204-5102-9

Cover design by Joni Holst

The paper in this book meets the guidelines for permanence and durability
of the Committee on Production Guidelines for Book Longevity
of the Council of Library Resources.

To my parents, Jack and Janie Segall

I have a sense that you are interested in the hidden curriculum of this teacher education program and its effect on student teachers and whether what we talk about and say we value in the program actually ends up being practiced. (Ron, student teacher)

You're trying to find out how we think about what we're being taught in this teacher education program. I think what you're going to come up with is students' inability to question what we're being taught and to look beyond what's being given to us. I mean, we're no different than students in high school in that we're accepting what's been taught and we're giving it back to the instructors and giving them what they want. . . . So when you're asking us all these questions, you're sort of looking at what and how we think and how that has changed throughout the program. It's funny, this interview is sort of a testament that it really hasn't changed a lot. [We're taught to] encourage students not to accept everything they read as literal proof, although we mostly did, which is why [he begins to laugh] it makes me think that we're probably not going to be very successful at it. (Jack, student teacher)

Table of Contents

Acknowledgments

This book comprises the contributions of many who helped inform, shape, and guide it. I would first like to thank the six student teachers—Jocelyn, Mary, Casey, Jack, Charles, and Ron—for sharing their experiences of learning to teach, for allowing me to use their stories, and for critically engaging my telling of those stories. Special thanks are extended to Simon, the instructor of the social studies methods course in which much of the study informing this book was conducted. I thank him for having the courage to invite me into his classroom, knowing the kind of "difficult" questions I would pose and the lenses through which I would go about answering them; both containing the potential to render his own teaching vulnerable. I commend him for practicing what he preaches and for believing in the importance of a critical study such as this to a much-needed conversation about practice, even when the subject of critique was his own practice.

Other friends and colleagues have contributed significantly to my work. John Willinsky and Peter Seixas have both been constant sources of support and inspiration. I thank them for the sober "reality checks" and humorous blend of encouragement and criticism that have pushed me to go deeper, further, and in new directions. I would also like to thank Brenda Trofanenko and Lisa Korteweg for reading earlier drafts of this book and particularly for encouraging me to pursue my convictions in spite of their potential (and often, actual) political ramifications.

I am also indebted to the Social Sciences and Humanities Research Council of Canada (SSHRCC) for supporting this work.

Last, but definitely not least, I would like to thank my partner of fifteen years, Ricki Goldman-Segall. Her ability to inspire and support has nourished and sustained my work. I am thankful for her continuous trust and friendship.

PART I

PREAMBLE

Chapter One

Disturbing Practice:
An Introduction

To further understand how we think and act in the world, we need to know not only where we currently are in the larger system of things but also how we got there and who we became in the process of "arriving." Informing us as much about the journey as they do about its destination, endings are therefore often opportune places to begin.

At the end of July 1997, soon after his final class of preservice teacher education, I asked Ron,[1] one of six student teachers whose experiences in preservice education inform this book, what he intended to do the first weekend following graduation. "I'll just go and sit somewhere," Ron said, "and try to unlearn everything that I have been doing. Not forget—that would simply be to deny," he emphasized, "but sit and reflect on it all and ask myself, Where am I now? What have I given up? What have I gained? And what do I want to do with it and about it all?"

That interview concluded my year-long ethnographic study of learning to teach. Ron's thoughts that weekend, as (or if) he found his "somewhere" to sit, unlearn, and reflect on what he had gained and what he had lost in the process of becoming a teacher, remain his own. What you will find in this book, instead, are responses to these and other questions Ron and five of his colleagues participating in this study chose to share with me as well as my own observations and reflections, as researcher, about those responses and the context that gave rise to them. Combined, they speak to the production of knowledge and knowing in (and about) preservice education: What and how is it that prospective teachers learn, do not learn, and learn not to learn in preservice education? How do the structures, discourses, and practices of preservice teacher education operate to "invite" prospective teachers to learn some things rather than others? And what implications do the above have for the kind of learning in which prospective teachers engage in institutions of higher education, as well as for the future of education in the public schools in which they will serve as teachers of others?

Anchored in a secondary social studies methods course at the University of Western Canada (UWC) and following 6 of its 37 students through their 12-month university- and practicum-based experiences, this book examines how particular versions and visions of education, teaching, and learning are made possible in preservice education and what they, in turn, make possible for students learning to teach. Put otherwise, and borrowing from Britzman and Pitt (1996), this book explores how knowledge in teacher education is made, and in the process, what that knowledge "'wants,' what it 'forgets,' and what it 'costs'" (p. 119).

The Socializing Effect of Preservice Education

Preservice teacher education comprises only a small part of beginning teachers' understandings of, preparation for, and socialization into their roles as teachers. Years of primary, secondary, and tertiary schooling as well as interactions outside of school with the media and other socializing environments have already provided student teachers with a multitude of experiences and images as to what it means to teach and be taught (Adler, 1991; Britzman, 1991; Bullough, 1989; Calderhead & Robson, 1991; Ginsburg, 1988; Hollingsworth, 1989; Liston & Zeichner, 1991; Shor, 1986).

While not introducing student teachers to the idea of teaching, preservice education nevertheless impacts prospective teachers' understandings of, and dispositions toward, the profession as well as the kinds of transformations they choose to make of those dispositions and understandings as teachers. Whether by challenging or affirming what prospective teachers already believe, teacher education is always active in organizing, facilitating, and promoting particular notions about what it means (and what one must undergo in order) to be considered a teacher.

The body of knowledge that comprises the curriculum of teacher education and the body experience of being schooled through the apparatus of teacher education "are not separable from each other" (Lewis, 1993, p. 186). Through its explicit, implicit, and null[2] curricula, teacher education overtly, covertly, and by omission imposes a particular version of educational purpose (Kincheloe, 1993, p. 12). It does so by what it elevates to be considered knowledge, by the ways and spaces it chooses to represent and engage that knowledge, and by the knowledge it chooses to ignore. The choice of materials, activities, and teaching strategies within preservice teacher education, the kinds of questions asked, "the ways in which answers are sought and validated, and what counts as an answer and on what basis" to use Doyle (1986; cf. McDiarmid, Ball, & Anderson, 1989, p. 196), all assign value and bestow meaning as they give definition and body to prospective teachers' experience, and provide shape and organization to their consciousness (Popkewitz, 1987, p. 340).

As is the case with any and all socializing environments, preservice education, to use Postman and Weingartner (1969), helps build the attitudes prospective teachers are enticed to assume, the sensitivities they are encouraged to develop, and the things they learn to see, feel, and value. They learn them, Postman and Weingartner suggest, because the "environment is organized in such a way that it permits or encourages or insists that [they] learn them" (p. 17). By that I do not mean to imply that student teachers are simply passive recipients of messages conveyed to them in teacher education. Prospective teachers are indeed agents of choice (Ginsburg, 1988), actively processing—modifying, negotiating, accepting, and/or rejecting messages rather than simply acquiring them passively. However, their choices, as this book will illustrate, are not innocent. That is, they are implicated in, and in many ways determined by, the contexts of a teacher education program that makes those particular choices possible, even probable.

Although preservice teacher education occupies this significant socializing role, little is known about what actually takes place within teacher education classrooms and its impact on prospective teachers' educational imagination. In spite of the ever-growing body of knowledge on teacher education—short- and long-term research projects, books, journals, and conferences, even two generations of handbooks of research in teacher education—few provide descriptions or analyses of the day-to-day practices of teacher education/educators and the experiences they render possible (Adler, 1993; Armento, 1996; Banks & Parker, 1990; Feiman-Nemser, 1983; Zeichner, 1986). Contrary to public schools, which have, for some time, been the subject of critical investigations by external researchers, teacher education programs—and for that matter colleges/schools of (and faculty in) education in general—have maintained their extraterritorial status, remaining free from such investigation. In other words, while the doors of public school classrooms have been opened to external researchers (many of them teacher educators), university classrooms have, to a large degree, remained under lock and key. Teacher educators, as educational researchers, tend to investigate their own practices or those of others; they are not, by and large, the subjects of (external) investigation themselves. Not surprisingly then, there is relatively little that critically describes or assesses teacher education programs or provides a critical examination of the teaching/learning interactions that take place in them.

As debates about teacher education reform persist, however, teacher education programs can no longer afford the "luxury" of masquerading as an invisible, innocent context within which prospective teachers naturally build ideas, knowledge, and skills (Feiman-Nemser, 1990; Lanier & Little, 1986; Sarason, Davidson, & Blatt, 1986). While explanations by educational researchers for the inability of prospective teachers to institute and maintain change "are often grounded in attributions to the culture of schools or the personal biographies of prospective teachers," writes Armento (1996), they "tend to ignore the fact that [student teachers] are actively involved in a teacher preparation program that might, could, or should have an effect on prospective teachers' beliefs," dispositions, and understandings (p. 498). As a host of national reports continue calling on teacher educators to examine, rethink, and change existing program policies, structures, and practices, more knowledge is necessary about what actually occurs in teacher education programs and how those occurrences influence prospective teachers' practice (as students and teachers) in particular ways.

In part, this book is intended to fill some of that conspicuous void. Its approach to teacher education and its study is inspired by, borrows from, builds on, and extends two previous critical ethnographic studies of preservice teacher education: Mark Ginsburg's (1988) *Contradictions in Teacher Education and Society,* which analyzes how student teachers' teacher-identities are constructed, in part, through the contradictory messages presented in the explicit and implicit curriculum of the teacher education program at the University of Houston; and Deborah Britzman's (1991) *Practice Makes Practice,* which focuses on the contradictory realities and cultural myths of teacher education and how those shape, and are shaped by, student teachers' knowledge about (and in) education.

While departing from those two studies in foci and emphases, this book nevertheless shares the desire exemplified by Britzman and Ginsburg to explore not only how student teachers are encouraged to engage ideas and theories in teacher education classrooms but also, and more importantly perhaps, how the ideas and theories in those very classrooms manage the student teachers attempting to engage them. My interest, then, like theirs, is to discover how teachers' ways of being are dependent, in part, on student teachers' ways of becoming as they go through and are constructed by the apparatus of teacher education. In order to examine the complex relationship between the knowledge student teachers are given and the knowledge they produce, this book focuses not only on what happens to student teachers during preservice education but also on "what they make happen because of what happens to them" (Britzman, 1991, p. 56). In other words, this book does not stop at describing what student teachers choose to say or do in preservice education but examines what structures and directs their particular choices and actions.

Reading and Writing Teacher Education as Text

As indicated in its subtitle, this book is an attempt to read (and, hence, write) the teacher education program at the University of Western Canada as a *text*. (In the process, the use of the term "disturbing"—both as verb and adjective—in the title will also gain meaning.) Traditionally, the word *text* has been used to distinguish written words from other forms of communication (Graddol, 1994, p. 40). Over the last two decades, however, the notion of "text" has expanded to include "any aspect of reality that contains encoded meaning" (Kincheloe & Steinberg, 1996, p. 184). Moving from the physical to the semiotic materiality of the text and regarding texts "not as 'things' but as meaning," Lemke (1995) explains, a text becomes any object, event, or action insofar as it is endowed with significance and symbolic value (pp. 9, 15). From that perspective, a teacher education program, the interactions that go on within it, even the characters partaking in those interactions can and should be considered texts (Stables, 1996).

To view social institutions as "readable," claims Geertz (1983), "is to alter our whole sense of what interpretation is" (p. 31). The promise of these new interpretations, however, does not derive simply from identifying something as a text but (as Geertz would surely agree) from the theories and understandings (mostly from literary/critical theory) that go along with such an identification. Broadly, those theories emphasize that the meaning of a text, which derives from its very construction as one, does not precede its reading. Rather, all three—meaning, construction (writing), and reading—infuse and are infused, construct and are constructed, by each other. That is, while we speak of an educational (any) event as a text, its textlike materiality does not exist prior to its interaction with a reader. A text, then, is the creation of the reader; it is not an already encoded reality waiting to be deciphered.

What implications might this have in the context of this book? First, perhaps, since different researchers read and write their texts from different reading/writing positions, what you will encounter in this book will undoubtedly differ from that which might be offered by any other researcher studying the very same teacher education program (Flinders & Eisner, 1994; Hammersley, 1992). Second, it implies that there is no one, single, authorized text of any phenomenon—in this case, that of the UWC Teacher Education Program—from which to start one's (different) reading; no agreed-on version on which to base one's investigation. Hence, I speak of reading the UWC Teacher Education Program or the social studies methods course in which the study was located *as* texts rather than reading *the* text of either.

Stating that there is no *one* official text of this teacher education to be read does not, however, preclude the existence of *an* official text with which to do one's reading. This latter text is created by the reader (myself) who both, and at the same time, determines what constitutes this official text and then reads with, into, and against it. The author of the text is therefore the reader who, through the act of reading, becomes its author (and authorizer). From that perspective, and as the Second Text (which I elaborate on later) will demonstrate throughout the book, there were as many official texts of this teacher education program as there were readers participating in this study—student teachers, instructor, researcher— each constructing their own text and making different interpretations of it. The text I refer to as the subject of my reading in the remainder of this book is thus a combination of what I chose to read of and into this teacher education program; a version I not only constructed but, also and simultaneously, subjected to my critical reading (See, e.g., Britzman, 1995; Denzin, 1995b; Derrida, 1976; Young, 1981).

Reading Positions

The reading of the teacher education program at the University of Western Canada offered in this book is not only constructed but constructed from particular constructing positions. Those, it should be emphasized, are not (nor do they intend to be) neutral or objective. On the contrary, the readings offered are personal, positioned, often passionate and judgmental. The "false division between the personal and the ethnographic self, [which] rests on the assumption that it is possible to write a text that does not bear the traces of its author," Lincoln and Denzin (1994) claim, "is impossible." "All texts," they add, "are personal statements" (p. 578;

Smyth & Shacklock, 1998, p. 1), and mine is no exception. Indeed, the theories, assumptions, interests, values, language, and life experiences I bring to my work play an active role in guiding what and how I studied. Inevitably, what I attend to and the questions I ask are a reflection of what I take to be important (Flinders & Eisner, 1994, p. 350). Though researchers and authors are never fully aware of all the reasons for their actions, non-actions, and interactions (Ellsworth, 1989), I have some obligation to explain the perspectives, positions, and understandings that generate my claims to knowledge (Simon, 1992, p. 16) in this book, and provide reasons why I see things as I do (Lemke, 1995, p. 20).

The theories, assumptions, and perspectives I bring to the reading of the UWC Teacher Education Program are based on my experiences in education and those I have derived from (and often against) that education. Thus, in the same way that I set out to study how student teachers partly become a product of their education, I recognize that I, too, am a product of my own history in/and education. I am a Jewish white male in his mid-forties, born and raised in Israel, where I not only was educated but also educated others for three years as a secondary social studies teacher. Having taught in Israel without a teaching certificate, I was required to enroll in a teacher education program in order to be eligible to teach in Canada. In 1992, two years after moving to Canada, I entered the secondary teacher education program at UWC—the same program I am now to explore as a researcher.

Growing up in Israel, where education (and culture in general) is, more often than not, based on active participation, contestation, doubt, dispute, and dissent, and where students, by and large, tend to voice opinions, even if, perhaps because, theirs differ with those already present in the classroom, I was struck by a learning environment at UWC that was characterized, primarily, by serenity, agreement, politeness, civility, and courtesy. All, no doubt, are beneficial to learning. They do, however, carry a price tag, especially when compliance, conformity, and consensus—as process and product—are elevated to a desired goal. I found that while prospective teachers may be encouraged to ask questions about content or pedagogy *in* their teacher education courses, they are rarely encouraged to ask similar questions *of* those teacher education courses. Or, they are actively discouraged when confronted with the "political" consequences of continuing to do so.

Education that is premised on, embedded in, and promotes the mechanisms of a priori agreement about the process and culture of learning, Tyler (1991) explains,

teaches—indirectly, accidentally, and unbeknown to itself—the terror of CON-
SENSUS. . . . The great end of all consensus is to bring discourse to an end in the
silence of agreement, in the elimination of difference, and the reduction of all
opposing voices to a single, disembodied voice that having spoken in the authority of the all falls silent. (p. 82)

Within such a consensual learning environment, not only were the critical
questions I, as a student teacher, was asking of my own teacher education
program not answered, they were often not even considered questions
worthy of an answer in the context of learning to teach. In many ways,
then, the study underlying this book is an opportunity to revisit those
questions; this time, however, as a researcher—a position that allowed
me not only to ask those questions but ensure they were actually addressed. In other words, while this book is about the UWC Teacher Education
Program of the 1996–97 calendar year, it is probably as much about the
one in which I participated, as a student teacher, several years earlier.

Why a Focus on Social Studies Preservice Education?

The reason for focusing this book on social studies (rather than English or
mathematics, etc.) teacher education is twofold. First, my academic subject area background is history. I have taught social studies in high schools
in both Israel and Canada, and I now teach prospective secondary teachers how to become social studies teachers of others. Second, and more
importantly, such a focus derives from the very demands put on social
studies teachers—perhaps more than on teachers in any other area—to
help students critically engage—read and write—the world. Wineburg
(1991), for example, having studied how high school students and histo-
rians read historical texts differently, calls on teachers to move students'
readings beyond the literal and inferred text and to engage the text's subtext.
That is, to see texts as socially constructed speech acts, to explore not
only what texts say but also what they do. Teachers, according to Wineburg,
must use what they already know in order to foster that kind of reading
among students. But what is it that teachers already know? And how are
they being prepared to know? What role do the context and culture of
teacher preparation play in producing teachers who not only are able to
foster such readings among students but who also know how, value, and
are inclined to do so themselves?

Such questions become pertinent because reading the subtexts of historical texts is not an isolated endeavor. Rather, it is embedded in and
dependent on a variety of other educational and pedagogical texts, subtexts,
and contexts, as well as on the values they carry, the expectations they

convey, and the dispositions they promote. Thus, while Wineburg was surprised that the best high school students read acceptingly rather than critically, the question that needs to be asked is what constitutes "best" (students and readings) in the current culture of education—whether in schools or in schools of education. Do we count among our "best" those who produce critical, questioning, and oppositional readings or those who reproduce and paraphrase what teachers/instructors and textbooks/course readings already consider as fact? Do we reward students/prospective teachers who challenge or those who comply with the authorial invitations, instructions, and intentions of the authors of texts and those of the educative environment in which those texts are read? If, as Wineburg suggests, it is upon teachers to foster students' critical readings, what kind of critical readers are they? How, if at all, do the practices of teacher education position those learning to teach to read the (and their) world? How and what is it that preservice education invites student teachers to read and not read while learning to teach? And what do prospective teachers carry with them from their experiences as student teachers when they become teachers of others? Thus, and returning to a question I raised earlier: What do the practices of teacher education make possible for student teachers learning to teach and what do student teachers, in turn, make happen because of what happens to them in that context?

Lenses, Discourses

Any discussion about the purpose and process of learning to teach is grounded either implicitly or explicitly in particular views about what teacher education is, about what it ought to be (Borko, 1989; Doyle 1990). The study informing this book borrows from and is grounded in a variety of discourses—i.e., postmodernism, poststructuralism, feminisim, postcolonial theory—providing its particular lenses with (and through) which to read and write the pedagogical world of initial teacher education. Those discourses can be best defined as "critical." Critical discourses use critique as a conceptual and strategic tool to challenge the innocence of existing knowledge and knowing and highlight the "insufficiencies and imperfections within so-called finished systems of thought" (Kretovics, 1985, p. 56).

I wish to focus here on two communities of discourse in particular—cultural studies and critical pedagogy—that gave rise to the specific structure, syntax, and process of the study reported in this book. My intention is not to provide a comprehensive account of either[3] but, rather, to explain—

epistemologically and ideologically as well as strategically and pragmati-
cally—why and how both are (and were made to be) useful for the purpose
of this particular study.

As areas of study and as methodologies with which to study, cultural
studies and critical pedagogy prove beneficial to my work as both share a
common interest in "how knowledge, texts, cultural products [and prac-
tices] are produced, circulated, and used" (Giroux, 1994a, p. 280) as well
as with what (and who) they produce, circulate, and use in that process.
While engaging different venues of inquiry—critical pedagogy mostly in
and about institutional education, cultural studies primarily outside of it—
both infuse and are infused by a critical theory of pedagogy.[4] That is,
both cultural studies and critical pedagogy share a common interest in
exploring the pedagogical nature, process, and effects of cultural practices, discourses, and texts on the negotiation of power, knowledge, sub-
ject-position, and identity.

Cultural Studies

Drawing on postmodernism, post/structuralism, and postcolonialism, and
combining ideas, methods, and concerns from literary theory, anthropology, sociology, history, and media studies (Sparks, 1996, p. 14), cultural
studies raises important questions for educators and educational researchers—questions I use continuously throughout this book—in order to rethink the nature of educational theory and practice (Giroux, 1996, p. 44).
Challenging, as I do, the interests underlying the questions not asked
within pedagogical encounters, cultural studies invites educators and researchers to expose how existing absences and silences governing teacher
education ignore the link between knowledge and power and "refuse to
acknowledge the particular cultural practices they help produce, circulate,
and legitimate" (Giroux, Shumway, Smith, & Sosnoski, 1996).

Seeing cultural and pedagogical practices as texts (and vice versa),
cultural studies is not so much concerned with what texts mean as it is in
how they come to have meaning (Giroux, 1996, p. 44). Its aim, thus, is to
study a text not for itself but for the subjective and cultural forms it helps
realize (Johnson, 1996). Seeking to question the self-evidence of meaning (Mohanty, 1986) through analyzing procedures, traditions, discourses,
and practices for how they function to include or exclude certain meanings, produce or prevent particular ways of being, behaving, and imagin-
ing (Giroux, 1996, pp. 48–49), cultural studies provides educators and
researchers with tools with which to read cultural practices (texts) not
only in context but also against their context. That is, to illuminate a text

as it cannot show itself and highlight the conditions of its making about which it is, and prefers to remain, silent (Eagleton, 1983).

Critical Pedagogy

Critical pedagogy is the result of the encounter between critical theory and education (Kincheloe & Steinberg, 1997, p. 24). Based in the writings of Paolo Freire and the Frankfurt School and, more recently, incorporating aspects of postmodernism, poststructuralism, feminism, deconstruction, and postcolonial theory (McLaren, 1997, p. 1), critical pedagogy provides educators and researchers with the means to critically examine the interests structuring current notions of educational theory and practice.

Critical pedagogy poses a counter discourse to the prevalent, depoliticized discourse in most colleges of education. It challenges mainstream schools of education for taking what Aronowitz and Giroux (1985) define as a narrow instrumentalist approach that emphasizes the "how to," the "what works," and the mastering of the "best" teaching methods. Such an approach not only introduces student teachers to rules and regulative practices that have been laundered of ambiguity, contestation, and cultural politics (Giroux & McLaren, 1987, p. 273), it also reduces learning to teach to a problem of finding a correct technique (Britzman, Dippo, Searle, & Pitt, 1997, p. 16). Rarely, states McLaren (1988), do teacher education programs provide their students with opportunities to analyze the ideological assumptions and underlying interests that structure the way teaching is taught (p. 42; see also Arends, 1991; Britzman, 1986, 1991; Giroux, 1988b; Giroux & McLaren, 1986; Greene, 1986a; Kincheloe, 1993; Smyth, 1989; Zeichner, 1983).

Rather than produce what Freire called a "culture of silence" (McLaren & Giroux, 1995, p. 32), critical pedagogy encourages prospective teachers to critically analyze and challenge the origins, purposes, and consequences of the "constraints and encouragements embedded in the classroom, school, and societal contexts in which they work" (Zeichner & Liston, 1987, p. 1).

Teacher education from the perspective of critical pedagogy should, according to Giroux and McLaren (1986), link

> critical social theory to a set of stipulated practices through which it becomes possible to dismantle and critically examine preferred and officially sanctioned educational discourses and traditions, many of which have fallen prey to an instrumental rationality that either limits or ignores the possibility of creating alternative teaching practices capable of re-configuring the syntax of dominant

educational and/as political, social, and cultural systems of intelligibility and representation. (p. 229)

This book incorporates the approach to teacher education advocated by Giroux and McLaren and other critical pedagogues and does so at two levels. First, as will soon become evident, I am an ardent supporter of critical pedagogy. Labeled too ideological and political by most teacher educators and therefore ignored in many colleges of education, critical pedagogy is the direction toward which I, as a teacher educator, believe preservice education should (and must) move if we wish to make education (and society in general) more democratic, equitable, and just.

The second (and a consequence of the first) level in which this book incorporates critical pedagogy is in the research methodology of the study reported in it. That is, the issues and concerns raised by critical pedagogy about teacher education underlie and direct the questions and issues concerning this study.

But it is the combination—perhaps infusion—of those two levels that constitutes one of the main contributions of this book. While critical pedagogy has provided powerful, poignant critiques of preservice teacher education, the language of possibility critical pedagogues hope to generate within teacher education students through that critique seems to be directed primarily toward the culture of schooling, teaching, and learning in schools, not toward those of teacher education itself. In other words, while the venue for such critique is teacher education, its substance, more often than not, is the education student teachers will find in schools, not the one they themselves receive in the process of learning to teach at a university. How, then, one might ask, are prospective teachers to move from a language of critique (in teacher education) to a language of possibility (in schools) if the two remain disconnected in the process of learning to teach, if rethinking the essence of teacher education itself is precluded from the discourse of critique advocated within it?

Attempting to make that connection apparent, this book uses the lenses of critical pedagogy not only to examine preservice education but also to have prospective teachers use those very lenses to critically examine their own process of learning to teach. In doing so, this book redresses another absence in the literature in critical pedagogy. While critical pedagogy has provided an abundance of significant critical analyses of teacher education, most have not been grounded in or accompanied by "thick" ethnographic descriptions (Geertz, 1973) about actual practices in teacher education classrooms or "the web of meaning and action involved in the process of becoming a teacher" (Ginsburg, 1988, p. 3. See also Kanpol, 1998, p. 191).

The Structure and Order of the Book

This book is in three parts. The two chapters in Part I introduce and outline the issues examined in this book as well as contextualize and frame the study informing it.

Part II focuses on how specific discourses and practices commonly found within preservice education position future teachers to know. Chapter Three briefly discusses the pedagogical nature of discourses. Chapter Four examines the impact of the discourse of planning and organization on prospective teachers' educational imagination: What does such a discourse emphasize? What does it tend to ignore? And how do the two work together to construct prospective teachers' conceptualizations of teaching and of "good" teaching in particular? The relationship—too often the separation—between critical thinking and thinking critically in preservice education is the focus of Chapter Five: What, when, and how do critical thinking/thinking critically mean in teacher education? How and when are they employed and toward what (and whose) ends? How do the meanings ascribed to each help direct student teachers' understandings about teaching and learning? Chapter Six examines how "difference" is given definition, purpose, and body in preservice teacher education through the discourse about, and the practice of, gender and multiculturalism: How, where, with whom, and to what pedagogical ends is difference inf/used while learning to teach? Who is difference for? What and who is it about?

Part III revisits the study and teacher education in general in light of this study. Chapter Seven reexamines the study described in this book, this time asking what and how it disabled/enabled its participants. Chapter Eight revisits teacher education itself in light of issues raised in previous chapters and outlines a reconceptualized preservice teacher education where prospective teachers learn about teacher education by publicly learning from it. It proposes experiences that engage teacher education courses not as preparation for practicum but as practicum environments in and of themselves where practice as-it-is-practiced gets theorized, and theory considered not only *for* practice but is indeed practiced. Rather than provide solutions to what this book has identified as problems, dichotomies, or contradictions within preservice education, Chapter Nine uses the issues underlying those problems, dichotomies, and contradictions to further the conversation about preservice education. It invites teacher educators and educational researchers to use that conversation to rediscover that which we all believe we have already discovered about preservice education, to unlearn that which we have already learned, and thus learn further by learning again.

Uniting the different chapters of this book is not only a shared focus on the production of knowledge and knowing in preservice teacher education but also their use of critique as a common epistemological and methodological approach to the investigation of that production. Critique, Zavarzadeh and Morton (1994) emphasize, "should not be confused with criticism" (p. 62). While criticism tends to end discussion by handing down a verdict, critique attempts to open it up. Criticism, Barthes (1981) explains, seeks to discover the hidden meaning of a work. Critique, on the other hand, "impugns the idea of a final signified. The work does not stop, does not close. It is henceforth less a question of explaining or even describing, than of entering into the play of the signifiers" (p. 43). In that fashion, critique is invoked in this book not in order to criticize or devalue what took place in the teacher education program at UWC but rather, to critically examine "the tensions between and within words and practices, or constraints and possibilities" in preservice education by questioning "the consequences of the taken-for-granted knowledge shaping responses to everyday life and the meanings fashioned from them" (Britzman, 1991, p. 13). The purpose of such an examination is not to solve any imperfections, dichotomies, or contradictions this study highlights in the work of teacher education but, rather, to engage them publicly in order to bring more of what is done (and how what is done, by definition, creates that which is not done) in teacher education into the fold of the discussion; a discussion not only about but also *in* teacher education.

This form of discussion—a critical conversation about practice—is facilitated in this book in two ways. First, through a combination of the questions I pose, the responses they generate among the study's participants, and the analyses I provide of the relationship between participants' responses and the context that made such responses possible. Another means to facilitate a discussion about teacher education within this book is provided in the form of the "Second Text," identified by an icon **[ST¶]** and appearing in italics throughout the book (beginning in Chapter Two). Hoping to constitute a conversation about teacher education not only within the book but also about it (that is, about how I, as researcher, read and wrote about teacher education), the Second Text invited participants, after the (research) fact, to add to, comment on, and critique my analysis and interpretations about their words and actions within the world of preservice teacher education.

As a form of metadiscourse about the discourse presented in the First—running—Text, the Second Text incorporates participants' comments (and sometimes my comments about their comments) about my text, about my textual constructions of them as actors in my text, about their experience with, of, and in the text, about their readings of my research and my role as researcher as texts. Despite my authorial urge to respond to their comments, to cohere, to clarify, and justify my work, I tend to mostly stay out of their way. Rather than devour participants' comments into my text (as researchers often tend to do with the results of member-checking), leaving no apparent traces of participants' objections, additions, or comments, the Second Text allows participants to speak in their own words (which are presented unedited and in full) whereever they chose to insert them.[5]

Such a process not only positioned participants differently in relation to the researcher (and as I will explain in Chapter Seven, to themselves as participants and to the issues being researched) but also the research text in relation to the research process. At the level of participants/researcher, this process allowed participants a space where they are not merely interrogated but where they interrogated, posing questions rather than merely providing answers. At the level of research text/process, the Second Text opened the research—running—text itself to critique, thereby making it part of the research process rather than only a summation of it. In that sense, the existence of the Second Text extended research beyond a report about "findings" to the politics of "finding" and of textualizing one's findings. My hope is that opening my study to that form of critique will serve as an invitation to readers of this book to do the same; to learn not simply from what my research purports to report but from the ongoing conversation within it and from the conversations you as readers, from your own reading positions, engage with it.

Chapter Two

Framing the Context

The UWC Teacher Education Program

The Secondary Teacher Education Program at the University of Western Canada (a large, reputable, public research university located in Cantoria, one of western Canada's most populated cities) is a twelve-month postundergraduate program.[1] [The University of Western Canada (UWC) and Cantoria are both pseudonyms.] It comprises two components—university-based course work and a school-based practicum—which take place over three semesters. The first (fall) and last (summer) semesters are devoted to courses provided at the university. Sandwiched between them is the second semester, which takes place in public schools in and around Cantoria and provides the setting for student teachers' practicum.

The first university-based semester of learning to teach takes place from September to mid-January and is interrupted by a short two-week—mostly observational—practicum in mid-October. During that semester, "prospective teachers are introduced to the theoretical bases of modern educational practice and to strategies and methods of teaching, both in general and in relation to the subject(s) they are preparing to teach" (UWC Calendar, 1995/96, p. 169). To accomplish that, student teachers are required to take the following courses: *The Analysis of Education,* which focuses on gender equity, anti-racism, multiculturalism, and First Nations issues in education; *Education during the Adolescent Years,* a course that deals with physical, social, cognitive, moral, and emotional growth of the adolescent learner; *Development and Exceptionality in the Regular Classroom,* emphasizing the teacher's role in enabling an integrated learning environment for exceptional students; *Communication Skills in Teaching,* where students study and practice interpersonal and communication skills required in the secondary classroom; *Principles of Teaching,* which pertains to issues relating to the role of the teacher, instructional planning, teaching strategies, classroom management, and assessment and evaluation; and two methods courses relating to each student teacher's specific teaching concentration(s). Another course—*School Organization in Its Social Context*—spills into the beginning of the second semester (immediately before the practicum). This course focuses on the organization and administration of the education system in the province, including issues in governance, finance, and professional control.

The second semester of the teacher education program at UWC (from January to April) is devoted to student teachers' 13-week practicum, conducted in a variety of Greater Cantoria public schools. Having completed their practicum, prospective teachers return to the university for the third and final semester of the teacher education program (May–August). This part of the program is designed to put student teachers' "teaching competence in a more comprehensive framework of knowledge and understanding. An opportunity is provided for them to enhance their subject-matter and/or pedagogical competence" (UWC Calendar, 1995/96, p. 169). Students are required to enroll in the following courses: *Learning, Measurement, and Teaching,* a course that deals with principles and practices of assessment; *Language Across the Curriculum,* where students analyze oral and written language from various curriculum areas and its implication for teaching and learning; and at least one of four educational studies courses: *Educational Anthropology, History of Education, Philosophy of Education,* or *Educational Sociology.* Students are required to take two additional courses (six credits) in order to fulfill the academic requirements of the program. Those usually comprise either another methods course (within the College of Education) or a "content" course (outside of it), both normally pertaining to students' particular subject area specialization.

Following the satisfactory completion of the program requirements (both coursework and student teaching), students are awarded a Bachelor of Education (Secondary) degree and are eligible for a teaching certificate, a document required in order to teach in the public school system in the province.

While the university-based portion of the UWC Teacher Education Program comprised two-thirds of learning to teach, it was no doubt the third portion—the practicum—that was deemed its most significant. Much of everything done before the practicum was seen by instructors and students alike as more than preparation for the practicum; the very success of university teaching that preceded or followed the practicum was, in many ways, measured against it. As such, the first semester at the university—the one preceding the practicum—became the more important of the two university-based semesters. While the last (Summer) semester was often considered superfluous by prospective teachers ("We've already taught in schools for three months, what can the university still teach us?"), the significance of the first semester at the university was not questioned, as it was the one preparing them for the practicum. As such, the first university-based semester of the program is the one my research focuses on most.

Certainly, all the courses provided in the first and formative semester at the university related directly to teaching and, in combination, played an important role in highlighting both general and specific issues pertaining to the educative endeavor. It soon became apparent, however, that in the minds of the six student teachers participating in this study there was a clear hierarchy among those courses; the litmus test, by and large, determined by their applicability to teaching, to what a teacher needs to know in order to make instruction possible, sufficiently operational, viable, profitable, and, ultimately, according to participants' continuously evolving definition, "educational."

The two educational psychology courses, which focused on developmental characteristics of the "normal" and exceptional adolescent learner both inside and outside of the "regular" classroom, seemed, in the view of this group of student teachers, very much peripheral to what they actually needed to know and, more importantly, *do* as teachers in classrooms. While adding important perspectives to the understanding of education or the learner, these two courses were often seen as irrelevant to the actual act of teaching. They might have been interesting and informative, students argued, but they were not essential. One could—indeed one did, they claimed—teach just as well without them. Labeling these courses (as they also did with regard to their communications course) as "redundant," "boring," "irrelevant," and "a waste of time," participants could not come up with one example throughout the six interviews I conducted with them as to how those three courses might be important or beneficial in informing them as social studies teachers. **[ST¶ Ron:** *I may have said at the time that the ed. psych. courses seemed peripheral or irrelevant, but I think that I was reacting more to the way material was presented than to content. Later on, in the summer, I found my knowledge of Piaget and Kohlberg to be very valuable in the Philosophy of Education course. Also, upon reflection on my first year as a teacher, I wish I had learned more procedural knowledge in the educational psychology courses: how to deal with ADHD kids, how to recognize* *warning signs of abuse, learning about disabilities, depression, etc. But now, another question occurs to me: Given all of the fuss made over critical thinking not only in social studies but in all courses, why did none of us challenge the definitions of "normal," "exceptional," and "regular"? I think we were all paralyzed by the fear of "Oh God, what if I get one of THOSE in my classroom?"* **Casey**: *Having taught for a while, I can now make a strong connection to the relevance of these two courses, especially in terms of "troubled teens," since I have seen quite a few extreme cases myself. At least the ed. psych. courses made one cognizant of the potential for problems with students. Sometimes as teachers, we tend to focus on assignments and curriculum, critical thinking, etc., and forget the students and that to some of them, at a given moment, what we do focus on is the least of their concerns. This is important, and in some cases, I think students need to be given latitude. We should not forget the psychological turmoil that often goes along with being an adolescent.*]

Much higher on student teachers' "relevancy list" was *The Analysis of Education,* an educational studies course focusing on issues such as gender equity, anti-racism, and multiculturalism in education. Yet while students recognized this course as extremely important and relevant to what a teacher needs to *know,* it seemed less relevant in relation to what a teacher actually needs to *do* (I address this dichotomy in more depth in Chapter Six). The courses prospective teachers found most significant and those they continuously referred to both positively and negatively while commenting about the teacher education program as a whole were *Principles of Teaching* (*POT*) and the various methods courses, especially the social studies methods course in which this study was conducted.

Principles of Teaching introduced students to "principles and instructional procedures related to classroom management, instructional planning, and the assessment of learning as applicable across grade levels and subject matter fields" (UWC Calendar, 1995/96, p. 398). The social studies methods course, as methods courses normally do, focused on issues of curriculum and instruction in social studies. For better or for worse, these two courses seemed to be at the center of the teacher education program for this group of students. As they viewed it, these courses were directly related to teaching, to what student teachers should learn, to what teaching (and more importantly, as I will show, what "good" teaching) is fundamentally about. [ST¶ **Ron**: *Look at the title of these courses:* **Analysis** of Education, **Principles** of Teaching, **Methods** courses. *These titles* suggest "doing something." To me, the title Principles of Teaching privileges this course because it suggests action. I think what needed to be questioned is the obsessive nature in which the entire course called Principles of Teaching centered around unit planning. One catch phrase I have heard lately talks about the need for "leaders" or "managers." Yes of course, every teacher should know how to organize learning, for what purposes and with which desired outcomes. And all I really wanted was a simple, basic model of how to do it—like learning a filing system. I think something like that should take maybe a week, at the most. All I do now, having taught for a year, is to draw up a chart on a big piece of paper and fill in what I want to do, how I'm going to do it, and how I'm going to evaluate what's been done. So I think the POT class was the biggest waste of time.] (This issue is considered in depth in Chapter Four.)

I present this hierarchy not as a statement about what I believe is the significance—actual or potential—of any of the courses offered in the process of learning to teach but, rather, as testimony to what prospective teachers themselves thought was important in that process. As such, this hierarchy becomes useful in highlighting two interrelated points relevant to the remainder of this book. First, this hierarchy is by no means innocent or coincidental. Beyond their focus on the "practical," *Principles of Teaching* and the methods course found their way to the top of students' lists due both to the structure of the UWC Teacher Education Program (in the case of *POT*) and to the disciplinary organization of knowledge and learning in schools (in the case of the methods course). *POT* became significant for this group of participants not only because it provided the foundations for teaching across subject areas—engaging issues such as the role of the teacher, planning, instructional strategies, classroom management, and assessment and evaluation; issues pertinent in and to all the other courses—but also due to the special role it played as the liaison between the teacher education office at UWC and student teachers (in a way, functioning like a homeroom in schools). *POT* is where the associate dean of teacher education addressed prospective teachers; it is where they received their sets of "official" documents from the ministry of education and other professional organizations; it is where they fulfilled requirements by the library and other administrative structures in the program (insurance, etc.). As such, what was done in *POT* often had significance beyond the boundaries of the course itself. In many ways it represented "the program" and served as its mouthpiece, acquiring special status and authority in the process.

As for the methods course, the idea that content-area courses are more important than general courses that focus on the learner is structured on the expectations about teaching with which prospective teachers come into the program (Britzman, 1991). These expectations are based on prospective teachers' previous educational experiences, whereby teachers teach content rather than learners. Teachers, accordingly, are defined by their subject area and are measured by their creative organizational skills to convey it, often in abstraction from the effects the discipline and its organization have on those who are made to engage it.

Yet the hierarchy presented above is not simply the result of what prospective teachers brought with them into the program; it was just as much the effect of a teacher education program that not only refrained from interrogating the assumptions with which student teachers came into the program but, by doing so, might have actually reinforced them. Such a reinforcement occurred when educational issues normally examined in those "irrelevant" or "less relevant" courses (i.e., *Analysis of Education* or the two educational psychology courses) were mostly made irrelevant in the courses that seemed to matter most—the "practical" courses—such as *Principles of Teaching* and the methods courses.

The second point to be made about the hierarchy of courses prospective teachers constructed is its utility in the context of this study. In order to examine, as I claim to do, how the discourses of teacher education position student teachers to engage education in particular ways, one must first identify which discourses student teachers listened to, which they valued, and what they valued in them. Identifying what courses were significant in prospective teachers' eyes is a first step to knowing where to focus one's attention as a researcher. Indicating that *Principles of Teaching* and the social studies methods course were at the heart of the program, the messages conveyed by those courses and the discourses engaged in them, one might assume, had the largest influence on the final images of teaching with which students left the program. Regarding these courses as more important than others, what was said and done in them ultimately made a (more) lasting impression on students' conceptions of education, teaching, and learning. As their courses of choice—courses where they focused much of their attention and from which, according to them, they gained the most—the discourses in those courses carried more weight in their eyes, conveying messages about what it means to teach, how one should go about (and what becomes significant in) learning to teach.

The Social Studies Methods Course/An Overview

The Social Studies Curriculum and Instruction course (the methods course, as I tend to refer to it, or Simon's course, as students chose to name it) was one of the various methods courses offered to student teachers in the first semester at UWC. It was a required course for all student teachers whose teaching concentration (either exclusively or in combination with another) was social studies. The course, which convened three times a week (Mondays, Wednesdays, and Fridays) for two academic hours per class, emphasized issues of curriculum and instruction in social studies—that is, curriculum organization and principles and methods of instruction applied to its teaching (UWC Calendar, 1995/96, p. 393). The particular focus of the methods course (and its subtitle) the year this study was conducted was "Reading and Writing Texts." This, explained Simon, the professor teaching the course, "is based on a conception of what it means to know, and to learn. If teaching is about helping students to know and if we come to knowledge (learn) from reading texts and then writing our own, then learning to teach is about becoming able to help others learn how to read and write texts. Hopefully," he added, such an approach "will enable us to explore [the following questions]: How do we know things? How do we teach [high school] students to ask questions about how they know things? How do we stimulate students to want to ask the kinds of questions that will get them to know more?"

The course was divided into four conceptual themes (units). The first—an introductory unit—included: (a) a discussion about the nature of social studies and the purposes of teaching it; (b) an examination of the provincial social studies curriculum—its purposes, goals, objectives, and proposed approaches for instruction; (c) an exploration of critical thinking and its role in teaching and learning; (d) an examination of the ways in which history textbooks present themselves as neutral and authorless and how that might position students to engage the past in certain ways rather than others.

The second unit/theme of the course, which focused on reading historical texts, began with students exploring four issues: What is history? What is a fact? What, if at all, is the difference between history and fiction? And what, if at all, is the difference between a primary and a secondary source? Using a variety of historical texts and forms of textualizations (i.e., print, photographs, video, etc.), student teachers then explored: (a) ways to encourage students to more critically and thoughtfully engage history not as a presentation of the past but as a discourse about it; (b) elements of historical thinking—significance, continuity and change, progress and decline, empathy (perspective-taking) and moral judgment, and agency—and how those do and could play differently in history education. The use of film as historical representation concluded that unit and provided a bridge to a third unit, which focused on the media. Here, students examined and interacted with popular media texts and media professionals (a former editor of one of the two local daily newspapers in Cantoria) as they explored the following questions: What are the media and how do they affect/influence/enable an understanding about the world? How do different media present the same world differently? How do the media help frame public/controversial issues (Werner & Nixon, 1990)?

Landscapes and the built environment as texts were the focus of the fourth unit of this course. It included the educative possibilities embedded in environmental, economic, political, and social issues pertaining to urban development. As a class, students constructed a unit centered around the impact of converting a forested area around UWC into a residential complex that would answer the financial needs of the university as well as the growing demand for housing in Cantoria, one of the fastest growing cities in Canada.

A specific emphasis throughout the course was put on using primary sources as tools for enhancing students' thoughtful, critical, and reflective inquiry into social studies issues as well as the organization of such inquiry into modules (lessons and units) of instruction around concepts, themes, or controversial public issues. (Students' evaluations as to how the different components of the course came together to educate are discussed later in this chapter.)

Methods

> We often do not know what we are seeing, how much we are missing, what we are not understanding or even how to locate those lacks. Fatal contingencies, deceitful language, the self-deceptions of a consciousness that does not know what it acts toward; it is the experience of consciousness in its very limits that I inscribe here. (Lather, 1999, p. 4)

The study described in this book comprised four phases and took place over a two-year period—from the beginning of September 1996 to the end of December 1998. The first and most substantial phase took place in and around a 13-week secondary social studies methods course at the University of Western Canada, which convened for two hours, three times a week, September 4 to November 29, 1996 (with a two-week break at the end of October for a short, observational practicum). With the purpose of examining how (and in which direction) the discourses and practices within the methods course and the teacher education program in general helped construct prospective teachers' understandings and dispositions toward education, teaching, and learning, data collection combined: a) observation, field note taking, and audiotaping of all sessions of the methods course; b) three "official" one-on-one in-depth interviews with six of the student teachers participating in the methods course, who volunteered to be part of this study's focus group, and two interviews with the course instructor; c) examination of all documents, resources, and readings pertaining to the methods course, as well as all texts (assignments and final exam) written by the six student teachers participating in this study.

The second phase of the study was carried out in six Greater Cantoria public secondary schools, while student teachers were on their 13-week practicum (February–May 1997). This part of the study was not aimed at exploring the practicum as a site of learning to teach in and of itself but, rather, the degree to which (and how) what took place in the first semester at the university impacted prospective teachers' educational imagination about practice while in, and within the constraints of, the practicum. Two interviews with each of the six student teachers were conducted following visits to their classrooms in order to contextualize references they made to their teaching during our interviews.[2] To learn more about what student teachers were working for, with, and against during the practicum, one-hour interviews were conducted with their sponsor teachers.[3] Data collection in this phase also included documents—i.e., lesson and unit plans and other materials and resources—pertaining to the practicum that student teachers chose to share with me.

Phase three of the study took place during the summer of 1997, as prospective teachers returned to the university following their practicum for the final, summer semester of their teacher education program. The intent for data collection at this stage was to consolidate the study by allowing student teachers, at the end of their program, a space from which to reflect about the program as a whole, and to make connections among courses and between the university-based and the school-based portions of the program.[4]

The fourth and final phase of this research (August 1997–March 1999) focused on "post"-fieldwork data analysis, interpretation, member checking, and writing.[5] This phase also provided the opportunity to incorporate participants' comments about the First Text into the Second Text of this book.[6]

Methodology

Any study is always more than the sum of its methods. What gives it meaning and direction is not its methods but its methodology—the theories and pedagogies it assumes and utilizes for (and during) the process of conducting that research.

As a critical ethnographer, my intent was to move beyond traditional practices that ask participants to articulate what they know to "having them theoriz[e] about what they know" (Lather, 1986, p. 264). In that sense, I was looking not only to observe, record, and interpret participants' "thoughts and meanings, feelings, beliefs, and actions as they occur *in* the *'natural'* context of the research" (Schumacher & McMillan, 1993, p. 407, my emphasis) but also to have them articulate their thoughts *about* that context and what it was in that context that generated particular thoughts, meanings, feelings, beliefs, and actions. My research, then, did not stop at observation, recording, and analysis of occurrences in the "natural" context of the research, but moved its participants to investigate the very idea of "naturalness" in that environment. Interviews seemed the most natural environment in which to explore those issues.

The six in-depth, one-on-one interviews—some lasting more than two hours—conducted with participants throughout their university- and practicum-based experiences were opportunities for them to reflect on what went on in the methods course, and to make connections between the methods course and the teacher education program in general. Participants were also able to articulate their thoughts and understandings about the culture of teaching and learning; about the need for and the role of social studies education; about their wants, expectations, and aspirations as well as those put upon them both as students and teachers; about the structures and conditions of schooling; about the goals of, and their own goals for, education.

Reading the UWC Teacher Education Program as a text and inviting participants to do the same during interviews meant examining *how* that text meant, not only *what* it meant (Birch, 1989, p. 21). Analysis, Macherey (1978) offers, "does not remain within its object, paraphrasing what has already been said; analysis confronts the silences, the denials, and the resistance in the object—not that compliant implied discourse which offers itself to discovery" (p. 150; cf. Birch, 1989, p. 17). If, then, as Fiske (1990) claims, "what is absent from a text is as significant as what is present" (p. 96), research attains its critical promise only when it carefully listens to silences and makes them speak (Sultana, 1995, p. 119). Identifying the silences, gaps, and absences in this teacher education program and having them measured and spoken against its utterances (and how utterances construct silences and yet do their best to conceal their existence and their implication in bringing them to life) meant bringing those silences and absences into the open, exposing and deconstructing them for what they yield, for what they attempt to conceal.[7]

The traditional, unidirectional model of interviewing "as a one-way passage of knowledge from interviewee to interviewer" (Limerick et al., 1996, p. 456) would not have been adequate for such a task. Instead, and using the methods of the Active Interview (Holstein & Gubrium, 1995), interviews were conducted in a form of collaborative, interpretive practice, involving respondents and interviewer as meaning-makers rather than as asker and tellers. Such a model rejects the image of respondents as "vessel[s] waiting to be tapped in favor of the notion that the subject's interpretive capabilities must be activated, stimulated, and cultivated" (p. 17).[8] While not intentionally leading students to preferred responses (but nevertheless leading them *to* respond), interviews encouraged respondents to enter into and shift positions in order to consider alternatives. Rather than search for the best or most authentic answer, claim Holstein and Gubrium, the aim is "to activate ways of knowing—the possible answers—that respondents can reveal, as diverse and contradictory as they might be" (p. 37). In that sense, and as you will find throughout this book, I, as researcher, intentionally provoke participants by problematizing the taken-for-granted in everyday practice and indicating—even suggesting—positions and frameworks with which they could enter a critical, dialectic conversation with their situation in order to transform it. For research to be praxis-oriented (Lather, 1986), it cannot be only about participants; it must also be for them in the sense that it allows them to do, learn, and/or do something about/within the research context that they would not be able to do without it. (I discuss the praxical aspects of this research in Chapter Seven.)

Introducing the Participants

The six student teachers participating in the in-depth part of this study shared several characteristics. Casey, Charles, Jack, Jocelyn, Mary, and Ron were all white, middle-class, Canadian-born and educated, and they all spoke English as their first and (with the exception of Jocelyn and Ron) only language. All six were remarkably polite, considerate, willing, dedicated, and enthusiastic (characteristics that, as I explain in Chapter Seven, also drove them to participate in this study). Except for Ron who was in his early thirties, all the others were in their mid- to late twenties. Charles was the only student teacher in this group who enrolled in the UWC Teacher Education Program right after receiving his B.A. All others had spent time either working (Casey, Mary, Jocelyn, Ron) or learning a profession (Jack) prior to entering preservice education.

Enrolling in a teacher education program for this group of aspiring teachers seemed to be directed more toward gaining professional competence, accreditation, and certification in the educative system as it currently is rather than challenging and actively reforming it. Although issues of equity and social justice were very much at the center of their thinking, those, most believed, could be well addressed within the current system of education—by tweaking and slightly modifying it—rather than by challenging its underlying core conventions, purposes, assumptions, and structures. **[ST¶ Jocelyn**: *Challenge and reform seem to be what you believe a teacher education program should promote. But I'm not sure that one can challenge and actually reform a system without first knowing the system. As learners of education—or as students learning to function as "the other half" (teacher)—I think we, or at least I (since I should not speak for everyone), first wanted to understand the system before I could begin to challenge it.*]

While each of the participants was no doubt his/her own unique teacher, visits to their practicum classrooms and the interviews that followed illustrated a variety of shared pedagogical approaches. They all went well beyond what Goodlad (1984) or Cuban (1984) describe as teaching governed by teacher-dominated lecture, textbook assignments, and recitation lessons coupled with an avoidance of controversial issues. More often than not, and incorporating much of what was emphasized in the social studies methods course, they presented knowledge (and had students, mostly in groups, consider such knowledge) as socially constructed and historically situated and framed topics as controversial public issues, making sure to keep controversy at the surface by having students engage a variety of different perspectives, interpretations, and textualizations. Together (and, in most cases, individually as well), participants infused teaching with primary and secondary sources, including film, video, newspaper articles, novels, poetry, art (mainly reproductions of painting), artifacts, posters, cartoons, advertisements, photographs, and, naturally, historical documents. Still, there seemed to be a difference—at times a dichotomy—between what participants said social studies education should be and how they went about teaching it during their practicum (Goodlad, 1984). However, contrary to prospective teachers described in other studies of learning to teach (see Cochran-Smith, 1991; Cole & Knowles, 1993; Feiman-Nemser & Buchmann, 1986; Kickbusch, 1987; Lanier & Little, 1986; Zeichner, 1986, 1992), however, those involved in this study were very much aware of such differences and spoke often about the frustration resulting from trying to implement such changes in the realities of student teaching. [ST¶ **Jocelyn**: *The reason for the gap between what we wanted to do (or felt we should do as good social studies teachers) and what we were able to do was mostly the result of fear. Those who were in charge of the practicum report—sponsor teachers and faculty advisor—had first to be pleased, paychecked-out, if you will. What did they want? To what would they respond positively? In the end, they hold the strings to a glowing report, a satisfactory one, or a failure.* **Ron:** *I may very well have been told that I was free to employ whatever innovations I wanted during the practicum; I did not experience myself as very free. While my sponsor teachers repeatedly told me to try whatever I wanted, I was also aware of the tremendous risks involved in doing so. On the one hand, I was aware of my sponsors' desire that any experimentation I undertook should not set the class behind schedule or disrupt the order which he had worked to build. On the other hand, I was also aware that trying a personally inspired innovation and then failing carried with it the risk of appearing not to embody the qualities of an effective teacher in the eyes of my practicum supervisor, who had the power to decide whether I passed or failed the practicum.*]

Jack

Those who knew Jack while he was growing up in a small town in northern Ontario would have been as surprised as he was when he entered preservice teacher education. As a kid, Jack never cared much for school. Easily getting bored when "things didn't move along quickly enough," he "would start socializing and having fun"—seeking attention, as Jack put it, "by goofing off." In grade ten, and as a consequence of that constant "goofing off," Jack was sent to a private boarding school. It turned out to be "the most positive experience of my life."

> There were a lot of rules and regulations, but I certainly had a good time and was able to express myself even within the boundaries. I hated being told what to do in school: I've always not liked authority but at the same time I rely on it to keep me in line. Otherwise I wouldn't accomplish what I want for myself. Structure and discipline are important because people by nature are lazy. People will choose to do nothing, especially kids, and they have to be taught against their nature. If

you're disciplined and you think the right way then you will begin to reap the benefits of your discipline and be happier than if you were a lazy slob.

At high school, Jack told me, "we were geared to look for careers where we would make money. Men with suits would come frequently to talk about their careers and prep us to become important, powerful people: lawyers, doctors, finance managers, and brokers." Consequently, and having received a B.A. in political science, Jack began studying to become a broker but soon realized

> that I didn't really care how much money I made. It was something my mom had pushed me toward and the school and all my friends whose respect I wanted. This realization sort of opened me up to what I wanted to do rather than what I needed to do in order to make money. I realized that I would *really* like to teach. I really love to be with kids. I realized that I could teach social studies—which is what I like—and have a whole career around it. I looked back at boarding school and thought that if I can have an effect on some kid the way my teachers had on me, then it would be worthwhile and that I would get more satisfaction from teaching than from anything else. And satisfaction is much more important than money.

One of the more vocal students in the methods course, Jack regularly asked questions and shared comments publicly. For Jack, there was more to social studies education than, "Let's bang out some content; here's a neat way of doing it; oh, let's do a worksheet; OK, they've got that information, let's move on." But turning social studies education into the critical engagement of public issues from multiple perspectives that he hoped it could be within the realities of school was "much tougher and harder than I thought it would be." This transformation was Jack's main focus and struggle throughout the study. Although receiving nothing but praise and encouragement from his sponsor teachers and faculty advisor for his innovative approaches to social studies education, Jack never felt fully comfortable with what he was doing. Setting extremely high standards for himself, Jack always believed he could have been more prepared, chosen better resources, or used different pedagogical approaches to better—that is, more actively, critically, and thoughtfully—engage his students.

Jack currently teaches social studies in a private high school in Cantoria. He is also the school's soccer coach and was recently invited to be on the Canadian National Soccer Team.

Charles

While not remembering much of his high school years, Charles did recall always having "a comment for everything. I was bored so I talked a lot, disrupted everybody. I mean I was a good kid, but I had my moments. . . . I was disruptive but not disrespectful." After high school Charles began studying commerce at a community college. He never thought he'd become a teacher, but in his second year there, he got an opportunity to coach a grade-eight boys' basketball team. Coaching that team was a turning point for Charles.

> We were a horrible team. We only won about two games the entire season. After we lost our last game, I walked into the locker room expecting to find a lot of sad faces but instead I got dunked. It felt really good because although we lost, they were all smiling. And I figured: "Hey, I must have done something right!" I tend to feel comfortable around kids. I've had pretty good experiences coaching. I never had any kids who did not enjoy my coaching. I don't know what it is. I guess I just do it right. I try to keep things fun and keep everyone involved. So as I was thinking about my future, I thought to myself: "I have coached sports for much of my life and teaching is almost the same."

Deciding to become a teacher, Charles left commerce and refocused his studies on human kinetics and history. Four months after receiving his B.A., Charles began his teacher education program at UWC, with a double concentration—physical education and social studies. Mostly quiet and reserved, Charles rarely participated in the method course's large-class discussions. He was, however, somewhat more forthcoming in our conversations, though even in those occasions he was never a "big talker." Few issues could disturb his calm and when they did, he tended to respond with a witty, cynical, almost dry sense of humor. While he very much enjoyed the methods course, Charles thought the course tended to be too theoretical and wanted to spend more time on the "basics"—constructing lessons and units for instruction, engaging the actual social studies high school curriculum. It was thus often difficult to move Charles beyond the "practical" in our conversations, not because he was unable to do so but, rather, because he did not wish to. Charles did everything possible to resist discussing theory and its implication for practice. This resistance, however, I soon discovered, was mostly a veneer. For when I persisted, a whole new Charles evolved, whose responses were just as theoretical as those of others. Yet it always took a while to get there, often, as his words throughout this book illustrate, with him "kicking and screaming" along the way.

During his practicum, Charles taught only one social studies class (his other classes were all P.E.). This one grade 10 class, however, proved quite a challenge. Almost half of the students were recently arrived immigrants whose level of English did not allow them to read the textbook (or any other grade 10 level text) nor feel comfortable participating actively in class discussions. Another quarter of the students were what school administrators had already determined as "students with learning disabilities (some of them, quite serious)."[9] Attending to the needs of this very diverse classroom, Charles most often had to rethink the curriculum, supplement it, and implement less than traditional methods to meaningfully engage all his students with the subject matter.

Following the completion of his B.Ed., Charles returned to his hometown, where he now has a part-time position teaching Career and Personal Planning (CAPP) and social studies.

Mary

Mary's memories of high school conjured mostly unfavorable images—both of the institution and of herself as a student. "I was hardly a student," she said. "I was there only for the required time—for the time I *had* to be there in order not to flunk the course. The rest of the time I was at the bar. I don't think I was the average student, that's for sure."

After school, Mary worked as a secretary. She

> was going to be the world's greatest secretary. But I soon realized that you have to have postsecondary education to get anywhere in life. E-v-e-r-y-b-o-d-y around me had their degree and they all had more responsibilities than I did. I realized I had to get better qualified. And if that meant going back to university to get a degree, then that's what I was going to do.

In 1991 Mary began studying geography at a community college. Her decision to go into teaching occurred in her second year. "What was I going to do with a bachelor of arts? I wanted to prepare for the future so I planned to enroll in a teacher education program as soon as I got my B.A." But there was another reason pointing Mary toward teaching:

> My mother is an elementary teacher so I have sort of an inside view of the pros and cons of teaching. There are a lot of benefits to teaching besides the obvious ones. I think one of the most important ones is helping young people by guiding them in making their own decisions. If my teachers had given me a stronger academic upbringing when I was in school, if I had a better education, I think I probably would have gone onto university right after school instead of doing the secretarial thing, which was a complete waste of time.

Two weeks after receiving her undergraduate degree, Mary began her teacher preparation at UWC. Never hesitating to say what was on her mind, Mary often surprised her colleagues in the social studies methods course with her sharp observations and her appended punch lines, bringing to light the humor and irony in most every situation. As one of the three declared "geographers" in the course, Mary was somewhat anxious about having to teach a curriculum overwhelmingly dominated by history. Yet her practicum experience was overshadowed not by her unfamiliarity with history—in fact, her sponsor teachers' comments in that regard were always positive and encouraging—but by external demands requiring her to first change schools and then move from one sponsor teacher to another. Mary was nevertheless determined not to allow these factors to stand in the way of continually providing her students with a critical and thoughtful learning environment. Mary's passion was antiracist education, which she continually infused

> whenever it was relevant. Whenever I could throw some stuff in there about groups that were discriminated against or whenever there was a stereotype or a myth that could be debunked, especially about immigrants—because I know there's a lot of racism in the school—and if I can have any say in getting rid of that, then I will.

At the end of the teacher education program, Mary left Cantoria and returned to her remote home community, where she substitute teaches in its three high schools.

Jocelyn

Born in a small town nestled in the Rocky Mountains, Jocelyn remembers doing well in school, though she was always "more interested in sports than in anything else, spending most of my free time in the gym." Wanting to become a teacher, according to Jocelyn, was not the result of a particular critical moment or turning point in her life. Rather, it was something she always saw as a natural progression of who she was as a person—someone who loves to learn and share with others in their learning. From her previous experiences in coaching, tutoring, and teaching summer and theater school, Jocelyn realized that the most rewarding job—both personally and professionally—would be one where she learned herself and then turned around and taught and mentored others.

Though most of her high school social studies education consisted of "worksheet after worksheet, map after map, which you never had to think about again . . . sit down, get out our atlases, and count the number of provinces in Canada and locate their capital cities," Jocelyn began to love history as a result of her grade 11 teacher.

> He was very much into showing us why what we were doing was important and engaging us in conversations and challenging our thinking: "Well if you don't think it's important, why?" "What do you think *is* important?" He was really

open and understanding and thought that anything could, with a particular focus, be brought to bear on what we were studying. It was the first time I actually enjoyed social studies and that's where my love for history started.

After receiving a degree in English and history from UWC, Jocelyn moved to Japan, where she taught English as a Foreign Language for three years. It was there that Jocelyn learned to appreciate the cultural nature of knowledge and knowing. For the first time, "I could experience how my own education presented me with versions of the world that were constructed from a particular perspective."

When she returned to UWC in order to begin preservice education, Jocelyn was, in some ways, already a seasoned teacher. One of the most outspoken students in the course, she was often first to have her hand up, first to make a comment or ask one of the "hard" questions waiting to be asked. That also translated well into her teaching. Stating that "language dictates how we see the world and affects what we think is possible," Jocelyn continuously engaged her own students during the practicum with the historically constructed nature of knowledge/language and the inevitable language base of history and of historical texts as well as with the need to examine the gendered, racialized, and class-based nature of the curriculum and the learning environment in which it is presented.

It's important to understand that the materials we're studying in a Western history class will be different from what is being studied in Japan. It's the same chronological time, but different issues are discussed. It is important to understand that what we call history is *our* interpretation. And how do you even begin to communicate that to students if you don't first of all talk about multiculturalism, about different perspectives, different ways of looking at things. Gender can affect that, age can affect that, culture can affect that, society can affect that, class can affect that. You can't separate those things from content; they are the content.

Having received her B.Ed., Jocelyn got a full-time position teaching humanities, social studies, and Japanese in the same school in which she did her practicum and has been teaching there (successfully, I hear) ever since.

Casey
A good, hard-working student, Casey liked school and did fairly well in it, though she definitely remembers knowing how to enjoy adolescence to its fullest. Casey began her undergraduate studies at UWC focusing on English. But a seven-month study-trip to Israel at the end of her first year at university, which included an intensive seminar on the Arab-Israeli con-

flict, redirected Casey's academic interests to International Relations. After completing her university studies, Casey spent three years working as an insurance agent in her father's business. That, however, did not seem to provide the level of intellectual stimulation she was after. Casey had initially thought about becoming a teacher when she first started tutoring in high school. She enjoyed "explaining concepts that others found difficult and seeing the message get across. Teachers can have a good influence on others," she added, "and there's a lot of satisfaction in a job where you can do that." Deciding it was time to leave the nest and establish a career of her own, Casey enrolled in the teacher education program at UWC. She decided to specialize in social studies because "I think that's one of the only school subjects where you can actually teach something." As Casey explained:

> If you look at the world in the last 100 years and the amount of change that has happened in our society and the effects that it has on people, I think it's extraordinary. And I think it's important that people who are living in this society have some idea of how it's changing and what's happening so they can hopefully function in it. We live in a democracy and I think it's important to be informed, to be able to critically analyze the commercials and whatever you get bombarded with and to hopefully have the confidence not to believe everything that is put out at you but to question it and have some background knowledge so you can make informed decisions.

This was something Casey had been exposed and accustomed to at home, where public issues and how those were engaged in the media were regularly discussed around the dinner table. Casey's teaching during the practicum not only encouraged students to critically examine texts already present in her sponsor teacher's classroom but also broadened the definition of what might constitute a legitimate text in the social studies classroom. Incorporating, for example, a variety of popular culture texts—video, film, music, magazines—as part of the curriculum that needs to be read and written critically, Casey made the curriculum more relevant and immediate to students' lives and also had them critically examine the texts they normally engage outside of, and see as separate from, the social studies classroom.

Casey currently substitute teaches in two school districts around Cantoria and is actively seeking a full-time position. Meanwhile, she still helps out in her father's insurance business, though she has also been taking undergraduate science classes at the university in preparation for studying medicine sometime in the future.

Ron

Ron was considered by all a good student, and his recollections of school, of his teachers, and of social studies education were mostly positive. Coming from a family of educators—his grandfather a headmaster in Wales, his mother a secondary French teacher—Ron was destined to follow suit. At university, Ron majored in anthropology and archaeology, though the latter part of his studies comprised mostly history, philosophy, English, and literature courses. Having spent three years teaching English in Japan immediately after graduation, Ron returned to Canada and decided to enter the UWC Teacher Education Program.

While Ron didn't speak much in the methods course, he was very reflective, open, and forthcoming during our interviews and used them as an opportunity to ask questions—mostly of himself and of the program—as much as to provide answers. Ron was no doubt the "philosopher" among the group. Commenting, for example, on an initial working title of my study—"Subjecting the Objective Center"—Ron opened our first interview by discussing the need to move away from "the subject/object dichotomy and begin speaking more in terms of meaning and experience." What such a dichotomy proposes, claimed Ron, is that

> there is an independent eye that is the subject and is aware of its own thoughts, but those thoughts are somehow disconnected from an objective outside world . . . separating the body from whatever is around it and then worrying about breaching that gap in a kind of Hegelian sense. How do you interpret experience? What meaning do you attach to it—experiencing your own thoughts, your own process, experiencing the meaning you attach to experience and participating in shaping the world as it also shapes you?

Consequently, while most other participants saw the teacher education program as a place to receive answers as to how to become the best teachers they could be, Ron, as illustrated in the opening section of this book, was more in search of questions—those pertaining to his own understanding of the program and what it did and did not offer him as a prospective teacher.

Moving beyond social studies' traditional goals of "forging some kind of Canadian identity and assimilating students into it by providing an official history and interpretation of our society," Ron focused on the need to

> look at society critically and build a more just society by recognizing and redressing some of the injustices that are still structurally there toward First Nations people, women, non-whites or non-Anglo people in Canada; to come up with

some solutions for some of the inequities of wealth and access to education, power, and the like.

Throughout the first semester of his teacher education program, Ron kept asking himself, "Am I going to be the idealistic, interesting, exciting, and effective teacher—the kind of teacher I believe I am—when faced with the demands of the provincial curriculum and those of the school schedule? How long is it going to last before I sort of throw up my hands and whip out the worksheets?" Faced with a sponsor teacher whose expectations were mainly "to get the material covered, keep the interest up, keep the pace up, keep them working, and stress punctuality and attendance," Ron, in what may be a perfect example of the "dumbing down" effect of teacher education, could hardly recognize himself in the teacher he was turning into. "It's kind of frustrating," he said, "to recognize the difference between what I had wanted and thought about in the university and then finding myself doing almost the opposite [in the practicum]. Somehow I've fallen into this idea that there is X amount of material that has to be covered in X amount of time and it's my job to get through all of that."

After graduating from the UWC Teacher Education Program, Ron found a long-term temporary position teaching grade 7 and 8 ESL and Japanese classes in a private school in Cantoria. He is currently working as a substitute teacher for several school districts and is teaching ESL to adult learners.

Simon

Simon, the professor teaching the social studies methods course in which much of the study reported in this book was conducted, is an established, mid-career professor and the coordinator of secondary social studies education in the College of Education at UWC. With a B.A. in history from a prestigious private university in the United States, a master's in the history of education from UWC, and a Ph.D. in history from the University of California, Berkeley, Simon taught social studies in Cantoria high schools for 15 years before coming to UWC. Since then, he has taught a variety of methods courses in the teacher education program as well as graduate seminars on the politics of, and the relationship between, historical representations and historical understandings.

Presented with the idea of this research project, Simon embraced it immediately and wholeheartedly. He was amenable to allowing me access to his classroom and was also enthusiastic about the kinds of questions I was raising about teacher education as a pedagogical endeavor and the perspectives and lenses I was bringing into this study. While having a "critical" reader in one's classroom might intimidate some, Simon thrived on our post-class conversations, often e-mailing me a "Nu?" if, for a day or two, I failed to raise poignant questions about what I saw happening in his classroom, and suggesting issues I did not see but might wish to examine.

In contrast to participants' mostly negative comments about the overall university-based part of their teacher education program—"An example of how not to do things" (Jocelyn); "Nothing was connected and the workload was outrageous" (Mary); "A whole lot of work to keep us busy until we actually go out to the school and learn stuff" (Charles); "So tightly packed that there's little time to reflect on what we're learning and doing. It just gets to be a matter of reading such and such a book and writing such and such a paper and then forgetting it and moving on to the next thing: factory production, assembly-line knowledge" (Ron)—students had nothing but praise for the social studies methods course.

Very soon it became apparent that Simon was not only an enthusiastic teacher, passionate about social studies education, but that he actually

> enjoys us as students . . . well not just as students. I really get a sense of being treated like his colleague, and I've heard other people say that too. It's refreshing. He's an excellent facilitator: He's good at moderating discussions and making sure everybody has a turn to speak without being heavy-handed and forceful about it. (Ron)

Ron's mention of class discussions was not coincidental; discussions (about "What is history?" or "What is a fact?" and so on) occupied much of the time in the methods course. Class discussions in which Simon often "threw his agenda out the door and said, 'Oh, that's an interesting question. Let's look at that,'" (Mary) were what the six participants liked and remembered most. Discussions, according to Mary, made present a broader spectrum of perspectives.

> Everybody has an equal opportunity to put up their hand and speak their piece, which gets the discussions going and opens up opportunities for seeing things from different points of view. . . . There are so many different perspectives that I don't see, that people from other backgrounds see. How would I know those other perspectives unless I heard them in class? Whereas other teachers might say: "Well, no! We're getting sidetracked. You guys, come back!", Simon doesn't do that. So I r-e-a-l-l-y like those classes because I learn a lot from listening to other students. And having us teach each other is, I think, valuable, because [before that] I would have said, "Well, I don't want my students to teach each other. That's my job as a teacher." But no! I now understand that it's important.

Part of participants' respect for Simon grew out of the fact that his course seemed the one best able to "walk the talk" of the program—to reconcile its theories in practice. "While in other courses there was a difference between what we were talking about, what we were thinking about, and what we were actually practicing on a day-to-day basis, in Simon's class," according to Ron, "there was a correlation—first, between what Simon said and what Simon did, and second, between what other classes in the program talked about and what Simon actually did in his course." Students appreciated Simon's course because it encouraged them "to really think and question . . . as people who are analyzing society around them and thinking of ways to encourage students to think about that as well, to build a community of thinkers (Ron).

Moving students "away from the traditional read-out-of-the-textbook, memorize, do the questions at the end" and focusing instead on "critical thinking and high order thinking" (Jocelyn), Simon "provided us ways with which we can present things to students so that they're actually getting something out of it and critically analyzing things" rather than just "getting the information and regurgitating it back" to us (Casey). One of those ways, according to Ron, was an emphasis Simon put on questions—both in the activities and interactions in the methods course itself and in the lesson and unit plans prospective teachers were planning for their own students. The message in the course has been

> that the most important thing a teacher can be doing is asking students good questions. It's not a matter of us imparting our great storehouse of wisdom and knowledge. It's not even about information, but how to approach that information, how to question it, how to get it, how to understand it once you do get it. (Ron)

It was this particular focus that helped transform Jack's understanding of his role as a teacher. "While coming into the course I thought of the teacher more as the fountain of knowledge who knows everything, someone who stood up at the front of the class and dished out facts and told students what they needed to know, I now see it more in terms of the teacher guiding the students or presenting problems or cases or topics in an interesting and engaging way for the students to learn themselves." While Jack attributed his new approach to the kind of learning emphasized by Simon, Casey explained that the course had not so much offered her a new way of engaging education but rather affirmed and legitimated what she already knew as a student but did not believe she could ever do as a teacher. "I like to think that I've always questioned whether things are facts or not and not just taken everything as given. But I don't think I would have done as much of it with my students if we hadn't explicitly discussed it in Simon's class. Had I not taken Simon's course," she added,

> I might have been more focused on just giving students content, lecturing to them, not getting them to do as much of the work, not getting to think about what they're doing, not getting them to question the information, not getting them to question me or the textbook. I don't think I would have questioned textbooks as much. I mean, I think I did before but I'm not sure I would have had students do it as well.

The imbalance between students' mostly negative comments about the general UWC Teacher Education Program and their positive ones about the methods course is by no means coincidental. Rather, to a large degree, it reflects students' overall satisfaction with a course they saw as one of the highlights in a teacher education program most of them found to be less than desirable. Not only did the methods course fulfill many of their expectations pertaining to social studies education, it also seemed to embody what other instructors spoke of but rarely practiced. Paradoxically, then, and as different as the methods course might have seemed to participants when compared with everything else offered in the program, it was perhaps the best representation of what the UWC Teacher Education Program aspired to yet never fully accomplished elsewhere. An integral component of the UWC Teacher Education Program, the methods course was also very much implicated in it. Thus while the apparent differences between the approach taken in the methods course and that taken in other courses made it distinct in student teachers' eyes, a closer examination illustrates how underlying themes, approaches, and assumptions guiding the methods course were, at times, in fact, very much part of what prospective teachers identified as problematic in the overall teacher education program. That relationship and how it positioned students in the educative process of learning to teach is explored in more detail in the following chapters.

PART II

DISCOURSES AND THEIR IMPACT ON PROSPECTIVE TEACHERS' EDUCATIONAL IMAGINATION

Chapter Three

Interlude: The Pedagogical Nature of Discourses

Discourse is the maker of the world, not its mirror. (Foucault, 1972/1981, p. 49)

Any system of education is a political way of maintaining or modifying the appropriation of discourses, along with the power and knowledge they carry. (McLaren & Giroux, 1995, p. 37)

Discourses are the organizing structures that make the world—and one's ability to make meaning of and in that world—both possible and intelligible. Providing a "conceptual order to our perceptions, points of view, investments, and desires" (Britzman, 1991, p. 57), discourses order and regulate preferred forms and norms of thinking and being. Through that regulative function, according to Jackson Lears (1985), discourses play a powerful role in marking the boundaries of the permissible and discouraging alternatives. But discourses don't only define the boundaries of the permissible *and* discourage alternatives; they also do so *by* discouraging alternatives. And by inhibiting the creation of alternatives, discourses tend to reproduce themselves.

Discourses are inherent in any pedagogical endeavor. In fact, one might say, as Luke and Gore (1992) do, that discourses "define the classroom, the teacher and the student and are key to the production of subjectivity, identity and knowledge in pedagogical encounters" (p. 2; see also Phelan, 1994). Organizing knowledge and experience, discourses construct the imaginable in the educative process as they express what knowledge and knowing are of most worth, govern how teachers and students ought to go about acquiring them, and determine what can and cannot be said or done in the process.

Interested, as I am, not only with what discourses in the particular community of teacher education at UWC meant but, following Fish (1980), also with *how* they meant and ultimately with what they *did*, Part II of this book examines how discursive practices function "to include or exclude certain meanings, secure or marginalize particular ways of behaving" through the various means in which they actively and passively produce and mediate the context and content of teacher education (Giroux, 1996, pp. 48–49). To study the discourses of teacher education by examining their commissions and omissions, then, is to open "education and the language of experience" to its problematics, claims Britzman (1991, p. 17). For any discourse is defined not only by what it says, by the questions it raises, and by the actions it legitimates, but also by what it does not say, by the questions it cannot pose or answer, and by the actions it will not legitimize (Kretovics, 1985). Reading into the relationship between those two aspects, one can begin to examine the assumptions, values, and practices underlying preservice education, to explore how and why those particular values, assumptions, and practices dominate and persist over others, and what those assumptions, values, and practices make possible for those learning to teach.

With that perspective in mind, the second part of this book comprises three chapters, each dealing with a particular aspect of the impact of discursive practices within teacher education. However, while the discussion in the following chapters is about discourse, it is also through discourse. That is, the very investigation of discourse is, and can only be, conveyed through discourse—a meta-discourse which, as a mode of criticism, Barthes (1972) points out, is "ultimately, essentially, and in and of itself, a 'discourse upon discourse'" (p. 258).

A complex structure comprising a variety of ideologies, perspectives, and approaches both in and to education deriving from particular disciplinary and personal commitments of individual instructors, the UWC Teacher Education Program, as any other, did not speak of, or practice education in, a harmonized, single, monovocal fashion. Teaching to teach was often a fractured, discontinuous, and contradictory endeavor whereby a bricolage of discourses and practices crossed each other, were at times juxtaposed with one another, and were often unaware of each other (Foucault, 1972/1981, p. 67). Contradictions, fractures, and dislocations, however, are not only inherent in any complex, multi-discursive educative environment but, when brought to the surface, can provide means to unravel the weave that binds them together. For the very authority with which a teacher education program presents its vision is achieved, to use Cronon's (1992) discussion of history, through its ability to hide any "discontinuities, ellipses, and contradictory experiences that would undermine the intended meaning of its story" (p. 1349).

The story of learning to teach, therefore, must be examined both within and against itself, exposing its ellipses, contradictions, and silences and how those are made to speak—either by presence or absence—within that story. Contradictions emanate not only from the discontinuities within the combined overt curriculum of learning to teach; they are also part of the delicate relationship between the overt, covert, and null curricula of preservice education, between the declared goals of teacher education and its actual practices. The hidden curriculum, Ginsburg and Clift (1990) explain, does not necessarily mean that it is deliberately or explicitly hidden but that it is not part of the explicit curriculum. It comprises the content of the implicit messages transmitted to students through the structures, social relations, policies, and practices of teacher education beyond those conveyed by the stated curriculum (Glatthorn & Coble, 1995, p. 29), as well as through the contradictory messages of the overt curriculum itself and those emanating from the dichotomies between what is advocated and what is practiced. Distinguished from the explicit and implicit curricula is the "null curriculum"—the nonrandom, structured absences within a curriculum that work to silence and thus eliminate the existence of alternatives through their non-coincidental (perhaps deliberate) absence (Erickson, 1991). While the pedagogical framing of the explicit curriculum—made apparent by a teacher or text physically there for students—is more visible in the educative process than those of the hidden and null curriculum, the latter, as Bernstein (1996, p. 28) points out, never cease their pedagogical functions. In fact, claim Ginsburg and Clift (1990), they possibly communicate "a stronger and more persuasive set of ideas about teaching, pedagogy, [and] curriculum" than the "publicly stated and intended goals of teacher education" that they accompany (p. 450).

With this perspective in mind, Part II of this book explores the following questions: How do the multiple and contradictory discourses and practices of teacher education—each making different claims about the purpose and conduct of education, teaching, and learning—come together to educate? How do students (or do they?) make sense of them and the existence of discrepancies among them? How do these different discourses and practices position student teachers to conceive of, think through, and act on education—their own education as students and the education they are to provide their own students in the future? And how do the discourses and practices provided student teachers influence their educational imagination and the pedagogical constructions they do and do not produce as a result?

Chapter Four

The Discourse of Planning and Organization: A Study of Con/sequences

One of the most powerful and prevalent discourses in preservice educa-tion—perhaps an overarching meta-discourse through which other dis-courses are made available—is the discourse of planning and organiza-tion. Emphasizing lesson and unit planning as means for conceiving, organizing, and assessing instruction, the discourse of planning and orga-nization plays a prominent role in preservice teacher education class-rooms (Brown & Wendel, 1993; Clark & Peterson, 1986). So taken for granted is its significance in learning to teach, it has assumed an almost extraterritorial status. While scholars/teacher educators might disagree as to how one might best go about teaching prospective teachers how to plan-to-instruct (for a variety of models, see Clark & Peterson, 1986), the centrality of planning-to-instruct in initial teacher education has mostly been left unquestioned.

Many would argue, "for good reason." Planning—making decisions about and organizing—instruction, claims Arends (1991) is "among the most important aspects of teaching" (p. 55). A process through which teachers link curriculum to learning (Clark & Yinger, 1987), planning "is a major determinant of what is taught . . . and how it is taught" (Arends, 1991, p. 55). "Purposeful planning and the organization of instruction," Arends adds, give teaching and learning a sense of direction. Occupying such a prominent role in the process of learning to teach, the importance of teaching novice teachers how to plan has generated much research, with several studies looking into how they go about doing their planning (Borko & Niles, 1987; Brown & Wendel, 1993; Bullough, 1989; Grimmett, 1991; Kagan & Tippins, 1992; Koeppen, 1998; Sardo-Brown, 1993a, 1993b). Too often, however, the desire to enhance prospective teachers' ability to plan is so embedded in the discourse and practice of preservice education that little time is devoted either by prospective teachers involved or the teacher education program busy "involving" them to consider not only what is accomplished in that process but also to examine its consequences, to contemplate what gets disabled in that otherwise enabling endeavor.

With that in mind, the focus of this chapter is not as much on the particular discourse (or discourses) of planning and organization used in this teacher education program (though that will ultimately come through) but on how that use (and, as I will show, possibly overuse, at times even misuse) positioned its prospective teachers to know. While not questioning the inherent need to teach prospective teachers how to thoughtfully plan for instruction, this chapter attempts to illustrate the (mostly unintended) effects on students' educational imagination—that which pertains to planning and that which goes beyond—of immersing them so intensely into the discourse of planning.

Planning as the Organizing Discourse of Experience

A month into the UWC Teacher Education Program, its prospective teachers had already fully encountered the discourse of planning and organization. Fifteen of their 24 weekly instructional hours were spent in courses focused primarily on planning to teach. By the end of that first month, prospective teachers had already been required to produce four lesson plans in *Principles of Teaching* (POT)[1] and one in each of their two methods courses, and were working on three unit plans, one for each of those three courses.

To illustrate the impact of that planning on student teachers' understandings about planning and its relationship to teaching, I turn to an excerpt from a discussion in the methods course that took place while students were working on the above-mentioned unit-plan assignments. Having heard from students in his other—earlier in the day—section of the methods course that they were finding it difficult to reconcile the requirements for the unit plan assignment in *Principles of Teaching* with those in the methods course, Simon began this class by asking students if they too were encountering similar difficulties. Almost three-quarters of the students raised their hands to indicate that they were.

> Simon: That's pretty major and I think we'd better sort that through. I'd like to hear a bit more about the nature of this discrepancy in expectations for what is put forward as good teaching. . . .

Student #1: We're having big contradictions on the length of a lesson. In *POT* it's strict: You do not go over 70 minutes, and it's [usually] somewhere between 40–70 minutes. There are several people in here who might have gone over 70 minutes because of what we got in this class. We backed it up with relevant things we will be doing in that lesson but that was just not accepted [in *POT*].

Jack: Just to add to that, our units are not allowed to be more than six to eight lessons [class sighs, "Yeah!"] and every concept, issue, or theme we've talked about in this class are designed around month-based units, which seems reasonable to me. However, God forbid, if we ever handed that in as part of our unit in our *POT* class, we'd probably be failed on it. . . .

Jocelyn: Since there's no way I can fit my unit into seven lessons, I'm saying in my unit plan that these seven lessons are *part* of my unit. And if the *POT* teacher takes issue with me, then [she says with a sense of defiance] I'll go talk to her!

Class [in what seems a combination of respect and disbelief at Jocelyn's "unruly" approach]: Oooooohhhhhh!!! . . . .

Simon: You can see that these kinds of questions: "How long is a lesson?" "How long is a unit?" are not deep pedagogical issues.

Student #2: But they appear to be for [our *POT* instructors].

Simon: If your *POT* instructor says that the lessons turned in must not be longer than 70 minutes, and there's no flexibility on this, it seems to me that you produce 70-minute lessons for that class. . . . But that shouldn't be the source of confusion about what is a lesson or what is a unit. Some teachers have units that are always 10 lessons long, and that's fine. And if someone insists you frame your unit that way, then you'll have to turn in something different there than you would here. But these are not underlying differences in what it means to teach.

Student #1: It's more than inconveniences because we have to go out into, say, the practicum and they're going to ask us, "What do *you* think?" And we're going to be going, "Well, we had so and so who said this, and then we had our other methodology instructor who said this," and then . . .

Simon: But that's an answer to a question: "How long do you think a lesson should be?" [When you get into your school] you should be asking: "How long are classes in this school and do you consider a lesson something that is unified over two days or do you mean something that fits into that 60-minute block?" . . . But the problems raised [earlier] about how you were asked to use a "concept" in your lesson plans in POT seems more significant to me. Could somebody address that? . . . .

Student #3: Could we also know why it is important?

Student #4: Because that's what we are being marked on.

Jack: We're being forced to break down concepts in social studies into something so small that it can be dealt with completely—start to finish—within a lesson, and a lesson being one class.

Simon: I'm sorry. I can't help on that one. If you're going to have a concept that's useful for social studies, you'd probably want to move beyond . . . one lesson. . . . Not all lesson plans have to be organized around concepts. Did somebody tell you they do?

Student #3: No. But it seems as if we've been doing an awful lot of them!

Student #5: I can't speak for everyone but I feel that I'm not getting enough practice at writing lesson plans. I've only done a few in the month that I've been here and I have to go into the classroom in a week and a half [for the short, two-week observational practicum] and I don't even know how to write a really good one. I think that it's something we should all be doing more of. But [instead] I'm getting critical thinking in three of my classes. It's absolutely ridiculous!

Simon: Do you still have a future assignment [in *POT*] that deals with concepts?

Jocelyn: No. We have themes now. And, again, we have to do our themes and get through them in seven lessons. And that's not right either [class laughs in a manner that reflects as much discomfort and anguish as it does amusement].

The promise of this excerpt, from a discussion that was intended to last only a few minutes but, resulting from students' enthusiastic participation, took the lion's share of that particular class, is that it reveals as much as it conceals. What is included in the discussion is as much a reflection of that which is not. And what seems to cohere only unravels and falls apart as one examines what this excerpt represents and what is represented in and by it. **[ST¶ Casey**: *To me this discussion, in some ways, is a reflection of life in general and our educational system in particular. As one goes through the system, one realizes that different teachers teach the same things differently, and as a student teacher who wishes to do well, one must adjust accordingly. For me, I just adjusted and in the long run realized that I would present and design my lesson plans in a way that is right for me. In some way this could be viewed as a positive, as we were being exposed to different ways and methods about planning. I guess the problem arises because marks are involved. And when those are involved, if one disagrees with the way in which the instructor expects planning to be presented, that can become a problem.]* On the surface, this discussion appears to be about unit planning. A closer look, however, illustrates that it is about much more (and much less) than that. One can immediately recognize two different discourses about planning vying for prominence. The first—imported by students from *POT*—could best be defined as "instrumental." The other—summoned, albeit unsuccessfully from the look of things, by Simon—attempts to explore planning more pedagogically. While both discourses focus on the "how" of planning, the latter does not stop there. Rather, it connects the "how" to the "why" and the "for what" questions of teaching. Seen more as ends for instruction than as means to think about it, the former of those discourses no longer necessitates an exploration of epistemological and pedagogical questions embedded in those "why" and "for what" questions. Focusing only on the "how," this discourse substitutes them with (and in the process turns them into) questions of time management and organization. The concepts, language, and terms of this discourse are no longer (and can no longer be used as) tools to critically think about teaching. Instead, they become the focus, the very essence and embodiment of teaching itself. **[ST¶ Jocelyn:** *I think I'd have to agree. However, I wasn't at a stage to engage in this sort of discussion (that is, critically think about teaching) until I had some experience actually doing it!* **Simon:** *Student teachers, at this point, are inexpert at using the tools. And there is confusion stemming from the nature of the instruction they are receiving.*] Conceived that way, planning is not a space to think critically about teaching (see Kincheloe, 1998). Instead, it becomes embroiled in its own recursive process—planning for the sake of planning, with teaching taking precedence over learning.

And yet, as different as these two discourses are (and were in the context of this particular teacher education program), they nevertheless share a focus that emphasizes the importance of the exercise of planning in learning to teach. What becomes interesting, then, is to examine how prospective teachers negotiated and reconciled the differences between these two discourses while learning to teach and what effect the combined emphasis of those discourses on planning had on their educational imagination. The latter question is one I will pursue throughout this chapter. A partial answer to the former, however, may be provided by examining not only the kind of discourse about planning that students chose to invoke in this discussion but their relationship to it.

What students' comments seem to demonstrate is a dissatisfaction with, and a resistance to, a discourse of planning and organization in *POT*; a discourse that has reduced the discussion about, and the requirement for, teaching to the length of a lesson and the number of lessons in a unit. But do they really? And is that all they demonstrate? Discourse, Foucault (1979) suggests, is not only the instrument and an effect of power but can also operate as a potential "hindrance, a stumbling-block, a point of resistance and a starting point for an opposing strategy" (p. 100; cf. Young, 1981, p. 50). Immersed in a technical discourse of planning in *POT*, however, the ability (or desire) of students to resist becomes instead an instrument of validation. While they seem to disapprove of and ridicule the requirements put upon them in *POT*, their critique amounts to a desire for more conformity within the instrumental discourse of planning across courses rather than questioning the very concept of lesson and unit planning as the fundamental basis for learning to teach. In fact, as I will argue, students questioned the requirements in *POT because* unit planning had become so important in their thinking about teaching, not because it was insignificant, open to questioning. **[ST¶ Simon**: *You seem to be suggesting that students* should *question unit planning itself. Why? To what end?* **Jocelyn**: *I think my particular frustration with this class was just this—no one seemed capable of seeing the irony of* POT. POT *was a well-organized, planned-by-unit course and yet, in retrospect, it seemed the least relevant course we took. From the beginning, I knew that I could teach—I was never sure of my ability to select materials. Given a set of materials, I could organize it, dissect it, and transmit it. But was the "it" worth it? I still struggle with that question in my daily teaching at the present.*] Indeed, by the time this discussion took place, students had not simply been introduced to the discourse of planning but, through an intense preoccupation with it via a series of activities across courses, were in fact inculcated into it, subsumed in it, consumed by it. **[ST¶ Charles**: *Unit planning had overtaken what we were to teach. Especially in* POT, *the focus was on the exact science of unit planning, not the flexibility of teaching we got in the methods course. We were engaged in mostly "busy work," thinking about format, instead of focusing on the teaching.* **Ron**: *I question the amount of time spent obsessing about planning—which seemed to me what* POT *was all about. Where was the part of the course where we got to ask, "Why do we do education this way?" "Should we be doing it this way?" Doesn't the word "principles" [in* Principles of Teaching] *imply the questions "what?" and "why?" Yet* POT *had almost nothing to do with these questions and a lot more to do with "how."*]

Ron's questions—"Why do we do education this way?" "Should be doing it this way?"—were very much part of the general discourse in the social studies methods course, even when the focus was on planning. Yet as I will show, while the importance of these questions was emphasized in Simon's class and even as students made sure to incorporate them into their lesson and unit plans for that class, their significance did not, by and large, extend to prospective teachers' thinking about planning beyond that class. Rather, it was the "other"—instrumental—discourse that made an impact in that regard. Some responsibility for that, however, might actually be attributed to the methods course; a responsibility that derives not from how planning was engaged in the methods course but from the mere fact that it was engaged so extensively. That is, although very different in nature from the discourse about planning used in *POT*, the heavy preoccupation in the methods courses with planning ultimately, even if unintentionally, enhanced rather than displaced the overall powerful messages about planning sent to students from *POT* and other courses in the teacher education program. **[ST¶ Simon**: *The aspects of teaching that we can deal with in a university-based course are, indeed, thinking about the larger goals of teaching, and then helping students find productive ways of thinking about accomplishing those goals. We cannot go further, until they get to the school.* **Casey**: *To an extent, I agree with Simon because much of the implementation of instruction comes from actually doing it. Therefore, much depends on the sponsor teacher, the school, the students, etc. One can only plan so much, but planning cannot be in isolation from the three factors I mentioned above. Perhaps if this were spelled out more clearly to student teachers, there wouldn't be so much resistance to theory and thinking behind the lesson.*]

To be sure, the social studies methods course focused intensively on a variety of significant epistemological and pedagogical issues underlying the disciplines comprising the social studies and how one should go about incorporating them in teaching. Among those were an examination of "What is history?" "What is a fact?" and "What, if any, is the difference between primary and secondary sources, between history and story, fact and fiction?"; an integration of critical thinking in learning; an analysis of what comprises (appropriate) historical understanding and the reading of historical texts; a critical engagement of landscape, maps (that lie), and the built environment as texts; the role of the media in communicating a past and present; and the impact of popular media texts on students' historical understanding. Yet even as those (and many other) issues were a major focus of this methods course, the discourse of planning continued to underlie and often overshadow much of what actually took place in it. Thus, and as different as the discourse of planning might have been in the social studies methods course, its prominence within the course, regardless of form, ultimately contributed to the dominance of the discourse of planning and organization throughout the UWC Teacher Education Program, legitimating its supremacy in the process of learning to teach.

This became apparent from the outset. The language of planning was introduced to students in the first class as they were presented with an overview outlining the rationale, goals, and objectives of the social studies methods course itself. Those focused primarily on students setting goals and devising units for instruction and methods of assessment and evaluation to reflect and assess those goals. Using such terms both as the topic of inquiry and a lens with which to inquire, students devoted most of the second and third classes to examine the goals and objectives, the prescribed learning outcomes, the instructional strategies to fulfill those learning outcomes, and the strategies for assessment and evaluation advocated in the Social Studies Curriculum Guide of the province. With a continued focus on instructional planning, Simon presented students in the fourth class with two documents. The first, a chart entitled "Learning to Instruct," was divided into seven columns, each categorized by one of the following: students' prior knowledge and beliefs; main idea (theme, problem, issue); rationale; goals for the course; objectives for the unit and lessons; activities; learning resources; and assessment and evaluation strategies. The second document, "Scenes from the French Revolution," was an activity Simon had conducted with his own grade nine students several years earlier. Putting students in groups to think about the second document in terms of the categories presented in the first, Simon explained:

> The key things that I am interested in discussing right here are the goals and objectives . . . and some learning resources, and crucially, the assessment and evaluation strategies. And what I'd like to do is to see how the goals and objectives that you have thought through and the activities that are implied in this [document] and the assessment and evaluation strategies which you have thought of, how those fit together. . . . I am particularly interested [in] focus[ing] on the goals and objectives: how those mesh with these activities that are outlined here and what kinds of assessment and evaluation you think would be appropriate for measuring whether you have been successful in those goals.

As students gathered back from their group activity, Simon made what I found to be a rather telling comment: "If you can make goals and objectives which are linked to the activity [and] which can then be assessed in a reasonable way tied to those goals and objectives, *then you can teach.* That's the centerpiece of this" (my emphasis).

The pattern of engaging issues/topics in social studies education and framing them immediately thereafter within the discourse of planning as the ultimate, final, and concluding purpose for their engagement was a recurring pattern throughout the course. Dealing with primary sources, for example, led directly to an assignment to create a lesson plan centering around a question sequence in which high school students would engage that source. The geography section in the course (the geography "unit," as students referred to it)—one of the three major components of the course together with history and media—was also centered around planning a unit for instruction. Using a proposed plan to convert some of the endowed forestland surrounding UWC into a residential area, students developed a set of goals for a unit focusing on urban development. Each group of students was then responsible for constructing one of the lessons comprising that unit, including the articulation of objectives and assessment.

Further, while many in-class discussions were conducted, for example, on the nature of history and social studies or the production, mediation, and interpretation of textual representations, what students were actually evaluated on had less to do with any of those or other discussions (or the course readings leading to those discussions) but with lesson and unit plans. The evaluation of students was based primarily on three assignments, all of which focused on planning—setting goals and objectives and assessing their attainment during evaluation. The first of those assignments required students to design a lesson around the use of a primary historical source. The second assignment asked students to create a unit plan, paying special attention to "consistency among rationale, objectives, resources, activities and assessment" (Course outline).[2] The third assignment was the final exam, which consisted of three questions, two of which focused on planning. The first of those questions asked students to choose one of six provided primary documents (sources) and explain where and how it might be used to achieve certain goals and objectives. The second required students to choose one of eight given topics and design a unit of instruction around it. That is, to "define four to seven student learning objectives that you would pursue in a unit on this topic. Then describe the way you would assess students' attainment of those objectives. The assessment(s) should include specific criteria and should be directly linked to the objectives you defined." **[ST¶ Simon:** *I shaped assessment in this course to practices which teachers would need to master in order to teach well. Their ability to write a prose essay about their purposes for teaching would not, I believe, be an adequate* *measure of their competence. Ironically, the grounds on which you object to this assessment are that it does not assess what should have been the goals of the course (i.e., to have students think more critically about the nature of history, media representations, etc.). But such an argument would still be grounded in the very discourse that you are attempting to criticize.* **Avner**: *Your comment undoubtedly exposes the inconsistencies of any method of critique and the implication of critique with that which it critiques. I do believe that writing a prose essay about the purposes of teaching or the nature of history and representation and connecting that to what can be done in the classroom when history as representation is encountered (and when is it not?) can be a beneficial exercise both in theory and in practice as well as in theorizing practice, even if it is practice they themselves have yet to experience as teachers. I do believe that the purpose of teacher education is to provide structure for meta-thinking about practice as one constructs practice rather than simply practicing (in the sense of repetitive preparation) for (future) practice.]* (I discuss this issue more fully in Chapter Eight.)

Assuming the final evaluation of any course would measure what it considered most significant [as well as recalling Simon's earlier comment to students that "if you can do well on this exam, it means that you, in some way, will do well in the social studies class over a period of time," or that "if a student does well on the final exam that means they're prepared to start the process of teaching social studies"], I wanted to learn what messages students were given by the final exam about what it means to be, or what one needs to know, in order to become a social studies teacher. **[ST¶ Simon**: *If the assessment does not meet these criteria then there is a serious disjunction between the course and the school. Again, I don't see any other accessible ideal. In fact, the problem with too much teacher education is the disjunction between program task/ thinking and school task/thinking.* **Jack**: *I think Simon makes a good point. The tasks students are asked to do in the program should relate directly to what they do as teachers in schools. There must be a limit to theory!]*

Rather than simply have students tell me about the final exam or what the exam asked them to do, I was interested in having students read it as a text; that is, for what it was telling them through what it was asking of them. Without exception, all six participants shared the view that the final exam sent a clear message that what seems to be most important for social studies teachers is the ability to devise lesson and unit plans and ensure that one's assessment is connected to one's goals and objectives. According to Jack, this exam implied that what a social studies teacher needs to know most is how "to put together meaningful units and problems and themes for students, [and to ensure] that our assessment matches our objectives when we're creating a unit, that we're assessing the right thing."

The final exam, Jocelyn added, was designed to evaluate "whether or not we can take a topic and derive a set of objectives from that topic and assess those objectives." For Casey, the exam was an indication that prospective teachers "need to construct lesson plans with clear goals and objectives and be able to assess those lesson plans accordingly." But contrary to Jack and Jocelyn, who stated that in spite of the message coming out of the final exam the methods course also emphasized other—more important—aspects of social studies education (i.e., reading and writing texts, framing topics as public issues, and engaging students with multiple perspectives), when I asked Casey if she could think of anything more important about teaching social studies the final exam did not give her an opportunity to illustrate or discuss, her response, in many ways reflecting those of the remaining participants, was, "No. Nothing that I can think of." While other conversations with Casey and the remaining three participants illustrated that they all thought the methods course offered much more than a practice in planning, Casey's response—that she could think of nothing more important than the ability to plan units and lessons where goals and objectives tie to strategies of assessment and evaluation—gives some indication as to the power and effect of the discourse of planning, regardless of form, on student teachers' imagination. By the end of the first semester at UWC, at least four of the six participants were so caught up in the discourse of planning and organization that they found it difficult to think beyond it.

Planning: The Language of (Im)possibility

The numerous activities and assignments involving planning to instruct in the various courses in the program, and the discourse used as those were carried out, all provided students, to borrow from Foucault (1977), a "definition of a legitimate perspective . . . and the fixing of norms for the elaboration of concepts and theories" (p. 199). Their effect: making it virtually impossible for prospective teachers to think outside of them. As prospective teachers engaged the discourse of planning and organization, they also learned, to use Scholes (1985), "how to produce a specific kind of discourse . . . which requires [them] to be constituted as the subject of that discourse in a particular way and to speak through that discourse of a world made by the same controlling paradigm" (pp. 131–132; cf. Cherryholmes, 1988, p. 158). Embroiled so deeply in the discourse of planning, student teachers, as I will show, were no longer "merely located within the structure of language and the signifying system but, rather, [became] their effect (McLaren & Lankshear 1993, p. 385. See also Gee, 1987, 1990; Gee & Green, 1998).

As a result, by the second week of the program, students already had terms used in the discourse of planning and organization on the tips of their tongues. "Objectives," "goals," and "assessment strategies" were words they continuously invoked, not so much in order to engage a serious debate about teaching but as the embodiment of teaching itself, a way of speaking about teaching that no longer required a critical engagement with its underpinnings or with its consequences. As groups of students were working through the various tasks and assignments given by Simon—most often pertaining to the construction of an activity or part of a lesson or unit—much of the discussion in those groups revolved around determining whether a particular point or statement they wanted to incorporate was a goal or an objective. Often, these lengthy debates had to be resolved by seeking arbitration from another group so as to ensure that the ultimate "sin" of confusing goals with objectives (and vice versa) was never committed.

Intrigued by the degree to which students had become preoccupied with those terms so early on in the program, at how pervasive they had become in student teachers' discourse, and at how central they were in their thinking about teaching, I used the third set of interviews to ask how, if at all, such terms become important, beneficial in learning to teach, and what, in the process, do they enable and/or disable. Subverting my question and exposing its faulty supposition, Ron responded swiftly, "It's not an issue whether *we* think they are important; we are being *told* they are important." The difference between what students are told to think and the thinking that is a consequence of such telling was not as discernible to other participants. While none fully embraced those terms or the discourse of planning of which they are part, Ron was the only one who not only rejected what the use of those terms enabled but also raised the issue of that which was being disabled:

Both in the program and among ourselves, we talk all the time about goals and objectives and criteria [for assessment] and we're always worried about establishing the objectives and the criteria and also have our profs clearly lay out their criteria [for assignments] for us. But where have we actually talked about our own personal, philosophical goals and objectives—what we're trying to achieve as teachers and for ourselves as persons, as people who have something to contribute to society? We haven't really.

Though clearly objecting to the overuse (and the kind of use) of the discourse of planning and organization and the practices that accompanied it within the program, Ron uses terms from the very discourse he was attempting to resist in order to illustrate that resistance. In doing so, the word "goals" becomes both an object of critique and an opening of possibilities. In other words, even as he objects to that discourse, Ron finds it necessary to use it. "The discourse of critique" then, as this example provides and as Tyler (1991) explains, "is already and inextricably involved in what it criticizes"; it is already "committed to it, involved in it, and emasculated by its own desire to expose and correct, to prescribe and domesticate" (p. 91; see also Derrida, 1978, pp. 280–281).

Other participants, however, did not perceive the use and consequences of this discourse as problematically as Ron did. Unlike him, most explained the importance of, and the benefits provided by, these terms, even as they attempted to question them. While their questions provide interesting insights into the problematics of using some of the terms comprising the discourse of planning and organization, it is through their endorsements that one begins to gain a clearer picture as to the understandings they derived from the UWC Teacher Education Program about the purpose of clarifying goals and objectives in the process of instruction.

Echoing views held by the majority of student teachers participating in this study, Jocelyn spoke of the significance of learning, learning about, and using terms such as goals and objectives in education:

They're important for us in order to understand what it is that we're trying to do. If we don't have a clear understanding of what it is that we're trying to do then we really have no way of deciding whether or not we have accomplished what we've set out to do. We don't have any way of going back and asking, "What was it that I was trying to do and was that a good thing to do, was it valid and can I defend it?" So in that sense, before we even embark on a path, it's good to have some learning outcome or objective in mind. . . . [It] allows us to revisit what we had planned and ask, "Why did I choose that, what did that say about me or my perspectives at the time?" But that's not really essential. What's essential for us is to have an idea of where we started and what we intended to do so that when we get there, we can assess whether where we are at now is really where we wanted to be. [ST¶ **Jocelyn**: *I think this quote reveals my struggle to absorb a new language—to understand it before I begin deconstructing it.*]

Jack, too, thought the language of planning helped "in terms of learning how to build a framework [in order] to initially think about something." But while he mentioned the enabling side of the encounter with those terms, he explained they may also be restricting,

> because your activities have to relate back to your objectives and how do you know what . . . I mean if you're trying to get a student involved in a certain issue, then . . . if you're limiting yourself to the specific objectives you have laid out in your unit plan, then you'll also be limiting students in what they can learn at the same time.

Jocelyn and Jack highlight different aspects of the discourse of planning to teach—one its possibilities, the other its problematics. Yet their different perspectives demonstrate inherently similar understandings about the role goals and objectives play in the educative process. Both ultimately see the construction of goals and objectives as the guiding force, somewhat of a superstructure that directs (and therefore also limits) instruction and, at the same time, provides a way to evaluate it. Having what seems to be a life of their own once they are established, goals and objectives become the definers of instruction—limiting the possibilities of instruction beyond their original framing, in Jack's case, and providing a perspective from which to evaluate what one has accomplished, in Jocelyn's case. Rather than simply being a way of thinking about and organizing instruction in the direction one desires and abandoning them as soon as they become a hindrance to what one believes must take precedence as the educational endeavor unfolds—even if and even as what unfolds does not correspond to what was initially planned—the versions presented above see goals and objectives as authoritative structures to which teachers become responsible and accountable. Goals and objectives are no longer beneficial tools to think about and enable instruction but the very means to "understand what it is we're trying to do." **[ST¶ Jocelyn**: *This terminology was merely a tool for me. I did question the use of objectives and the rigidity of the* POT *class demanding one objective per concept. It is a way to "a tool" for comprehension; it's not comprehension itself.*]

The responsibility of teachers, it seems, is toward their own goals and objectives. What matters most, in the minds of these students, is that the end of the educational interaction corresponds with the goals and objectives determined at the outset, regardless of what those initial goals and objectives sought to accomplish. Jocelyn believed they allow teachers to revisit what they had planned and ask, "Why did I choose that, what did it say about me or my perspectives at the time?"; however, those questions, while perhaps beneficial, "are not really essential." Again, goals and objectives are no longer a reflexive way to evaluate what it is teachers chose to advance through their teaching and ask why they chose that particular topic in that particular way, what (and who) did that enable, what (and who) did it disable, and what does that tell about my own teaching, about myself as a teacher, about the structures in which I operate that lead me to advance such knowledge and knowing. The ability to revisit one's goals and objectives and examine the above-mentioned issues seems unimportant to Jocelyn at this point. This, of course, is not surprising since, as Ron noted earlier, little emphasis was put on those kinds of questions in much of this teacher education program. Instead, and in accordance with what *was* promoted in the program, Jocelyn stated that goals and objectives allow teachers to "have an idea of where we started and what we intended to do so that when we get there, we can assess whether where we are is really where we wanted to be." What Jocelyn says makes perfect sense, yet I question her use of the word "wanted." It is her use of the past tense that becomes problematic. According to Jocelyn, goals and objectives are not intended to measure whether where teachers are is where they want to be—a question every teacher must ask as he/she evaluates what has been accomplished as a way of looking to the future, to educational endeavors still to come. Rather, the use of the word "wanted" (in the past tense) indicates that goals and objectives are not as much used to examine where teachers want to be as they go ahead but rather whether where they are is where they initially wanted to be when their journey began. While this may seem no more than an issue of semantics, the difference is primarily pedagogical. The former looks forward, the latter backward. The past tense indicates a reflection rather than a projection; a way of examining correspondence to one's starting point, not a way of looking at where one actually is in the present, where one ought to be in the future. [ST¶ **Jocelyn**: *You cannot have reflection without "projection." In planning a unit, a lesson, even an objective, we are projecting. We haven't tried to go anywhere yet, but we plan to. Only then can we reflect on the process—once it's happened.*]

Rationale, goals, and objectives are terms educators often invoke as substitutes for questions such as: "*Why* am I doing this?" "Why am I doing *this*?" "Why am I doing it *this way*?" What needs to be asked in the context of a teacher education program is whether the way students are made to use those terms actually enables them to ask those questions while using their substitutes. Or does the use of those stand-ins actively work to obscure the possibility of having those questions asked? Indeed, can the use/overuse of these technical terms—often not actually thought about and thought through—still address the questions they initially intend to represent? Embroiled in the technical language of the discourse of planning and preoccupied with correctly articulating goals and objectives, those "why" questions often get left behind, silenced, pushed to the margins of student teachers' thinking.

Two examples serve to illustrate that point. The first derives from Jocelyn's response to a question about which courses she found most beneficial in the teacher education program and why. "The social studies methods course and my English methods course were f-a-n-t-a-s-t-i-c," she replied.

> Both instructors showed an incredible passion for what they were doing and in-depth understanding, and they had a vision and they had a purpose. I may have not always agreed with their purposes but they had a purpose, they communicated this clearly, and they went about to accomplish that purpose, their task. So I found those wonderful.

Apparently, it is not the kinds of goals and objectives presented and pursued in these two courses that brought about Jocelyn's recognition but rather the very existence of goals and objectives, the ability of the instructors to communicate them clearly and to continuously pursue them to the end. Though Jocelyn stated that she did not always agree with the purposes presented in those two courses, it seemed superfluous for this otherwise thoughtful student teacher to engage the why questions embedded in such purposes when there were purposes to state and tasks to accomplish. **[ST¶ Jocelyn**: *It wasn't that simple, Avner. If I have something to work with and question, then I'm satisfied—I can ask questions, I can try things on my own, I can learn myself. If I have no content, I feel lost. For example, in adolescent psychology, we read about and analyze case studies regarding students at a particular stage in their development. It was all speculation. Some students may feel this, some students may react that way; what would you do if . . . ? These were not helpful concepts, as every child is different, every class unique, and what I'd do today may not be the same as what I do tomorrow. The methods course had content and I could agree or disagree/engage or disengage in that content. I had a choice!*] Inspirational teaching is thus not measured by the philosophical, epistemological, or pedagogical issues underlying instruction—that is, whether one agrees with what is being done or not—but by the ability to pursue instruction, regardless of its consequences, its moral, ethical, or pedagogical implications. (By that, of course, I do not imply that the goals and objectives in either of the methods courses were any of the above but rather that such questions must drive one's relationship to the goals and objectives set out in those courses rather than the ability of instructors to simply accomplish them.)

The second example, again one from an interview with Jocelyn, comes from an exchange we had about another social studies methods course (*Curriculum and Instruction in Canadian Studies*) she took during the summer. Discussing that course, Jocelyn explained that the instructor regularly

> brought in *tons* of resources and said: "Here's a way that I've done it. How would you go about doing it?" He gave us a lot of opportunities for discussion and group work. . . . Sometimes he did that and sometimes he just gave us an assignment, like, "You *have* to teach *this*. What would you do?"

> Avner: Did you ever talk about why it is you had to teach that "this"?

> Jocelyn: No, we never did. Sometimes we would go off on a tangent when somebody would say they wouldn't use it at all and then we'd talk about why.

Preoccupied with devising strategies for teaching "something" and planning how to teach that "something," little time was left to examine the "why" questions I referred to earlier. Considered unimportant, perhaps, such questions were either never engaged, or at best, when they were, their consideration was thought of as "going off on a tangent," never the main route—the avenue on which a social studies methods curriculum and instruction course ought to embark. Not asking the "why" questions, teaching becomes what Popkewitz (1987) identifies as "the representation of stable elements in the curriculum." And "once content is identified," Popkewitz adds, "the instructional problem is to develop effective strategies by which to inscribe that content on . . . students." A teacher's responsibility is thus "functional, and it is technically defined" (p. 290).

The Discourse of Planning and Organization
and the Image of "Good" Teaching

It could, of course, be argued that it was not the discourse of planning and organization in the teacher education program that instilled in students the idea that teaching is fundamentally about lesson and unit plans, about coming up with appropriate goals and objectives but, rather, that students came into the program with those ideas already in mind, hence, fitting into the understandings students already had and the ideas to which they previously subscribed. While there is no doubt some truth in such claims (see Britzman, 1991; Ginsburg, 1988), student teachers' idea of what constituted good teaching at the beginning of the program appears to have had little to do with the notion of planning and organization. And yet, those were clearly stamped all over it by the program's end.

When asked at the beginning of the program what makes a good teacher or what, in their thinking, constituted good teaching, students' responses were as removed from the discourse of planning and organization as possible. In his response, Charles chose to remember a community college instructor who taught him prior to coming to UWC. "She was really lively and had a lot of energy," he said. "You could tell she really liked what she was doing and that got us involved, kept us interested. She was nice. She talked to us out of class and stuff like that. She was really good. I really enjoyed her class." Ron spoke of relevancy and interest. "Good teaching," according to him, was about

> bringing a relevance and immediacy to the subject matter; having a reason for what you're doing and making students aware of that reason (i.e., why we should or why we would want to study history or geography, or the economy, or political science). Being willing to participate in the learning process itself, that [is], the teacher should be able to learn as much from the students as the students learn from the teacher.

Jocelyn claimed that what makes a good teacher is the ability to integrate things and bridge subject matter to real life, to students' lives:

> To be able to show relevance and not keep the subject merely as a "subject," apart from life and having no bearing on life. A good teacher also needs to be concerned, to really care about what you're teaching and about the students you're teaching to. I think that's vitally important because students notice if the teacher doesn't care and that just puts them right off, at least that's the way I reacted. So, I guess what's important is to have concern, enthusiasm, and passion for what you do but not go over the top, not be too gregarious. You are not there to entertain, although that helps.

Casey emphasized the caring aspect of teaching—both about one's subject area and one's students. According to her, a good teacher was

> someone who cares about the subject they're teaching; someone who . . . gets the kids involved and actually thinking about what's going on and not just giving

them information and having them regurgitate it back. Someone who believes in teaching and who cares about the students.

To understand what good teaching meant to these same students at the end of the teacher education program (and, interested as I was in how the teacher education program positioned them to think about good teaching in particular ways), I asked participants what they thought good teaching meant at the very institution in (and through) which they were to construct images of good teaching. Hoping to engage students not with what they had been told good teaching was during their different courses at UWC, but rather with the messages they received as to what the UWC College of Education itself considers good teaching in its own instructors, I focused participants' attention to the evaluation forms they were asked to fill out at the end of every course at UWC. As a summative form of evaluation, created by the college itself, the SCETs (Standing Committee on the Evaluation of Teaching) not only ask students to evaluate university instructors' teaching but, by asking specific questions about some aspects of teaching and not about others, also send students both explicit and implicit messages as to what constitutes good teaching.

To find out what those messages might be, I asked participants what the numerous (close to 20) SCETs they had filled out throughout the program put forward as good teaching. That is: What does the College of Education at UWC think is important enough to ask course participants to measure? Since the issue was not to examine student teachers' ability to actually read the form but rather to examine the accumulative effect of those forms, I did not bring an actual SCET to these interviews. Instead, I asked student teachers to read them from memory. Not having an actual SCET with which to do the reading did not seem to pose a problem. I soon learned, as Casey, the first student I interviewed in that round, said with a chuckle, "I've done so many of them, I don't need the form. [By this time in the program], I know it almost by heart." What is it then that Casey and the other participants "knew"?

The teacher education program at UWC, no doubt, supported and encouraged each and every one of the attributes of good teaching students mentioned as they entered the program. That aspect of the program was recognized by all of the participants in this study. Yet while students' comments about what attributes UWC valued most according to the evaluation sheets (SCETs) included many of the attributes they themselves stated at the beginning of the program, they now all mentioned one more—organization. Not only was organization included in the list; it topped it. Four of the five students asked[3] ranked organization as the most important issue asked about or reflected in the UWC SCET forms (the fifth student put organization in second place), with "preparedness" coming in a close second.

What Mary remembered most from the SCETS was that, as a good teacher, "you have to be organized, you have to be prepared, willing to answer questions, be available." Jack responded by saying that the SCET "asks about the organization of the course. It asks students about the motivation of the instructor and their interests and how they presented themselves, not in terms of clothes but how they spoke and things of that nature." Jocelyn, in a similar fashion, said that the SCETs ask the following about teachers: "Are they organized; are they prepared; do they present materials in an interesting and intriguing way; are their assignments helpful." Casey was the only one who did not put organization at the top her memory list. For her it was: "Content, organization, being in tune with students' needs, being interesting, having knowledge of what you're teaching." Putting organization back at the top of the list, the first thing that came to Ron's mind as he tried to recollect what the SCETs were about was: "Was the teacher well organized? Did the teacher respect students' opinions? Was the teacher interesting? Was the course material relevant? [long pause] I can't remember more than that, and yet that would make a very interesting text, wouldn't it?" Indeed it does.

Interestingly, although participants thought organization/the need to be organized the number one (or two) characteristic of a good teacher according to the SCETs, when one examines an actual SCET form it becomes apparent that only 2 of its 30 questions deal directly with organization—one about the organization of the course as a whole, the other about the organization of class presentations in the course. The message about the importance of organization was therefore something student teachers projected on the SCETs rather than something they actually found in them. While speaking about the importance of organization in the SCETs, they were actually speaking about its importance in the program as a whole, the very program the SCETs are intended to evaluate. In a program that continuously invoked the discourse of planning and organization and one in which planning and organization were also the object of study while using such a discourse, students simply (and not uncharacteristically) reversed the evaluating measure with the object of its evaluation.

The notion of organization, then, generated by the activities done in class and the assignments students were required to produce in class, also became the implicit message about the instrument of evaluation—how students evaluated the program, how they thought the program evaluates itself, and, ultimately, how they evaluated themselves as teachers. Or was it that the idea of organization was so embedded in the way prospective teachers were taught that when asked by the end of the program to read the SCETs, organization had already become the only organizing discourse through which they could read them, the only language with which they could speak about them? Regardless, the consequence is identical. Whether it was the SCETs or the teacher education program as a whole, organization and the importance of being organized were undoubtedly what this group of student teachers received as the predominant message about what counts for quality teaching.

But the impact of such an understanding was not only on how student teachers viewed good teaching at UWC. It also impacted the way they thought about teaching in general and their own teaching in particular. When I asked Jack at the beginning of the program what, in his view, makes a good teacher, he said it would be someone who challenges kids, someone who "turn[s] on the light and makes sure the kids sit there and learn something not because they'll get tested on it or because they'll get into trouble if they don't, but because they become passionate about the issues they are being taught."

In a conversation we had during the practicum, Jack said that he felt a lot of pressure to be a "good" teacher. I asked, "What is a good teacher?" Jack responded, "To be organized . . . to have something planned that engages students, that keeps them busy for an hour." Although he immediately qualified his statement by adding that "keeping them busy" entails "keeping them doing something worthwhile and thinking and that keeps everyone engaged for an hour," the initial requirement—what first sprang to his mind about "good" teaching, his own good teaching—was an image of organization, of being organized.

When I asked Mary at the beginning of the program what she thought were the attributes of a good teacher, she responded by saying that it is someone who is a facilitator more than a lecturer. Someone who "facilitates students' own decision making by presenting them with the necessary facts and figures and then helps them make their own decisions." In a later conversation, when a similar question came up, Mary added that she thought good teachers

> educate kids not to think only one way by introducing them to controversial issues because [presenting issues to students in such a manner] . . . makes them think in more than one way. If students look at a controversial issue and can't understand why it's controversial, then we haven't done our job. As educators, our goal is to make these kids think . . . teach them how to think so that they can solve

not only the problems that we give them but the problems that life gives them. And by looking at controversial issues, I mean, that's perfect, isn't it? It's philosophy and it's moral studies, and, my gosh, it's everything rolled into one.

Visiting Mary several months later in her practicum classroom and talking to her after observing a few of her classes, I asked her to tell me of a lesson or a unit she was particularly proud of, and why. Mary chose to describe a lesson—a problematic one in her view—that she had just concluded with her grade 11 students. Learning about Canadian society at the turn of the century, and specifically the section in the history textbook that dealt with immigration at the time, Mary's class engaged issues of racism through the exploration of immigration policy at the beginning of the century and then connected those to current immigration policies and the kinds of immigration policies her own students thought should be implemented in Canada today. Exploring immigration policies as a political, economic, and cultural issue, always embedded in controversy and change, Mary had her students, working in groups, role-play and advocate a variety of perspectives, many of which students personally opposed, in order to critically understand the motives that led to the establishment of specific (and often racist) immigration policies at different times in Canadian history. Interestingly, Mary said, she found that while many of the students in her classroom criticized the restricting policies imposed on minority immigrants entering Canada since its beginnings as a nation, many similar restrictions—an immigration fee, a head tax, or the need to be proficient in English prior to immigration—were apparent in the immigration policies her own students (mostly non-white and immigrants themselves) were advocating for today.

True to her own definitions of good teaching, Mary did not lecture nor tell her students what to think. She engaged her students with a public issue that was not only controversial but was also made so in the classroom—with and by students. She also ensured that students "don't see things only one way" by having them both advocate and oppose a variety of perspectives often different than their own. But when I asked Mary why she was particularly proud of this specific lesson, she said,

Well, it was well organized. Nothing caught me off guard. They were stimulated. They were *very* actively engaged. Everybody was on task. They liked it and that's hard to do, that is, give them something they like to do. It met all of my objectives. It just worked out really well.

Although Mary incorporated all of what she believed constituted good teaching at the beginning of her teacher education program, when she tried to explain why she was proud of this one particular lesson, she said: "It was well organized." Mary was not particularly proud of the time spent on dealing with "official" racism and an important public policy issue. Nor was she especially proud of introducing students to a controversial issue and making them think "both ways," although those were exactly the things she did. What became the prized object of good teaching was the fact that everything was well organized, that students were on task, that they were actively engaged, that she had met all of her own initial objectives.

How is it, then, that in spite of all the efforts put forward by many (perhaps most) involved in this teacher education program to enable students to imagine otherwise, organization emerged as its prized attribute? Or, to put it more boldly, what is it that went awry in this teacher education program that at its conclusion, what students believed this program values, above anything else, is organization?

The message of organization as the panacea for good teaching was obviously transmitted to students in a variety of ways, mostly, as I have argued, through the discourse of planning and organization that ultimately overruled various other discourses that might have positioned students to think otherwise. And while I have focused much of my attention on how that discourse influenced students' thinking in the direction of what they ultimately found, when I spoke to Jocelyn about it she mentioned another aspect, another level of influence I had neglected to consider. It pertained not only to the kind of discourse with which students were engaged or the kinds of assignments they were asked to produce but to their very being in the teacher education program. The whole program inculcates organization, Jocelyn said.

> You have to juggle six courses in the first semester, you have to do this in your practicum, and you have to come back in the summer and juggle some more. And you have to have 9,000 assignments that are due and they're all due at different dates and you have to keep this organized and that organized. If you're not organized, it's a lot more work. So I think the whole program inculcates that.

Organization was thus not only a discursive practice that affected how one thinks about what is being studied; it also became a way of *being* in a program that provided a framework from which to begin one's thinking about what is studied. In other words, one needed to be organized in order to even begin thinking about what it was one ought to have organized. Organization was therefore not merely an epistemological and/or pedagogical aspect of this program but also an ontological one.

Immersed in this triple bind, it is not surprising that when this group of students read the SCET forms, organization emerged as that which the

UWC Teacher Education Program valued most. And while organization was by no means the only attribute of good teaching they mentioned, when one takes a closer look at their lists, what seems equally interesting and/or alarming is not only what students included in those lists but also what they did not. I will begin with what they did. Besides organization, which appeared to top the list, there were other—and I would argue more significant—aspects of good teaching mentioned as well. Those included (in order of ranking): being prepared, motivated, interesting, intriguing, relevant, helpful, available, in tune with students' needs and respectful of their opinions, and willing to answer students' questions. What was most striking for me, however, was not what found its way onto their lists about what this teacher education program valued most but what did not. For while all of the above are important attributes any good teacher should strive for, one ought to question a teacher education program whose students, only a week from graduation, mention no aspect of teaching that moves beyond the delivery of content or the technical aspects of teaching. None of the students mentioned ethics. None mentioned equal opportunity, equity, and social justice. None mentioned questioning, challenge, reform, and change. None mentioned thinking critically about one's world. In short, none said anything about education as a political and social endeavor for making the world more of what they themselves (and many instructors in the program) had said they wanted it to be—more democratic, equitable, inclusive, and just. Instead, it all came down to the technology of teaching and the performance of governance and organization, which, by its very (political) nature leaves many other discourses beyond the limits of its imagination, exploration, and articulation. Indeed, as Banks and Parker (1990) caution, "by narrow attention to questions of what methods are most effective, focus is fixed on the means, or technology, of teaching and kept away from questions that could change the status quo" (p. 682). [ST¶ **Jack**: *After one and a half years of teaching experience at the intermediate and secondary level in social studies, I would have to say that the single most important key to success is being well organized. This is not to suggest that other things are not also very important. However, I am so busy at my school with teaching, administration, and extracurricular responsibilities, that I need to be very organized. Perhaps it is the nature of the profession that led the program to emphasize this skill or characteristic.*]

Chapter Five

Critical Thinking and Thinking Critically in Learning to Teach: A Tale of Contradictions

Prevalent within the explicit curricula of the different courses comprising the teacher education program at the University of Western Canada and the discussions taking place within them was a discourse that stood at the cusp of educational innovation. Eschewing the traditional teacher-centered approach underlying existing school practices where unquestioned knowledge is transmitted to (mostly passive) students, this discourse called for learning based in inquiry and discovery, where students get to actively and critically question the knowledge they encounter and produce in (and, as a result, hopefully also out of) classrooms. This was particularly the case in the social studies methods course, entitled *Social Studies as Reading and Writing Texts*. There, a questioning stance toward (or an ability to critically read—i.e., question) curricular texts was advanced as a method of moving social education beyond its heavy present-day reliance on memorization and regurgitation, with the purpose of fostering a citizenry able and inclined to critically read and write their world.

One of the approaches most frequently considered a pillar of such a vision within this teacher education program was critical thinking—referred to in most of its courses not simply as an arsenal of predefined steps and procedures to assess the validity of a given statement but an umbrella term for "quality thinking" (Case, Daniels, & Schwartz, 1996). This form of critical thinking, it was argued, should be used to question the assumptions and values embedded in messages conveyed through curricular and other texts brought into the classroom. As critical thinking was incorporated into almost every course, often to a point of redundancy (Case et al.'s article was assigned in three of the program's six courses during the first semester), students soon became suspicious that its widespread inclusion was the result of nothing less than a conspiracy orchestrated from above. "Why else could they all be focusing on critical thinking," asked Mary, "unless somebody had been talking about it at some meeting somewhere along the line? Either that, or it's a buzzword in the industry. I just don't know which." Although the appearance of the same reading in three different courses might refute the conspiracy theory (unless, that is, we give the conspirators more credit than they deserve), what ought to be examined is the relationship between what Mary termed the well-orchestrated effort to parade critical thinking so prominently and the possibility that critical thinking might be considered more of a buzzword in teacher education than a method governing its own practices, a tool made possible to those learning to teach in order to think critically about it.

To pursue that possibility, this chapter examines how, when, and where critical thinking and thinking critically—often as separate methodologies—were engaged in this teacher education program. I conduct that analysis at two different levels, each with its own constituency and purpose in mind. The first focuses on student teachers' ability to create learning environments that initiate, maintain, and foster critical thinking with their future students in school. The second explores student teachers' ability to think critically *themselves* about the content and context of their own learning in teacher education, making pedagogical connections between how the ways one teaches and learns structure and determine what is learned. The former externalizes learning in teacher education for its application elsewhere—in schools; the latter connects the process of learning about teaching at the university with how one might be positioned to teach in that elsewhere of schools. The difference, then, pertains not only to who should be thinking critically and where but, resulting from their integration, also to the substance of critical thinking. The distinction I propose for this analysis is not meant as an endorsement of that separation but as a strategic tool in order to problematize it. Its utility as a method of inquiry derives from the fact that it represents and follows the inherent complexity of teacher education, which, through a double helix, does not simply teach prospective teachers how to teach others but also, and simultaneously, through the explicit and implicit messages embedded in the process of learning to teach, teaches them what it means to teach and be taught.

Levels of (Dis)engagement

Throughout his teacher education program—as student and teacher—Jack saw critical thinking as the panacea for many of the current ills of education. Critical thinking was a way of enabling students to become what Jack called "thinkers," questioning rather than accepting predefined, textbook answers. A "thinker" himself, though, Jack was at times confused about the manner with which critical thinking was engaged in his own teacher education program. Crediting, for example, the social studies methods course for highlighting critical thinking as an important, necessary, and powerful teaching tool for students in schools, Jack had reservations as to how it was used as a learning tool for student teachers in that course. "Interestingly," Jack commented,

> while as student teachers we are asked to ensure our students think critically, we've done very little critical thinking ourselves in the methods course. We haven't really analyzed approaches to anything. We read all these articles in which we're being told which approaches to use in the classroom: like to think critically about historical texts or "What is history?" but we don't really . . . we aren't really able [given encouragement? permission?] to criticize the content of what we're reading. It's like we're not really practicing it.

Jack's critique begins to shed light on how critical thinking was and was not engaged in the methods course—when it was (not) used, with whom, and for what purposes. But Jack's account tells only part of the story. In contrast, Jocelyn believed the methods course provided a wide range of opportunities for student teachers not only to talk about critical thinking but to actually experience it. "Simon's approach," Jocelyn offered,

> is very different than the traditional read-out-of-the-textbook, memorize, do the questions at the end. He's really tried to promote critical thinking and he's really tried to promote high order thinking. I think his premise is that it can happen at any grade level; that it should start at the earliest grade level possible and should continue on through and that that's part of our job as social studies teachers. So I think that part has been really good, especially because his activities have also promoted critical thinking within us and have given us lots of opportunities to engage in critical thinking. I think his hope is that if we are critical thinkers then our courses will be and if our courses are based on critical thought that will encourage critical thinking in our students.
>
> Avner: How has Simon done this? How has he focused on critical thinking?
>
> Jocelyn: Well, the way he structures his classes and the way he structures his activities for the class. They are all based on critical thought. I mean the readings that he asks us to read as well are all . . . I mean the Roland Case article and others. I just think that he encourages it in his materials and everything he does or the assignments that he gives, the questions that he poses. They're all open-ended and higher-order thinking questions.

Speaking on the same day, Jack and Jocelyn tell very different stories about whether or not the social studies methods course encouraged its student teachers to think critically. The difference between these two versions, however, stems not from the fact that they are two opposing points of view about a similar course, but rather because each addresses a different level of critical thinking which was (or was not) engaged in it. Jocelyn emphasizes the fact that Simon created a learning environment that stressed both the need for student teachers to create opportunities for their own students to think critically and, at the same time, for student teachers to think critically themselves about the content they may be called on to teach and the pedagogy through which they were to teach that content as teachers. Jocelyn's description of the learning environment created by Simon was supported by all other five participants in this study, including Jack, who on numerous occasions expressed similar views. What Jack was addressing in this particular case, then, is not the level of critical thinking in the methods course that engaged student teachers with their future role as teachers but rather with their current role as students learning to teach. His comment refers to the level of critical thinking students were expected to assume not toward what they will teach in schools but toward what they were learning as students in this course, two roles Jack seems to think inform each other and are therefore inseparable. In other words, these two seemingly opposing stories are complementary rather than contradictory. In fact, to better understand how critical thinking was dealt with in the methods course, one needs to examine the connection between these two perspectives and how one made way for, or occupied the space of, the other.

To do so, I go back to the beginning of the methods course, to a particular class in which critical thinking was addressed specifically and for the first time. Having asked students to read an article about critical thinking (Case et al., 1996) at home, Simon chose to structure class around two activities. The first was a somewhat brief discussion of critical thinking, consisting primarily of Simon's enthusiastic endorsement of the benefits of critical thinking for education as described by the authors of that paper. **[ST¶ Avner** (to Simon): *Why did you choose to overtly support the position advocated in the article or take any position at all at the beginning of class rather than allow a discussion to unfold as you have in all other classes? Why did you not encourage students to critically think through the article itself? Did you intentionally choose to avoid a discussion as to what critical thinking is, why critical thinking is defined the way it is (rational, etc.) or who it privileges, what kinds of ways of knowing it privileges, etc.? Why did you choose not to make explicit the connections between how the definition of criti-*

cal thinking we subscribe to affects/determines what we teach, how we teach, and who we connect with (and who we ignore)? **Simon**: *Ah—wonderful. I am not going to offer a defense of what I did, rather a genealogy: How did the class come to take this form? The term "critical thinking" is ubiquitous in curriculum documents and materials, and often, I'm afraid, quite meaningless. This short article gives me a relatively simple way to present something I found meaningful to teachers and student teachers. My reading of this piece, this fall, offered more promise than either of two presentations I have heard Roland [Case] give, and certainly more promise than other definitions have offered. There are many ways to engage an article like this. One is to discuss the article itself. Another is to attempt to apply it to a lesson-planning task, and then discuss what emerges. I chose the latter, mainly because, in the short time we had, I also wanted to give the students a first experience in thinking through a lesson plan. You ask why did I choose not to make the connections between the theoretical and the pedagogical. If I understand what you mean by this dichotomy, I think that is exactly what I attempted to do, though not simply by discussing the article. Well, perhaps that is a bit of a defense after all.*] As soon as that brief discussion was over, Simon quickly oriented students toward the second part of that day's class. In it, students were to: (a) examine a social studies textbook; (b) find a topic addressed by the textbook in a way that does not require students to think critically (not too taxing a task for those who are familiar with social studies textbooks); and (c) create an activity or a mini-lesson around that particular topic that *will* engage their future students in critical thinking. As Simon began distributing the textbooks, I moved to sit with Jocelyn's group. This was the first time in many years that any of the group's four members had held a social studies textbook. Encapsulated in those textbooks were memories of days past and anxiety of those to come. Both were very evident in students' comments and body language as the two books the group had received kept changing hands. While I was disappointed that the class had moved to an activity in which critical thinking was to be applied without a sufficient discussion about what and who critical thinking does and does not enable,[1] students thought otherwise. According to Jocelyn,

> It was nice not to dwell so much on what is critical thinking—because it has already come up in a lot of my courses and I don't think it's something that can be resolved—and say, "All right, whatever we think critical thinking is, how can we encourage it with our students when we use a textbook (which often doesn't)?" So without dwelling too much on it—on the "What is it?" stuff—we actually applied it.

Tired of what student teachers often term "theory" and instead desiring the "practical," Jocelyn found it refreshing to no longer simply talk about critical thinking but actually apply it. It is difficult not to empathize when a practicum looms. The question remains: To what degree can critical thinking be applied without first understanding that which one is attempting to apply? And what does application mean in an unresolved (and, according to Jocelyn, unresolvable) context? Coming at those questions from Jocelyn's perspective more than from mine, Jack suggested two obvious benefits emanating from applying critical thinking through that activity rather than continuing to dwell on it.

> It showed us that as a good social studies teacher, you're going to have to take this book of facts and challenge students to make them use their brain rather than just memorize these chapters or just having them read those chapters and then quiz them on content. That's not good enough. And because textbooks aren't usually designed for that, you have to do it yourself and formulate questions or activities to challenge the students and force them to think so they will benefit from the course or the unit. It also established for us how we need to translate critical thinking over to our students, because while all of us in this course are familiar with it, we can't assume that the students we're going to get are going to be critical thinkers. So it was worthwhile to familiarize ourselves with the concepts, because we're going to have to instill them in our students and make sure they get transferred to them.

Anyone would be hard-pressed not to recognize the importance of that activity even if only from the lessons Jack says he was taught by it. From his evaluation, it appears that the activity did not substitute theory with application but brought theory into the open through that application, connecting what social studies teachers need to know with the "why," the "how," and the "with whom." Nevertheless, I question Jack's a priori assumption that student teachers already think critically and all they need is to learn how to translate that thinking in order to instill it in their own students, who don't. Charles's evaluation of the activity highlights the need to question that assumption.

> Charles: I thought the activity was beneficial, for sure. But I don't think it was an exercise in critical thinking for us.

> Avner: It wasn't?

> Charles: To a point. I mean I guess . . . well, maybe the two tie together . . . I guess he wanted us to learn how to translate our [critical thinking] so we'll be able to enable students to think that way about whatever text we give them.

What Charles, albeit with some difficulty, was attempting to connect are two different activities or, more accurately I believe, two interconnected sides of the same activity. The first, and the one he believed this activity did not focus on, was student teachers thinking critically themselves. The second, which he thought was emphasized, was teaching student teachers how to translate their own critical thinking (which he claimed wasn't activated) so that their students might learn to do the same. The same as what? Thinking critically as student teachers did not? Or not thinking critically as they did? While this was obviously not the intended message of the activity or the one Charles meant to convey, there's something intriguing about student teachers thinking they were not thinking critically while working on activities that were supposed to promote critical thinking in others. To be sure, and bringing into account Charles's other comments about this activity, what he meant was not that student teachers were not thinking critically as part of the activity but that they were not thinking critically *about* it. **[ST¶ Jack**: *I think we were thinking critically during that activity if thinking critically is defined as "quality thinking." We devised activities for students, then discussed their effectiveness as a group. Granted, we were not thinking critically about the benefit of the process itself.*]

This connection (or disconnection, if you will) is best demonstrated in an exchange I had with Jocelyn a day after this particular class. Recalling the difficulties Jocelyn and her group encountered in order to complete the assignment in a meaningful way in the short time allotted them, I began our conversation with a question about the activity per se.

Jocelyn: I found it difficult, very very difficult because . . . well, number one, there wasn't enough time to really look at that textbook. It was the first time I had seen that textbook and to try to determine what are its problems and what are its strengths and weaknesses, that was hard because I didn't have time to really read it. So how do I know what's good or bad about it? That was sort of a very difficult task to do. And then to pick out an activity that encourages critical thinking and develop a mini lesson plan, again, the directions [?], it was difficult in that short amount of time, but I thought it was worthwhile.

Avner: Well, I sat in on your group and I didn't hear you say any of that to your group members or in class. In fact, I didn't hear anybody else say anything to that effect in class.

Jocelyn: Well, we had a task to do. Our task was: "Do this!" Yeah, we didn't assess if this was a good task or a bad task and we didn't ask, "Why are we doing this?"

Avner: I'm confused. You are doing an activity to encourage students' critical thinking and you have critical thoughts about it, thoughts you've just expressed, and yet you thought you had to hide them or that they were irrelevant to a task of doing critical thinking?

Jocelyn: That is true. Yeah, that *is* true!

Avner: Why?

Jocelyn: Well, because we were given a task [she laughs]. It's like Pavlov's dog: "Here you go!" "Here's your stimulus, here you go!" Of course I thought all of that but I just chose not to say it. It's not that I thought it was irrelevant but I thought that the purpose wasn't for us to engage critical thinking. The purpose was to learn or think about how we can encourage our students to engage in critical thinking.

Avner: Do you think it's possible for a teacher not to engage in critical thinking and yet create opportunities for their students to engage in it?

Jocelyn: [laughs] Of course not. Even when we were discussing what we were going to do we were employing critical thinking . . . but it tells a lot. Without even knowing it, it's been inculcated in you when is a good time to question what you're doing and when is not. I mean I questioned what we were doing but I thought, "Well, OK, whatever." Simon has asked us to do this so I gave him the respect that there was some reason for doing this: "All right, we'll go with this." But of course you question that and it's almost automatic whether you voice it or not. It's inculcated in you that there are times to ask questions and there are times to voice the questions you are thinking in your head and there are times that aren't. **[ST¶ Jocelyn**: *Interesting! Now I find that some of my greatest classes come from students who are willing to question why! We are often sidetracked but this is always a pleasant surprise.*]

Avner: Was there anything in Simon's actions that sent you a message or gave you the impression that you should not be asking or voicing questions at this time and that you should just get on with doing the task?

Jocelyn: I don't know what gave me that message. I don't really know. I think maybe it wasn't even a message from him at all. Maybe it was just the nature of the classroom, the nature of education, and of my experiences in education. When a teacher asks you to do something, unless it's profoundly wrong, you do it because you assume that there's a point to this and that by doing the task you'll get to that point. It's like you become a willing participant and you give the person who is leading the benefit of the doubt that they have a place that they are going to lead you to and that you're going to get there. So when a teacher stands up and says: "OK, we're going to do this activity, here is the outline of what I want to do and we'll have a discussion afterwards, then I think, "Well, I may not agree," but the fact is they've asked me to do this so I'll do it and then maybe in the discussion we can get to some of the points I disagree with. So maybe it was my interpretation more that anything he [Simon] did or did not do. As a teacher, I would want cooperation from my students if I ask them to do something. I don't want them to ask "Why?" every minute and I don't want to spend 90% of the time explaining why and what are the reasons for what we're doing. I would hope that they would assume that I have good reason for choosing what I have. If they don't, then they can ask, but I've still got things that need to get done. So [I'll tell them], if you give me the benefit of the doubt, hopefully I'll produce for you, or you'll produce for yourselves and it will all work out. That's why I think I didn't analyze the activity. That's not what I was asked to do. I was asked to do something else. **[ST¶ Simon**: *Without this level of assent from students, it is impossible to teach: The process comes to a standstill.* **Ron**: *This is true. We do need the assent of students in order to teach. We need them to trust us. But that also denies the agency of the teacher. Don't we learn when we interrogate? And don't we learn when we are interrogated?*]

Jocelyn's comments raise a variety of issues that are fundamental to any examination of teacher education, and to this discussion in particular: How and what are student teachers positioned to learn? How is the process of coming to know related to the knowledge being produced? What and when do student teachers question, and what structures inform that? What is the relationship between the ways in which student teachers are en/dis/couraged to think critically and question as students, and their ability to become critically questioning teachers? What appears to lie at the heart of Jocelyn's comments is a particular notion of when student teachers think (and believe they are encouraged to think) critically—that is, to question—as well as what they are urged to (or feel they can) think critically about. **[ST¶ Simon**: *Certainly by Case's [1996] definition of critical thinking (and you have not objected to that), the tasks that students faced in this class involved critical thinking. But what you are calling for is a relatively simple—and I would even say pervasive (among adolescents)—disposition toward formal learning.*] Whether from Simon or from her previous experiences as a student (though she tends to pin it on the latter), Jocelyn nevertheless received the message that the purpose of this activity "wasn't for us to engage critical thinking. . . . The purpose was to learn or think about how we can encourage our students to engage critical thinking." Jocelyn thus illustrates not only the existence of the two different levels of engaging critical thinking in this program—critical thinking as an activity designed to initiate critical thinking in others, and critical thinking that is practiced by those who create (and *as* they create) opportunities for others to think critically—but also, and more importantly, their separation. Although Jocelyn had a variety of critical thoughts about this particular activity—thoughts she articulated in our discussion—she chose not to raise any of them either within her group or in the large-class discussion that followed. This, she states, was because she believed it was high school students' critical thought this activity was designed to activate, not her own or those of her colleagues. In making that separation, Jocelyn points to a second dichotomy, which, in the context of teacher education, has more profound pedagogical implications; a dichotomy that separates the text student teachers are writing (for their students) from the text they are reading (about their own experience of producing the text for students). Moreover, the distinction Jocelyn points to divorces the products of learning to teach (the lessons they prepare) from the process of learning to teach (the lessons they learn about teaching and learning while producing lessons for their students). This, by definition, excludes an examination of the product—the learning tool—from the pedagogy that made it possible. In other words, and according to this example, what critical thinking amounted to in this program was something at once spoken about, incorporated in student teachers' assignments and lesson plans, even directed at what prospective teachers will be needing to teach others, but not something with which prospective teachers themselves should think *about* the process in which they learn any and all of the above. Accordingly, what Jocelyn says in this excerpt does not contradict what she said earlier about Simon's actions that promoted critical thinking and the avenues he opened up for student teachers to think critically in the methods course. At the same time, however, it also corroborates Jack's assertion that student teachers were not encouraged to think critically about what they were provided with in the methods course or about the learning context itself in which they learned how to become teachers who think critically.

As Jocelyn's experience shows, and as Beyer (1987) has said before, "[b]eing a student teacher means acquiring . . . knowledge and learning how to use it in a context that does not include criticism and has little patience with analysis" (p. 22). According to Jocelyn, she refrained from analyzing the activity because "that's not what we were asked to do. I was asked to do something else." "We had a task to do. Our task was: 'Do this!' Yeah, we didn't assess if this was a good task or a bad task and we didn't ask: 'Why are we doing this?'" **[ST¶ Simon**: *A poor program is far more likely to stimulate this question—as a poor textbook is more easy to deconstruct.* **Avner**: *It is indeed more difficult to stop and question a good program, a good course, a good instructor (which I argue the course has been and you are). But does that mean that we learn from poor instruction by deconstructing it and from good instruction by emulating and following? I would say not. But in order to* *learn meaningfully from good instruction, it too must be put to a test, not in order to undermine it but in order to understand what makes it good and how one can learn from it and apply that learning to other—different—contexts and situations.*] It seems this analytic question—"Why are we doing this?"—was a question students not only did not articulate publicly but one they did not even entertain privately, since this did not appear to be their task. And in a task-oriented curriculum that also prepares prospective teachers for a task-oriented career, one performs one's task rather than question or analyze it. But this "little" question—"Why are we doing this?"—the question school students like asking most and the one teachers tend to therefore like least (and ignore most), is perhaps one of the most significant questions in education, especially, I would argue, in teacher preparation. What seems equally interesting, therefore, is why that question was not asked. Beyond the idea that Jocelyn believed asking such a question was not part of the task at hand (we were asked to do something else), and that when one is given a stimulus one reacts to it rather than analyzes it, Jocelyn also mentioned that asking such a question would disrupt the flow of the class, would derail learning, and would destabilize the authority of the teacher, who needs the cooperation of his/her students in order for learning to take place.

The fear of having a "Why are we doing this?" question disrupt the flow of learning to teach was also part of Ron's experience in his *Principles of Teaching* (*POT*) class. In a conversation I had with him a few weeks into the program, Ron told me of his frustration in attempting to reconcile the dichotomy between what was preached and what was practiced in that *POT* course.

Ron: I am a little bit critical of some of my courses, like the *POT* course, because it's all very teacher- or lecture-centered. Whereas the expectation seems to be that when we get out into the schools we'll be doing more cooperative learning, where the teacher is one of a group of learners in the most ideal extreme and that the idea of knowledge being constructed rather than conveyed or transferred.

Avner: So what you're doing in *POT* doesn't seem to correspond to what you're talking about in *POT*?

Ron: There seems to be a discrepancy, yeah.

Avner: Did you say anything to that effect in class?

Ron: I probably will, very soon. I've been talking a little bit about it but my POT instructor . . . I started to get into it but I think she was concerned that, you know, we only have two hours to get through all this stuff so she signals she gets the point I'm trying to make and then restates it and then goes on to somebody else without really spending any time on it.

Avner: Did anyone else in class raise that issue or follow up on your question?

Ron: Not really. Well, I didn't really raise it in a way that would have generated that. I think I'm going to try to do that a little bit more although I am also hesitant to do that because I'm aware of the demands of the course and what people want to know and the information that we want to acquire, and to start saying "Why are we doing this?" would disrupt that flow.

Disrupt the flow of what? Oddly, both Ron and Jocelyn seem to think that "Why are we doing this?" is a problematic question in teacher education. I say oddly because, while this question is important anytime and anywhere in education, it becomes doubly important in teacher education and particularly in a Principles of Teaching course. For in such a context, it is no longer simply a question that challenges the authority of the instructor (although that, I would argue, is always a positive stance in and of itself) or even a question about content. Rather, it is a question about the process of learning, about pedagogy ("Why are we doing *this*?" or "Why are we doing it *this way*?") and, inevitably, about the relationship between what one learns and how one comes to learn it. But when the process of teaching and learning in a teacher education program is excluded from its own curriculum, it becomes apparent why Ron and Jocelyn felt such a question might disrupt the flow. Still, it seems strange that a question about teaching would disrupt the flow of a course that focuses on teaching. What, after all, is teacher education about? How else can it reconcile itself with its own name? **[ST¶ Jocelyn**: *I often feel that if I'm going to ask "why" and question the effectiveness of a certain approach, I need to provide an alternative. I didn't always have one and hence was reluctant to voice concerns.* **Avner**: *Isn't the very act of asking that question already an alternative? For the beginning of an alternative is a question about that which one feels ought to change, even if the precise direction of change is still unclear.***]**

Part of what distinguishes teacher education from teacher training is an exploration not only of what but also of how one comes to know and the politics through which the one frames, determines, and builds on the other. At a more specific level, this means a critical reflection on how student teachers themselves come to know in teacher education and what they come to know from (and through) it. Divorcing the ways in which student teachers are taught to teach from a discussion about how they should teach, student teachers become exiled in and from their own experiences in learning to teach. That is, while living the program and living in it, student teachers are nevertheless exiled—both epistemologically and pedagogically—from the materiality of their own education as they learn about education.

The Declared and Enacted Curricula: Learning, Living, and Negotiating the Difference

Across UWC courses and especially in the social studies methods course, instructors, using readings and class discussions emanating from those readings, encouraged student teachers to move beyond the current organization of school knowledge and knowing and the existing regularities of teaching and learning; to question the status quo and the practices of "things as they are"; to challenge the authority of curriculum designers and textbooks; to critically read all texts brought into the classroom and examine not only what they say but what they do with (and through) that saying. In all, a perspective that suggested teachers should question and challenge rather than comply and reproduce. Whether subsequently or not (one can never be sure) all six student teachers participating in this study frequently talked about the importance of questioning as an educative tool. Further, they believed the ability to question was the most valuable and powerful thing they received from the social studies methods course, and, subsequently, the most crucial and substantial perspective they could provide their own students. Yet as prospective teachers spoke of the importance of questioning, they themselves did very little of it as students. Intrigued by that contradiction, and wondering about its effect on them as teachers, I raised the issue with Jack.

> Avner: Having taken many courses encouraging all of you to encourage your soon-to-be students to question, how many students teachers do you think will actually create spaces for their students to question and challenge when they go into the schools?

> Jack: None.

> Avner: Why not?

> Jack: I don't know. I just don't think they will. It's too difficult. I think most of them are still left with their impressions of school. What they leave this program with is a lot like the impressions they came in with. I think some will, maybe. But most won't. **[ST¶ Jack**: *I don't like this quote. It suggests that I thought stu-*

dent teachers learned nothing from the program; that they will leave the program with the same ideas they entered with. Also, your question, now, doesn't seem clear enough. Were you asking me if the student teachers will create spaces for students to question and challenge student teachers' own teaching and methods or to challenge previously held notions of history or simply to critically think? If it is the former, then my answer would remain "No!" If, however, it is the latter, then I would like to change my response to "Yes. I think they will, to some degree."]

Though not making explicit the connection between why prospective teachers won't create spaces for their students to question and the culture of learning in preservice education, an implicit connection between the two is very much evident in Jack's comment. The reason for not creating spaces for high school students to question seems to be related to the fact that student teachers will be entering their practicum not having had the impressions of schooling with which they came into the program shattered significantly enough to provide alternatives. In accordance with other students' earlier comments, Jack was not speaking about the lack of alternative models advocated in this program but rather about models that prospective teachers could actually experience as they were considering the models promoted by the program. Indeed, as Ron put it, "There seems to be quite a difference between what we are talking about, what we are thinking about, and what we are actually practicing on a day-to-day basis in this teacher education program." When asked which of the two he thought would ultimately have a larger impact on prospective teachers' practice, as students and as teachers, Ron immediately responded, "No doubt the latter."

While pedagogical practices within teacher education should reflect those that teacher educators advocate for public education, the disparity between the advocated and enacted curriculum in the UWC Teacher Education Program was by no means unique. As Arends (1991) and Ginsburg and Clift (1990), among others, explain, contradictions between theory and practice are prevalent in much of the work in teacher (or any other) education. What then becomes of interest is not simply the existence of contradictions in the practices of teacher education but their possible impact on the educational imagination of those learning to teach and on the ability of what is preached to become a viable option for practice for those being preached. Speaking of educational innovation yet excluding much of it in practice, claims Arends (1991), teacher education does little to provide student teachers "with a sufficient repertoire to make serious departures from what they think they already know and can do well." Prospective teachers, he continues, "are introduced to countervailing ways of teaching but not in a powerful enough way to ensure their use later" (pp. 207–208). This, Arends adds, leaves beginning teachers without a sufficient repertoire to challenge the traditional behavioral regularities of teaching in any significant way; regularities they have, and are currently learning so well as students (p. 223). Remaining at the level of "theory," these countervailing aspects in the discourse of teacher education, Arends adds, tend to "serve as lip-service to educational innovation" (p. 212). As such, they are rarely seen as viable practical options for implementation in the "real"—high school or college—classroom.

In that fashion, while the UWC program spoke of a nontraditional education in schools, the education student teachers received in their school of education was very much a traditional one, reinforcing rather than challenging the existing nature of education and the roles students and teachers each play in it. Attempting to reconcile the differences between the declared and enacted curriculum was made especially difficult for prospective teachers, since the image of the nonconforming, critical, creative teacher advanced in the program seemed to fall on very receptive ears. Visits to participants' classrooms during their practicum and the numerous discussions I had with them about teaching regularly illustrated that they had adhered to, and attempted to live by, all of the above. That is, in their teaching, while with their students, not as students in the teacher education program nor when being evaluated by its representatives (university supervisors) while teaching during the practicum. While being questioning, creative, and critical were dispositions participants subscribed to, ones they believed would enable them to be the teachers they hoped to become, they had less faith that the teacher education program advocating those dispositions was actually enthusiastic about seeing them displayed by its own students. The reason, and Helsel and Krchniak (1972) provide it, is that although the official curriculum of teacher education "speaks of teachers as 'autonomous professionals'" who should question, the hidden curriculum often sends "an opposite message that participants need to be docile and to give those in charge what they want" (p. 90; cf. Ginsburg & Clift, 1990, p. 452).

Returning the "Gift": Giving Those in Charge What They Want

> We're no different than students in high school in that we're accepting what's been taught and we're giving it back to the instructors and giving them what they want. (Jack)

Jack was among the most critical students within that year's cohort of prospective social studies teachers and had a reputation as a risk-taker who often asked "difficult" questions about and of issues discussed in his various courses. During the practicum, Jack did his best to emulate the image of the "good teacher" projected through the discourse in this program and be creative, innovative, and experimental. But having "done" school for so many years prior to teacher education, and realizing that "school" in a school of education is not that different than the other schools he had done so well in before, Jack soon learned that success in the program had little to do with being creative, innovative, or able to question and examine the world critically. Instead, Jack said, succeeding and "getting good marks in the program only means you follow directions and that you are reasonably bright" doing so. Having learned how to "play the game," the very attributes Jack was proud of most during his teaching—being critical, creative, experimental, and knowing how to ask questions—were the ones he avoided while being evaluated, either as a student in the university-based portion or as a teacher in the practicum, by the very teacher education program promoting them. In those instances, such attributes seemed to come together in a constellation in which creativity was no longer a consequence of a critical perspective, of questioning, and of risk-taking but rather activated to suppress them. Creativity was used to mute questioning and criticality, to avoid risk-taking, to pursue the taken-for-granted, to provide that which is already tried and tested, that which he knew was going to "work." In other words, and to use those provided by Helsel and Krchniak (1972), accommodating a culture of docility and "giving those in charge what they want."

This came across clearly as Jack, speaking about what students need to do in order to succeed in education, brought up an exchange he had with his partner, who at the time was enrolled in one of the local community colleges. "She often talks about the things she thinks are important and how she would like to go with this topic and in that direction," Jack said. "And she's really enthusiastic about it. But she's in her first year, so I say, 'Don't do that. Write what they want to hear. Otherwise you'll get less marks.'" Recognizing the implications of saying that as a teacher (or of having me hear that from a teacher), Jack added, "I guess that's not what I should be saying, but it's true. I mean I found it to be true." This philosophy of "giving instructors back what they want" was not only one Jack recommended to others or one he found useful in the past; it was very much embedded in his then-current experiences of becoming a teacher.

> When I did my Unit Overview for Simon, I knew going in that I was going to get a good mark [he got an A+] because I had done exactly what he asked for. But other people didn't seem to have a clue. I saw some people walking in [to present their unit to Simon] who didn't have an overriding question or problem for the

unit, who didn't encourage critical thinking, and who didn't use as many different sources as they could find. So: "Like where have you guys been for the last four months? This is what he wants. This is what you're being tested on. Give it to him." And that's what I did when I put together my unit.

According to Jack, the primary reason for including an overriding question or problem in Jack's unit plan and for encouraging critical thinking or incorporating different sources (perspectives) in it—all issues Jack believed in and implemented in his own teaching—was not because he found them significant educationally but because incorporating them would give the instructor "what he wants." Giving instructors and supervisors what they want, complying with rather than challenging that which they want, even if and when that contradicts student teachers' own beliefs about education, was very much part of student teachers' experiences throughout their 12-month program of learning to teach. "I walked the walk," Jack told me as we spoke about his practicum following one of my visits to his school.

> When my faculty advisor (university supervisor) said stuff that I would find offensive, I didn't . . . I mean . . . I can play the game. I'll be anyone you want me to be. I had to get through that practicum and I wasn't going to jeopardize it. So I would sit there and do things I might have objected to, things my sponsor teachers did. And, believe me, there were things! Again, I didn't raise my objection because I had to get through my practicum. As a future teacher the practicum is valuable in teaching you different things but I couldn't do things I wanted to do. There was a lot of stuff I would have liked to have taught in ways I would have liked to have taught it but I didn't even *consider* trying because my sponsor teachers didn't buy into it; it wasn't structured enough [to their liking]. My faculty advisor would tell me when he was coming and I would plan the most boring sitting-at-your-seat completing-worksheets lessons for him because that's what he wanted to see. So the whole practicum was kind of restraining in that you had to follow these hoops and get through the checklist they had created to assess you.

Jocelyn, too, as did most others, spoke not of a mentoring environment that facilitated growth but one that stifled it in the name of rendition, tradition, and unquestioned practice. Referring to the ability to be creative, inventive, and experimental in one's practicum, as the teacher education program advocated, Jocelyn claimed that "when you are put under the authority of your practicum supervisors you are not encouraged to develop your own way of teaching. You are encouraged to emulate, to copy somebody else's and spit back to them what they are doing as a reinforcement. And that's when you get a good grade." Such understandings stood in contrast to much of the declared statements made in various courses throughout the UWC Teacher Education Program.

High among the list of dispositions promoted in the explicit curriculum of the program were creativity and experimentation. While those came up frequently in a variety of courses, they were primarily reserved for discussions about the practicum. Prospective teachers were repeatedly told by course instructors and faculty advisors that the school-based part of their teacher education program is a time to experiment and learn from experimentation, that one only learns what does and does not work by taking risks, by trying different things out, by being creative, nonconform- ist, experimental. All six participants, to a large degree, followed that pattern while teaching. Five of them, however, felt they could do none of that when their faculty advisor was around. Hence, the experimentation that was undertaken was enacted with students, not with the representa- tive of the institution that did its (verbal) most to promote it.

> Jack: When my faculty advisor is there I make sure I have something good, some- thing that I *know* is good and I know will always work. I won't try something new when he's here in case it didn't work. He wouldn't think I was a very good teacher if it didn't [work].

> Avner: But aren't experimentation and risk-taking important?

> Jack: Not to him, I don't think. I mean I would be creative once, two days before he came and if it worked, I'd do it again for him. But I wouldn't experiment when he's there. So while I think trying different things is what the practicum should be about, I never try anything new when he's here. I do what I know works well . . . and something he would like.

One of the only spaces in which students in this program felt they were encouraged to question and break the rules more openly was in their journals. Journals were required in many of the courses in the program and were intended, according to Ron, as a way for students to reflect on "course readings and class discussions and where that fits into our views on education." An institutionalized, mandated, and regulated endeavor, however, journal writing ultimately turned out to be less a point of resis- tance than a mechanism of validation. Ron's use of the words "and where that fits into our views on education" highlight that point. Not whether, not even how, but where what was read and discussed in class fit into students' views on education. The a priori assumption then, we learn from Ron, is that there necessarily was a "fit" between the two and what was left for students to figure out in their journals was *where* (not whether) that fit existed. Validation, as I will show, came not only through what was present in students' journals—where things fit—but through what was absent, through what prospective teachers felt they could not write about, through what ultimately did not and could not fit.

To explain, I return to a conversation with Ron I presented earlier in this chapter. In it, Ron spoke of his frustration with his *POT* class for not affording students learning to teach a space in which to discuss the teaching they themselves encountered as students learning about teaching. In contrast, Ron pointed to his *Analysis of Education* course, which made such spaces available to students through journal writing.

> Avner: You mentioned that in those journals you reflect on your readings and class discussions. But to return to your frustration with your *POT* class, do you also use those journals to engage the teaching that goes on in your *Analysis of Education* course as you are learning about teaching?
>
> Ron: No. I haven't yet.
>
> Avner: Has anybody?
>
> Ron: No. I don't think so.
>
> Avner: Why not?
>
> Ron: I think it's a paradigm that's really taken for granted. It's something we've been exposed to since kindergarten, that's 26 years or so for me, so it takes quite an effort to stop and say: Why is the teacher at the front of the room? Why this particular model of doing this? Can we do anything differently? It's tough.
>
> Avner: Is it tough for you to stop and ask that or have you already stopped to ask but find it difficult for you to articulate that?
>
> Ron: It's tough to do both. It's definitely tough to actually stop and verbalize and ask that, but it's even difficult to start thinking of that in your own mind. I think it's because of the nature of the program being one year and a huge workload that we have to crunch through and also the anxiety that we have of going out and facing our first practicum, you know, "going back to high school!"

While journals seem to have allowed students a space to reflect, teaching—what they were there to learn—appeared to be exempt from that reflection. The fear of "going back to school" Ron spoke of was used both as a weapon and a tool in a combined effort—unarticulated perhaps but fully understood and agreed upon—by students and instructors alike to avoid a critical discussion of the very essence of learning to teach. That is, one could discuss learning and teaching—separately or together—as long as the two were not implicated in the other in the context of the university setting. As a result, student teachers did not have to wait to get to high school to "do" school. The difficulty in activating the kind of questioning stance Ron described was inherent not only in the workload of a teacher education program but in its culture of education and the ability of that culture to keep itself unquestioned, perhaps unquestionable. Within that culture and under those conditions, "reflection," according to Jack, mostly took the shape of students telling instructors what they wanted to hear.

Hoping to use her various journals to explore what was actually on *her* mind while learning to teach, Jocelyn quickly learned that

> the professor was going to read it and you wanted to write on something impor-
> tant [*pronounced slowly and with irony*] rather than just: "I didn't like the way he
> approached what we did in class today." I mean when you come down to it and sit
> down with a pen and paper, and you know that instructor is going to read it,
> there's something in you that says, "Well, I could, sure! But is it worth it? He's
> going to take issue with this and I will have to go and defend myself. So OK, I'll
> write something else."

Avner: And how did you feel about that?

Jocelyn: It bothered me a little bit.

Avner: Why?

Jocelyn: Well, because I would like to be able to write what I want to write and I
normally would but with the constraints of the program, you do what you can do,
you know, and you get through it. They've got you around the throat like a boa
constrictor so you've got to do things to survive. And you do them to survive as
opposed to doing them because they are really of use to you and allow *you* to
learn.

Although Jocelyn might not have been able to write what she wanted in her journals nor learn the particular lessons she had hoped for while doing so, she nevertheless learned something from those experiences. She learned, as Ron did in the previous segment, that instructors and their teaching are granted an extraterritorial status in a program focused on learning about teaching (unless, that is, one is prepared to be summoned to explain why one has chosen to discuss this topic). Jocelyn also learned that the survival mode student teachers are made to assume while learning to teach may be just as much a way for a teacher education program to survive its students as for them to survive through it. But what Jocelyn, as well as Ron and Jack, learned most of all is a basic Foucauldian lesson of how power operates to regulate knowledge. The experiences they provide illustrate a pattern of regulation that pervades both the university and practicum settings and was part of student teachers' interactions with all three major levels of authority they encountered while learning to teach—university instructors, sponsor teachers, and faculty advisors. But as students learned one of Foucault's lessons, they also demonstrated another—that discourse is not only the instrument and the effect of power "but also a hindrance, a stumbling-block, and a point of resistance" (Foucault, 1979, p. 100. cf. Young, 1981, p. 50).

Regularly evaluated by a triad of supervisors with the power to determine—enable or terminate—prospective teachers' professional prospects, giving those in charge what they want seems to come with the territory. What prospective teachers point to in their accounts is a ritual enacted by those who receive and those who give; by those with the power to define the boundaries of that territory and by those confined in it, adjusting to its contours. As readers we learn it is primarily an industrious enterprise designed to maintain industrial calm, not the creative, experimental, questioning education it was meant to celebrate. Both sides of the equation appear to know this, yet they do little to publicly challenge its mechanisms and regularities; a mutually beneficial arrangement in which teachers and students each provide their share to preserve the comfort of the traditional teacher/student roles.

Interestingly, however, even as prospective teachers adopted this traditional student role of giving those in charge what they want, their explanations as to why they did so were not provided from the traditional student position. Instead of a naive acceptance or misrecognition of the workings of a system that prospective teachers believed required them to assume such roles, what comes across is a cynical and ironic stance that allowed students to maintain a distance from that system even as they participated in and contributed to its making. To use Zizek's (1989) discussion of ideology, students appeared to know quite well what they were doing, why they were doing it, and what that implied for their own learning as well as for the teacher education program as a whole. Knowing the falsehood of the enterprise and aware of the interests embedded in and served by it enabled students an ironic escape as well as a point of cynical resistance. Assuming that double-edged position, students could be two places at once—participating in the enterprise and distancing themselves from it, complying with the nature of the ritual and surviving what it attempted to do with and to them.

That double-edged position, however, did not appear to sustain itself throughout. Though evident in prospective teachers' understandings of the mechanisms of giving those in charge what they want, it seemed to dissipate, as we will see in the next section, when it came to *getting* what those in charge wanted them to get.

The B(l)inding Power of Authority
and the Suspension of Judgment

Periodically, I would ask participants to evaluate the social studies methods course, to say what they liked or found useful and beneficial in it as well as what they did not (always with a focus on why). In doing so, I had three interrelated purposes in mind. First, to have students ascribe value to class activities and, by having to articulate that value to me but mostly to themselves, to better understand their own values, perspectives, assumptions, and understandings about teaching and learning. Second, to have participants relate Simon's teaching to their own learning and, as a result, to think concretely about the relationship between teaching and learning—both in the lesson and unit plans they were proposing in the methods course as well as during their teaching in the practicum. And finally, to explore how (or whether) the theories advocated in the methods course about social studies education—in particular about critical thinking and reading and writing texts—were applied by students in the process of learning how to use those theories with others.

Having stated that the social studies methods course was one of the (for some, the only) highlights in an otherwise mostly uninspiring program, expressing what they liked and found beneficial in the methods course and in Simon's teaching of/in it seemed easy for this group of participants (for a sample of such comments see Chapter Two). All, however, had immense difficulty articulating questions regarding the pedagogical nature of the methods course or pointing to elements they did not like or find beneficial in the nearly 30 classes of that course. In fact, none could think of even one class, activity, interaction, or discussion they found problematic, or thought could and should have been done otherwise. What student teachers didn't say is obviously a compliment to Simon, a recognition of his teaching. It might be regarded as less of a compliment, however, when one considers that prospective teachers *could* not say anything to that effect. After all, as student teachers, they had to critically think through, analyze, and assess the teaching methods they proposed in their lesson and unit plans for the methods course as well as learn how to examine what did and did not work well, what was problematic, what might need to be done otherwise, or replaced, in their own teaching during the practicum. An unquestioning stance becomes doubly problematic in a course that encouraged prospective teachers to critically examine and question externally produced curricula documents, textbooks, and the pedagogies suggested in their accompanying teachers' guides, as well as other subject area texts brought into their classrooms. To what degree can one expect prospective teachers to do any of the above in school if they cannot do these things as students in schools of education? Can authority suddenly become questionable in one place if it has not been questioned in another? Can teacher educators expect prospective teachers to challenge authority as teachers in (and while in) schools if such a stance does not become an important part of their learning to be teachers? A partial response may be gleaned by examining student teachers' ability and inclination to question two aspects in their own process of learning about teaching: the teaching enacted with them and the theories derived in/through that teaching.

Questioning (and) Teaching

Two aspects Mary found most beneficial in the social studies methods course were its focus on reading and writing texts and its emphasis on critical thinking. In fact, Mary saw the two as one and the same. To read texts critically, she claimed, you need to apply critical thinking and to think critically you need something—a text—to think critically about. Discussing this double configuration, Mary explained that reading a text critically entails questioning:

> Question what you see. Is there a bias? In any case: Find the bias! and you're thinking critically. Question where it's coming from, who is writing it, what context are they writing it from. Read between the lines!

A fine definition, no doubt; one that also illustrates that the methods course had taught Mary what questions need to be asked and which strategies applied in order to read a text critically. Knowing that, what did Mary consider a text? And what kinds of texts did she, as a student teacher, believe required that kind of critical reading? While Mary initially considered a text only something written on paper, in conversations prior to this one she claimed a video, even a teacher could be considered a text since both, similar to a print text, convey information. To what degree, then, was Mary able to apply her critical stance toward reading texts to her reading of Simon—the one teaching her about the need to critically read and write texts—as a text? A partial response came about in a discussion I had with Mary toward the end of the methods course. In it, I asked Mary how, if at all, her understandings of social studies education had

changed having taken Simon's course. Although Mary came into the
teacher education program with degrees in geography and history, she
said, "I never really had a preconceived notion of what social studies was
when I came into the course. So everything Simon presented to us was
social studies as far as I was concerned because Simon was saying so."
Realizing from my prolonged puzzled look that I was in need of elaboration, Mary explained:

> Well, he's experienced, so I take his look at things and say [to myself], "What are
> we doing here [in class]? OK, I know there's a reason for it; just find the reason."
> If I'm confused about the reason why he's telling us something or why he's teach-
> ing us something, there is a reason. I just need to find the reason! It's my task,
> right? Otherwise I would become disenchanted, I'm sure. . . . I have no idea what
> his education is and whether or not he has his doctorate, or whatever, and I don't
> care. With other instructors I'm thinking, "Ah! Where is this person coming from
> and what qualifies him to be standing there and teaching me? Where do they get
> their authority?" To me all of Simon's authority comes from his experience.

> Avner: Experience in what?

> Mary: Teaching social studies in the classroom.

> Avner: In your classroom?

> Mary: No. In the public schools. I can tell by the way he's teaching us that he was
> as good a teacher then as he is now. . . . There's *no* doubt in my mind that he
> knows what he's talking about. He definitely knows what he's talking about. He's
> coming at it from like, "I know what you should be doing because I've been there,
> I've done it." His experience speaks volumes.

> Avner: Any weaknesses?

> Mary: If there is one I can't find it.

Any comparison between the questions Mary believed must be incorporated in order to read a text and the degree to which those questions
were absent from her reading of Simon as a text is striking, to say the
least. Blinded by the authority she attached to his experience, Simon's
teaching assumed an extra-territorial (perhaps, a *text*ra-territorial) status
in Mary's mind, no longer requiring the critical reading she would engage
with any other text. As such, Mary did not find it necessary to "question
what you see" in the methods course nor attempt to "find the bias."
Questions such as, "Where [is it] coming from? Who is writing this, and
what context are they writing it from?"—questions Mary believed were
imperative for "reading between the lines" of any text—appeared incon-

sequential when the agent providing her with information was Simon. With that reading (or non-reading) position in mind, Mary saw her role in Simon's class not as one of questioning, asking, "Why are we doing this?" but of finding the reason—"Just find the reason. It's my task, right?"—for what is already being done. In the absence of questioning, however, the "done" in teacher education tends to become that which is done *to* rather than *with* Mary. Submitting herself to Simon's experience, Mary chose to put the onus for finding reasons for why things were done the way they were on herself and in herself. Rather than question the curriculum presented to her as a way of learning to question educative purposes embedded in everyday practice, Mary chose to accept it unquestionably, relinquishing herself to the authority of its maker.

Whether it was Simon's experience or the quality of his teaching (or a combination of both), there seemed to be a reluctance among all students participating in this study to apply the very reading position advocated by Simon to Simon's own teaching. In a sense, an invisible wall was erected in students teachers' minds, one that separated the theories they were learning from Simon about how to activate one's critical reading and writing of texts and the application of those theories to their own reading and writing of Simon as a text. A conversation with Jack further illustrates this phenomenon.

Avner: I often heard students say that teachers can (and must) remain neutral while presenting topics and issues in the classroom; that they can avoid imposing views upon students. Students, they said, will objectively make up their own minds if we simply present them with a variety of perspectives.

Jack: I had trouble with that throughout the term.

Avner: Why?

Jack: I'll point at the obvious: You can't help but impose your view. I mean it's going to pervade everything you do, it's always going to be there. No matter how neutral you try to be, your slant is going to be there . . . and it's going to come out.

Avner: In what ways is it going to come out?

Jack: Well, in the materials you select, for one. Like you might pick more reasonable arguments to support your view and more ridiculous ones in order to show how wrong the other side is. . . .

Avner: So you think that even if a teacher doesn't specifically state his or her views, students can still sense what those views are?

Jack: I think they do sense it. So you might even be doing more harm if you try and hide it because students do sense it; the bright ones do anyway. I mean I do that when I write papers. I sense what I think teachers want to hear. . . . I mean, I probably do that with you too. So I think you might be smarter to come out and say, "Look [this is my view], but there are other valid perspectives and by no means are you expected to believe what I believe."

Avner: Did Simon impose his views on the class?

Jack: No. Not at all.

Any teacher, according to Jack, cannot help but impose his or her views on students simply because he or she determines the topics under study, the texts brought into the classroom to study, and the pedagogy for that study. Yet when asked whether Simon, whose position as instructor required him to do all of the above, imposed his views on students in this class, Jack's responded, "No. Not at all." Only after a long pause, much hesitation, and apparent discomfort due to my long silence, Jack half-heartedly suggested that maybe Simon might have done some of the above but immediately retracted by stating quite firmly that "Simon never imposed his position during class discussions." That is true. Any researcher sitting in the social studies methods class would have to acknowledge that Simon created a learning environment that was extremely open and demo-cratic, where students were invited to express their ideas, as divergent as those might have been from the ones proposed by Simon, and where they were made to feel comfortable doing so. As Jocelyn put it, Simon "encourages a very good and very safe environment. Nothing is discour-aged and nothing is wrong. You are not made to look silly. He always encourages you to say whatever it is and he always makes a point to show there was something good in it even if he doesn't agree with what you're saying." Even good and democratic teachers, however, impose their views. Such an imposition is inevitable; it derives from the very act of teaching, of making choices among a variety of possible learning opportunities for one's students; choices that advance some knowledge, knowing, and knowers over others. Regardless of one's intentions or abilities as a teacher, imposition is inherent in the teaching act—any (and anyone's) teaching act. Jack, as his comments above illustrate, knew that. Yet such knowl-edge seemed to evaporate when that teacher happened to be Simon—his own teacher.

Mary's and Jack's reluctance to see in Simon what they believed was present and thus should be questioned in any other teacher/text is a phenomenon that is not too out of the ordinary. Most students develop a "blind eye" when it comes to their own teachers, especially one whom they have learned to respect and with whom they have developed a special and trusting relationship. Such a stance does become problematic, however, when it is considered against the questioning stance prospective teachers were asked to assume as teachers in their preservice education program. Can one expect prospective teachers to be able to question the authority of curriculum designers as teachers in schools when they do not question the authority of the designers of their own curriculum as students learning to teach? Will the "blind eye" student teachers turn toward authority as students be transformed into a "critical eye" when they become teachers of others? And to what degree can a teacher education program count on student teachers enabling a critical, questioning stance among their future students when they have not done so themselves as students?

Questioning (and) Theories

> The emphasis in the social studies course has been on getting us to think on things critically, for sure, not just to take everything for what it is but to question it and look at it closely. (Casey)

Attempting to move social studies education beyond the traditional cycle of fact-finding, memorization, and fact-returning, Simon's overarching approach to the course focused on critical thinking as a method of reading and writing texts in order to enhance students' thoughtful, critical, and reflective inquiry about the world. What is the text trying to tell you? Why? Where is it coming from? How is it positioning you to know (and know what)? were some of the underlying questions prospective teachers were encouraged to explore in their future social studies classrooms. The positive impact such an approach had on student teachers' understandings regarding the purpose and process of social studies education cannot be denied. Students' comments about the methods course in Chapter Two, as well as the examples provided in this chapter, all serve as testimony to that. But if the purpose of that approach was for learners—not only future high school students but present prospective teachers—to become critical rather than accepting, to question rather than confirm, the viability of that approach as a meaningful educative tool might be reconsidered in light of the fact that the process of its adoption by student teachers left the approach itself mostly unquestioned. That is, it was accepted without scrutiny as the best and only approach to social studies education by the entire cohort of prospective teachers in this class. How is it, one may ask, that none of the 37 students in the methods class ever challenged (at least publicly, and the six participants in this study also semi-privately) an approach whose essence is to have students question and possibly reject? Can one uncritically adopt a critical tool and still retain its critical edge? Or does it become one in an arsenal of techniques teachers can pull out of a hat when necessary without being convinced of its critical pedagogical imperative?

When approaches to education are accepted by students not through a process of critical examination but because, as Mary suggested, one is compelled by the authority, experience, expertise, and artfully crafted teaching of the instructor, good teaching has the capacity to become authority teaching. No longer restricted by the presence of questioning, authority teaching can easily cross the line between example and imposition—even if that imposition is induced by the instructed rather than by one's instructor. Authority teaching—what Bakhtin (1935/1981, p. 342) calls authoritative teaching—binds students to ideas not because those ideas persuade them internally but due to the authority students attribute to the one advocating those ideas. Underlying the transformation of authority teaching into authoritative teaching is the reluctance to relate power to knowledge, accepting ideas without implicating that acceptance in a process that makes it possible, probable, at times even imperative.

An opportunity to engage that issue more directly came about as I continued my conversation with Jack (the one in which he stated that all teachers other than Simon impose their views):

Avner: From what I hear in class, we have over 30 student teachers who believe they are supposed to go into the classroom and encourage students to challenge what they see and read?

Jack: Yes.

Avner: And yet in the methods course there was very little dissent. Simon thought reading and writing texts and using primary sources are good approaches and although, as you said, he never imposed anything directly, everybody in class tends to think that those are the best approaches to teaching social studies. What might that tell you?

Jack: Well I suppose he *did* impose what he thought upon us. I mean if you look at it that way, he is telling us that using primary sources is the most important thing about doing social studies. Yeah, [what you're saying] is true. . . . Simon certainly has a lot of power in that he's pumped out 90 or so students [Jack is referring to students in all three sections of the methods course] that think that exposing students to primary sources is pretty darn important. Yeah. I guess it could be a problem. . . . You're right. I never thought of it that way. **[ST¶ Simon:**

So now, using your set of moves, we can see you teaching Jack, and Jack accepting what you say. Why didn't he question what you said? Is this the best (the only) construction of this exchange? No!

The problem, of course, is not Simon "pumping out" students who value using primary sources in their classrooms, but rather, Jack's inability to relate Simon's teaching in the methods course to the learning it produced, to realize the dependency of the latter on that which made it possible. Puzzled by students' refusal to make those connections explicit while learning about teaching and its relationship to learning, I raised that issue again, this time with Ron. Telling me about the kind of learning he would like to engage his students in during the practicum, Ron described a process that would incorporate primary sources and question sequences infused with critical thinking. Having heard many students in the course imagine their classrooms similarly, I asked Ron if he thought that was coincidental.

Ron: I was thinking about that a number of times and I was kind of struck by the number of students who do seem interested in engaging critical thinking. There was a very large number of people who were excited about this stuff and I was going: "Wow! That's neat!". . . . You know, you really don't find many people [here] who are into citizenship education or teaching history as fact.

Avner: Using primary sources or critical thinking are some ways to engage social studies and yet most students think they are the only ways. I understand they are exciting approaches. But when you think of the overall picture and hear everybody say, "We don't want to indoctrinate anybody," it's surprising that—

Ron [jumping in]: We all got indoctrinated. Sure, we get caught up talking about them because we don't talk about anything else. We don't have time to think about anything else.

Avner: What surprised me is not as much that everybody said the same but that they wanted to say the same and be the same. It seems to counter the very essence of what this teacher education program said it wanted to promote.

Ron: I think it's because we're all, by nature, very obliging, want to help, want to be agreed with, and want to agree with others. And if the pace is kept up like that [then] sure, we all just lock step and follow.

In a culture of consensus in which students, according to Ron, mostly wanted to agree and be agreed with, locking step rather than questioning appears to have directed students' engagement with learning. Wishing to conform to the thinking, saying, and doing of the norm left little room to inquire about the essence of the norm to which one was trying to conform. Conformity became its own self-regulating process, banishing questions to the sidelines. With that frame of mind, questioning, according to Jocelyn, necessitated too substantial a departure, too large a toll:

> When you have 40 student teachers who are pretty much "get out into the trenches and start the fight," maybe people felt . . . and I know I sometimes felt: "Well, this is really what I want to ask or say but I don't want to offend anybody and, sure, it would be great to explore that for a while, but am I obstructing what Simon would really like to have [done] in this class? And am I just baiting somebody or getting off on a tangent?

To be considered a team player, one who doesn't obstruct or offend, Jocelyn found herself not asking what she believed needed to be asked in and about learning to teach. Jocelyn's decision not to ask stems from the same stance that drove Jack to not think about teaching and learning "that way" and Ron to comply, lock step, and follow. Underlying these three actions (or non-actions) is a particular understanding not only of the role of questioning in education but of what it is one can and cannot question in one's education. To be sure, such understandings were not a direct outcome of any particular thing Simon did in the methods course but rather of what the teacher education program as a whole did not do: have student teachers use the theories promoted in it to make connections between what they were taught, how they were taught, and what and why they learned what they did as a result. That is, to critically read into the process of their own education and, consequently, to think more deeply about the education they will be providing others. While the degree to which the latter was absent from the practices of this teacher education program has been illustrated in the various examples I have provided throughout this chapter, it is made even more explicit by Ron as he reflected on the discourse and practice of critical thinking following the completion of his teacher education program. "The way critical thinking was dealt with in the program," Ron said,

> makes me feel that it wasn't practiced. We talked about it but we didn't do it. It just became yet another quick fix in our arsenal of teaching methods where, as student teachers, we went, "Oh yeah! Now *the* way to teach is critical thinking so I'm going to base my teaching on critical thinking." [Doing that], we are devaluing the meaning of critical thinking because for it to be meaningful it also has to be experienced and lived by those called upon to impart it.

Not having lived or experienced questioning as a viable option in their own education, it is not surprising to hear student teachers, as we have throughout this chapter, equate questioning with disruption (Ron and Jocelyn), with a possible offense (Jocelyn), with disenchantment and an improper role (Mary). With those adjectives in mind, and not having experienced questioning as a rewarding pedagogical tool in their own learning, prospective teachers' commitment to having their own students question seemed to become more tentative, perhaps even dissipate in the presence of resistance. As Jack chose to put it,

> In the methods course we were encouraged to frame things . . . to encourage students to sit around and question all the time. [But when we get into the schools], I think a lot of students will think, "Well, that's great for a class or two but I mean I've got to cover this curriculum. I have a responsibility to do that. And if I focus on having students question, I'll have to justify that to the principal and to the other teachers in the department and to the parents and to whomever." And if you just sit around making students into what you [Avner] might consider to be responsible citizens, a lot of others will say you're just creating these disagreeable young people. So I think most student teachers just won't bother.

Chapter Six

Gender and Multiculturalism: Additives, Sedatives, or Pedagogical Alternatives?

> Given the vast diversity of the student population in [classrooms]; the growth of the mainly white and middle-class teacher population; the persistence of equity issues surrounding schools . . . and children . . . ; the salience of curricular issues, especially in social studies, about the inclusion of all peoples and the role of multiple perspectives; and ongoing questions about "historical honesty" in the social studies curriculum, it is clear that the social studies teacher preparation research agenda should be very full and focused on a range of diversity-related issues. (Armento, 1996, p. 491)

How and to what extent are issues of diversity and equity addressed in teacher preparation? What knowledge and skills are prospective teachers learning regarding the issues raised by Armento? To what degree, as Ladson-Billings (1995, p. 749) asks, do multicultural issues drive, or get driven by, teacher education programs? How are teachers being prepared to address the challenges and capture the possibilities provided by the changing demographic and epistemological nature of a contemporary society? And what values, attitudes, dispositions, knowledge, and skills regarding diversity are prospective teachers able to transfer from their experiences in teacher education to their own classrooms (Gollnick, 1992, p. 67) and subject matter when they begin to teach o/Others?

To address these questions, this chapter examines the discourse and discursive practices surrounding issues of difference in the teacher education program at UWC. My interest here, as it has been in previous chapters, is to examine the relationship between the opportunities made possible for prospective teachers to engage issues of difference—specifically, gender and multiculturalism—and the opportunities they made possible in return because of what was made available to them. To do so, I turn to conversations I had with each of the six participants in this study about issues of gender and multiculturalism.[1] I conducted those conversations following the conclusion of the first semester at UWC (which also meant the end of the methods course), immediately before student teachers began their 13-week practicum in schools. I choose to present these exchanges almost in their entirety, since they encapsulate a variety of issues I wish to discuss in the remainder of this chapter. Further, situated between the university- and school-based components of learning to teach, those exchanges provide a way of looking back at how gender and multiculturalism were engaged in the first and formative semester at UWC as well as an opportunity to examine how students' experiences in that first semester positioned them to deal with such issues during the practicum.

"In some of your teacher education courses," I raised the point, "you talked about issues of gender and multiculturalism. Do you think those are important issues for discussion in a teacher education program, and if so, why?" In response to the first part—"are those important?"—students mentioned the following: "yes," "of course," "absolutely," and "definitely." Presented below are their responses to the second part of the question, "Why are they important?"

> Charles: [They are important because] they've been issues, they are issues, and they're going to be issues in the school system. I mean, gender equity is always an issue whether it be the teachers or the students themselves. And multiculturalism? It's obvious! Simply because of the vast different number of cultures we have in the schools today. You have to discuss it at some point.
>
> Avner: How, if at all, does it relate to social studies?
>
> Charles: First, because of the different students you have in your class. But it can affect the content too and how you stand on those issues. . . . You can decide whether you want to cover women in World War II or not, or if you want to talk about immigration in the 1960s or anything else you want to teach. I mean you can decide to talk about women in history or you can decide not to. So I guess it affects it in that way.
>
> Avner: And do you see yourself incorporating those issue as a social studies teacher?
>
> Charles: Oh yeah!
>
> Avner: In what way?
>
> Charles: Well, just like I said: women in history, it's obviously important.
>
> Avner: Why is it important?
>
> Charles: It's important because it's a part of history and it doesn't get talked about much, although it is getting talked about more. I guess it's important for me to know that my students are seeing some of it. One of my objectives would be for them to see, to be exposed to some of these other parts of history, like talking about Chinese railroad workers in the 1880s. I want them to see some of that instead of just seeing the Euro-

pean history that we always see. . . . I think exposing them to the different histories and cultures and stuff like that, will give them a greater appreciation for the way that all these different people and their ancestors had an effect on where we now live. I mean it wasn't just Europeans who built Canada; it was women and natives and Asians and Americans and British and all the other people who had an effect on how we live now, not just white Europeans.

Mary: Although [prospective teachers] might be more sensitive to issues of gender and multiculturalism than the average person, those issues still need to be spelled out because they are important for anybody who deals with kids in schools. Being sensitive to the cultural needs of others is something that all teachers should be aware of regardless of their faculty.

Avner: How would you incorporate those issues as a social studies teacher?

Mary: I would incorporate it into the history of the province and stuff. There's the historical racism that has gone on in our province that needs to be dealt with in social studies, for sure. We've got loads of information where that could be incorporated into a lesson plan. Like when we're teaching about the railroad, you can do: how the railroad was built and why it came to this province. Or, you could deal with who built the railroad and why did they build the railroad. You're still teaching about the railroad so you're fulfilling the IRP, right? But now you're also mixing in stuff about the Chinese workers and how they were disposable.

Avner: How, in your view, did Simon deal with gender and multiculturalism in this course?

Mary: I can't remember. I can't remember him dealing with it. . . . I'm sure he must have, though. Didn't he have a unit on that?

Casey: [Incorporating issues of difference is important] because we're going to be teaching students from different cultures, students of different genders, and there's a lot of empirical data that suggests there is a lot of bias where that's concerned. It's something I think we need to be aware of and I think it's absolutely necessary to teach teachers about it. As for gender bias, we discussed it in the *Analysis of Education* course and the instructor asked all the females in class if they ever felt discriminated against on the basis of gender. And we all said, "No!" And her remark was that maybe it's so entrenched in society that we don't even realize it's happening, but it is.

Avner: Do you think it's important to engage those issues in social studies?

Casey: Yes. I mean, it's part of social studies, it's part of history, it's part of our society. The whole gender issue, for example, with history, I mean, we study what we think are the significant events in history, which usually involve men. But there were also women who were involved in some way or another and I think, again, it's important to recognize that.

Avner: How do you do that in the classroom?

Casey: Well, we're sending these students into society and so I think we should, definitely, incorporate it and I think it would be a good idea for a teacher to have the students watch the teacher for one day and see if there is a gender bias when they're teaching, that type of thing. So it's relevant, it's right now, in their classroom and they see the importance of it.

Avner: Any other way?

Casey: I would want students to look at what's around them too, you know, in their own lives . . . with multiculturalism—getting to know the different students in their classroom: their backgrounds, their culture, where they came from, what they consider important, what holidays they celebrate, that type of thing, and to respect that and also be proud of their own culture.

Avner: How about gender?

Casey: Well yeah. I would like to teach about women in history. I think it's hard to find a lot of information and a lot of the information is more bottom-up because women weren't making, you know, a lot of important decisions. But I would want to use current events too, especially in Vancouver, because it is a multicultural city.

Avner: How were gender and multiculturalism incorporated in Simon's course?

Casey: I don't remember them being addressed directly.

Jack: [Those issues are important] because we should be aware that racism exists and that, as a teacher, you might want to engage it. I mean you want to be aware of it so it doesn't keep taking place or so that you can try and challenge those ideas if kids are racist or have racist leanings. I mean society is racist in general and knowing that can give you opportunities to challenge it. As for gender, sure! Gender inequality exists. I just read an article about a teacher who addresses the male students in the class X times more than the female students and it argued about the male evaluation system that women are forced to conform to. I thought it was all pretty interesting.

Avner: Is that important as a social studies teacher?

Jack: If you're ever going to engage those topics specifically, it would probably be in a social studies class. I mean it's something you can teach a unit on and make students aware of these ideas and that there is inequality.

Avner: So as a teacher you'll deal with issues of gender or multiculturalism in a specific unit?

Jack: Well, there's different ways to look at it. You could incorporate it in every unit to try and bring female perspectives in on topics that are usually dominated by these white males. Or, I guess, if you're not just dealing with gender then you can bring in other cultures' perspectives on different things, if you can and whenever you can. When you're doing the settlement of the West, you might want to look at women's experiences as well, not just the men's experiences and if you can't find [it in the textbook?] then just [use] diaries and whatever sources are out there that show how women felt about it. And then, if you want to do a specific unit on gender you can just look at how women are portrayed by society. . . . I think both approaches are valuable. I would take both.

Avner: So it's important for social studies?

Jack: Yes. Definitely.

Avner: I want you to think back on the methods course. How well do you think those issues were addressed in that course?

Jack: Well, they weren't at all [pause] were they? I don't think they were at all.

Avner: What message does this send to you as a social studies teacher?

Jack: I guess that they're not as important. But that's not fair because we looked at it in our other methods class. We looked at both multiculturalism and gender equity specifically and we looked at how we would shape units on it, at how we would do it directly. . . .

Avner: Of the articles you read for this course, how many were written by women?

Jack: Ahhh [pause] I don't know. Were any? I'm trying to think. [pause] I don't know if any were.

Avner: By people of color?

Jack: I don't know. They didn't have pictures.

Jocelyn: I think that if we're going to be doing anything about the social inequities which manifest themselves in an education environment—because education is a social environment, then we need to be, first, aware of them and, second, alerted to how we can rectify the problems or challenges. When I went into the school I was appalled at how much attention the boys received and how little attention the girls received. And then I thought, "You know, that's a comment not just on education but on society." Society comes through in the classroom; the classroom is made up of society and if we want to do anything about what goes on in society, we've got to start now, start young, start in the classroom.

Avner: Is it important for a social studies teacher?

Jocelyn: Incredibly important, incredibly relevant. They are relevant because your subject matter is society and when you come to a text you've got to be able to understand that the person's perspective on life is going to affect what it is they write and how their interaction with their environment made them write this. You also need to know that different people in your class are going to react differently to that very same text for a variety of reasons: gender, culture, language, all those kinds of things. So you can't get through your subject area material without talking about some of those issues. It's [also] important to understand that the materials we're studying in Western society, in a Western history classroom, are different from those being studied in Japan. It's the same history, supposedly, it's the same chronological time, but there are different issues involved. It is important to understand that what we call history is our interpretation and how do you even begin to communicate that to students if you don't first of all talk about multiculturalism, about different perspectives, different ways of looking at things. Gender can affect that, age can affect that, culture can affect that, society can affect that, class can affect that. You can't separate those things from the content; they are the content.

Avner: You were just telling me how important it is to address issues of gender and multiculturalism in a social studies class. How were they addressed in the methods course?

Jocelyn: Gender and multiculturalism? [pause and then a surprised] Ummmmmm [another pause and then another surprised] Ummmmmm. Gender really wasn't touched on, was it [she asks herself in a whisper]?

Avner: How do you think students coming out of the course will see issues of gender and multiculturalism relating to social studies?

Jocelyn: Well, I guess the same way as they saw it going in [to the course], unless they chose to actively take them on.

Avner: You said one can't write without one's positionality affecting what one writes.

Jocelyn: Right.

Avner: How many of the close to 20 articles you read in Simon's course were written by women?

Jocelyn: Two.

Avner: By people of color?

Jocelyn: I'd have to look at the whole thing again. It didn't strike me as [something to look at]. There might not have been anybody. I don't know. . . . You know, I hadn't thought of it, actually. It may be because we had talked about it and done so much of it in other classes, as things to be aware of, and after that it's up to you. And it *was* left up to us. Simon didn't give any weight to that at all.

Ron: [Dealing with issues of difference and positionality in a teacher education program is significant] because they influence how we teach and I think that's something we need to make explicit and really think about and discuss, especially if we have any intention of changing the way we run society or the way that we teach. If we want to teach students to be critical about society, about what they're learning, then, sure, we have to examine our own values. And I think also that there's no such thing as value-free education. Even the idea of being value-free is value-laden in itself. So yeah. I do think we have to engage these topics.

Avner: When you say "engage," what do you mean?

Ron: I think it's not enough to read a bunch of viewpoints about those issues. I think it's important to reflect and find out where we ourselves stand on these things, what we believe, what we're going to be acting on.

Avner: Is it important to also engage those things as a social studies teacher?

Ron: Yeah. I do think so. I mean certainly a part of social studies and history will be, at the very least, to look at gender roles and gender relations. And, again, if you're in a social studies class and you're talking about issues such as power relations, you're going to have to start dealing with it in terms of multiculturalism and gender and sexual orientation.

Avner: You said it's important to engage those issues in education and also in social studies. Were those issues engaged in Simon's course?

Ron: Not explicitly. . . . But I think they were engaged because they are part and parcel of the approach of critical thinking which the course focused on. I think that a critically reflective person will, at the very least, question these issues of gender equity and multiculturalism and think about them. And Simon seemed to model a kind of a democratic approach to learning in the classroom and I think that those values are part of that.

Avner: Did the words "gender" or "multiculturalism" ever come up in class?

Ron: Not really. No. . . . And maybe it would have been better if we had discussed them explicitly.

Avner: Who is multicultural education for?

Ron: Ideally it should be for everybody, but the cynical part of me wants to say that it's for mainstream Anglo-white people.

Avner: Were most of the students in Simon's class mainstream Anglo-white students?

Ron: Yes. [pause] So why weren't we talking about it?! Actually, as a friend of mine said, the problem with multiculturalism in Canada is that the French and English think they are above it.

Speaking about the role, place, and purpose of engaging gender and multiculturalism in education as well as to how those were (and were not) incorporated in their own education, students' comments begin to provide answers to some of the questions raised by Armento and others at the beginning of this chapter. Though I will periodically return to these individual responses as my discussion progresses, it seems that the power of the message generated by their words lies not in the differences between responses but in the commonalities among them. That is, in the answer their combined responses provides to the following questions: Why and how should gender and multiculturalism be included in social studies (any) education? To what and whose educative ends?

As this group of prospective teachers combines to speak about their understandings regarding the purpose of addressing issues pertaining to gender and multiculturalism in education and the degree to which they were engaged in their own education, several issues (and, consequently, corresponding questions) become apparent. First, perhaps, and in contrast to much of the literature in teacher education that states that prospective teachers enter teacher education very much indifferent to issues of diversity and with very limited cross- or intercultural experience (Ahlquist, 1991; Gomez, 1994; Haberman, 1991; Paine, 1989; Zimpher & Ashburn, 1992), the students involved in this study appear different. Though sharing a predominantly white, middle-class education with the (mostly U.S.) counterparts depicted in the literature, they had all spent most of their lives in primarily multicultural environments, not to mention in a country that since 1982 has incorporated multiculturalism into its constitution as a recognition of the diversity of Canadian culture. Two of the participants—Ron and Jocelyn—had each taught English as a Second Language in Japan prior to entering teacher preparation. Charles had gone to a school in which a large part of the student body comprised First Nations (a term used in Canada to refer to Native Americans) students. Casey had traveled to Europe and South Africa and had spent a summer in Israel while attending an institute about the Middle East conflict before beginning her teacher education program. In short, they were not the parochial student teachers Zimpher and Ashburn (1992), among others, describe.

A second issue stemming from participants' articulate and, to some degree, already thought-through answers is that diversity-related issues were not ignored in this teacher education program, that students had ample opportunities to discuss them prior to these interviews. Such discussions, however, as students made explicit, did not take place in their social studies methods course. How, then, and where were issues of difference engaged in this teacher education program? And what impact did their omission from the methods course and their commission elsewhere have on prospective teachers' understandings of difference in education? Third, these excerpts illustrate that while participants vary in their responses as to the purpose of including issues of difference in education, they are unanimous about the need for, the benefits of, and their own undivided commitment to such an incorporation. Indeed, throughout my six interviews with this group of prospective teachers, issues pertaining to gender and multiculturalism very often took center stage as participants—both as students at the university and as teachers in schools— continuously discussed their importance. Further, participants all demonstrate an understanding that difference is not only pertinent to the broad context of society and education but is connected to, and permeates (and thus should be addressed in) the social studies curriculum, and, more importantly, in the social studies classroom itself. Combined, they bring forth a variety of reasons for focusing on issues relating to difference. These range from the reality of a multicultural student body to the need to empower students, challenge societal inequalities, and combat misogyny, racism, and other forms of discrimination. How would such goals be achieved, according to these six student teachers? The connection between the past and the present is overtly apparent. By learning about women and Other in the past, participants unanimously argue, one not only exposes students to the contributions of those groups to our collective history and culture but also, by placing them as equally important contributors to our past, advances the possibility of seeing them as equal partners in the present.

Yet while participants' commitment to issues of difference is, by and large, unquestionable, a closer look at their responses (and those to follow) raises questions as to the nature of education about/for difference to which they are committed as well as its relation to the one they received. What constitutes an education about difference for this group of participants and in this teacher education program? How, when, and where was it (and is it to be) manifested? What is most striking, perhaps, is participants' recurring and, by and large, exclusive response to those questions. Unanimously, they emphasize the need to infuse the social studies curriculum with histories of and by women and Other. While few would disagree with the need to rectify a mostly Eurocentric, white-, and male-dominated history curriculum, it is questionable whether incorporating content about and by women and Other as a singular educative focus is sufficient to rectify the inequalities prospective teachers themselves claimed they wish to redress (see, i.e., Goodwin, 1994, 1997; Sleeter, 1993). Further, although what participants propose addresses the need to teach *about* women and Other by incorporating their stories (either in a specific unit or throughout the curriculum), there is no suggestion in their responses of using the different ways in which women and Other story the past (and the past they choose to story) as a pedagogy with which to inquire—a critical prism through which one might investigate everything and teach all. Focusing on the need to infuse new—previously marginalized—content, none of the participants explore difference pedagogically. That is, as a means to think differently not only about the "what" or even the "how" one teaches but about how both work with, on, and against the other to educate.

To think about difference pedagogically requires a perspective, a focus that, as Ramsey (1987) points out, is

> reflected in all decisions about every phase and aspect of teaching. It is a lens through which teachers can scrutinize their options and choices in order to clarify what social information [and formation] they are conveying overtly and covertly to their students. In a sense, it is a series of questions to induce educators to challenge and expand the goals and values that underlie their curriculum designs, materials, and activities. (p. 6; cf. Goodwin, 1997, p. 12)

This expansive pedagogical approach infuses diversity in all stages and levels of educational practice. The emphasis participants put on content rather than on pedagogy, indeed the separation they made between them, is perhaps not coincidental or innocent. Rather, as I will demonstrate in the next section, it can be attributed, at least in part, to the structure, discourses, and practices of this particular teacher education program.

Structuring Difference, Practicing Differently

Addressing difference in teacher education, claims Gay (1986), can generally be organized in two ways:

through the *infusion* approach, which integrates attention to diversity throughout the program's various courses and field experiences, or through the *segregated* approach, which treats diversity as the focus of a single course or as a topic
in a few courses, while other components of the program remain untouched.
While studies indicate a clear preference for the infusion approach, not surprisingly the segregated approach dominates. (cf. Melnick & Zeichner, 1997, pp.
27–28. See also Garibaldi, 1992; Grant & Sleeter, 1985; Martin, 1995; Zeichner
& Hoeft, 1996)

Incorporating a discussion about issues of difference in some of its
courses but not in others, the teacher education program at UWC was an
example of this latter, segregated approach.[2] The responsibility for dealing with issues of difference—that is, multiculturalism, gender, race, class,
and sexual orientation—was delegated primarily to a compulsory educational studies course, *Analysis of Education*. Bringing gender and multiculturalism in particular to the forefront, this course focused on how the
politics of difference and differentiation are always already inscribed in
education and thus also, and simultaneously, prescribe education. Discussing the various ways in which women and minorities have been (and
are still) marginalized—in society and education—students were made more
aware of the need to address and redress such marginalization in their
classrooms. Two other courses offered by the Department of Educational
Psychology and Special Education also engaged issues of difference, specifically *Development and Exceptionality in the Regular Classroom*,
which focused on the inclusion of "special" students. With an emphasis
on educational psychology and cognitive development, however, the contribution of these courses to the incorporation of difference was at the
individual rather than societal level, focusing on the importance of recognizing one's individual learners as different while at the same time accommodating their different needs equally.

Courses focusing on pedagogy, on the other hand, were mostly silent
about difference. The degree to which the social studies methods course
neglected to address those issues explicitly has already been established in
students' responses excerpted above (and will be demonstrated further in
the next section). But the silence on issues of difference in the social
studies methods course was not an isolated endeavor. Rather, it coincided
with the omission of difference from the discourse in *Principles of Teaching*
(*POT*)—the primary course about pedagogy required of all student teachers, regardless of their teaching concentration. In the five lectures students attended in that course—each focusing, in turn, on the role of the
teacher, instructional planning, teaching strategies, assessment and evaluation, and classroom management—issues of difference played no role.

Nor were they incorporated in any of the readings or the dozen case studies student teachers were asked to read, analyze, and respond to while discussing the above topics in the close to 20 seminar sessions following those lectures. Although the multicultural nature of the student body was often referred to in these case studies by mentioning Other students' "ethnic" names, difference was never addressed as an issue in any of those case studies. Nor did it present itself as an issue for consideration while thinking about pedagogy. Difference seemed to have no relevance in that course to prospective teachers' planning, teaching strategies, assessment and evaluation, or classroom management. Those all stood above and beyond issues of difference, never affecting or being affected by them. [ST¶ **Ron**: *I think that toward the end of one* POT *class, toward the end of the course, we all suddenly became momentarily enthusiastic about the need to address issues of gender and multiculturalism. And then left it at that.*]

While a third course on pedagogy—*Issues in Social Studies Education*—did focus on gender and multiculturalism, it did so primarily by emphasizing the need to insert content about the Others into the existing history curriculum (the "content" approach). In so doing, the argument went, prospective teachers will be able to illustrate to their own future students that although subjugated groups—i.e., women, Chinese-, Japanese-, or First Nation-Canadians—have been mostly excluded from and rendered silent in the chronicles of "official" history, they were nevertheless influential and active members of past communities. (Is it coincidental, therefore, to find these very examples in participants' initial responses?)

What emerges, then, is a structure whereby issues of difference were engaged primarily in foundations or "content" courses (or as content in a minor social studies methods course) while being excluded from the program's two main courses on pedagogy. And while the contribution of those "content" courses to student teachers' understanding about difference (and the need to infuse difference) in education is no doubt apparent in participants' initial responses, what these courses, by definition and purpose, did not provide prospective teachers is a pedagogy of how to engage issues of gender and multiculturalism in the classroom or how to engage a classroom or a curriculum with and through them. More than demonstrating to students that institutional commitment to cultural pluralism is territorial, segregated, and limited (Hidalgo, Chavez-Chavez, & Ramage, 1996, p. 774), that structure suggests that diversity is (and thus *can* be) divorced from pedagogy and pedagogy from diversity. [ST¶ **Jocelyn**: *I note the separation you observe and I agree. It's problematic,*

but I wonder how many currently employed teachers focus on the
"how" in their teaching along with the "what" in their courses. I'll bet
the number is very small.]

It is this separation between content and pedagogy that the next three
sections of this chapter examine. The first addresses the implications of
such a separation within the social studies methods course itself. The
second examines how that separation disabled prospective teachers from
connecting "content" they learned beyond the methods course to pedagogical issues relating to their own social studies classrooms. The final
section explores how the structured separation examined in sections one
and two enabled student teachers to both disengage from the ways in
which diversity was implicated in their own learning and to actively ignore
their own implication in a system that allowed, if not encouraged, them to
remain blind to such implications.

The Social Studies Methods Course

Two powerful messages come across as one examines participants' comments (or inability to comment) in the beginning of this chapter about
diversity in/and the social studies methods course. First, in spite of the
fact that all of the participants stated that issues of gender and
multiculturalism are inherently relevant to social studies education, those,
they claimed, played no explicit role within the social studies methods
course itself. Second, while participants believed it important to include
issues of gender and multiculturalism in the education they are to provide
their own students in the future, they seemed indifferent, at least prior to
my conversations with them, as to how (or whether) issues of difference
were incorporated in a methods course preparing them to teach others.
How do these two internally contradictory messages inform us about
what did and did not take place in the methods course, about students'
ability to disengage their own learning from the teaching they are to provide others? And what can we learn from them about the degree to which
content and pedagogy (and content as pedagogy and pedagogy as content) are able to remain disconnected in students' minds while learning to
teach?

Although the most salient message coming out of prospective teachers' comments was that the methods course did not incorporate issues of
difference, I wish to begin with the one student who claimed it did. Con-
curring with his colleagues that difference was not present in the explicit
curriculum of the methods course (and should have been), Ron suggested

that it was nevertheless always implicitly there in Simon's pedagogy. Ron gave two reasons for this assertion. First, Simon had repeatedly emphasized the need for prospective teachers to incorporate a variety of perspectives (texts) on any issue studied in the classroom. That is, while the focus in the methods course was on variety rather than diversity, students were indeed encouraged to include diversity in their variety; to incorporate peripheral histories that represent the past differently; to bring texts currently at the margins to the center of the curriculum in order to "view concepts, issues, and problems from diverse cultural perspectives" (Banks, 1991, p. 138. See also Banks, 1995, 1997; Edgerton, 1996). But the inclusion of difference in the methods course was most apparent, according to Ron, through Simon's modeling of a "democratic and egalitarian pedagogy," one that, according to Ron, was not only advocated *in* the process of student teachers' learning to teach but was also, and contrary to what took place in other courses, actually practiced *as* students were learning to teach.

When Ron spoke of Simon's open and democratic pedagogy he was also referring, I believe, to a learning environment that fits well within pedagogical approaches advocated in some of the feminist literature. This environment entailed, among other things, an atmosphere of self-reflection, trust, mutual respect, and community (Goodman, 1992; Hicks, 1990), based in/on egalitarian and cooperative structures (Schniedewind, 1987), and a teaching style that was constantly open to questioning (though little of it ever took place) through its tentativeness and pauses, inviting students to enter, critique, and reject, as well as support, add, and connect learning taking place in the classroom with their previous educational experiences (see also Boxer, 1982; Kenway & Modra, 1992; Shrewsbury, 1987; Sikes-Scering, 1997; Treichler, 1986).

That said—and as participants stated unanimously—issues of difference were never engaged explicitly. Not once in the almost 30 classes did the words "difference," "gender," or "multiculturalism" enter the discourse of the methods course. Granted, simply invoking these terms guarantees little. Excluding them entirely, however, necessarily gives some indication as to their value, or lack thereof. For silences are as informative as are the utterances surrounding them; they always work with, through, and against the latter to educate. **[ST¶ Jocelyn**: *I agree. However, I think that these issues surround us in everything we do and therefore we need not "talk" about them—we live them. No one articulated this in class but I know I thought/felt them.* **Avner**: *Isn't it exactly because these issues are all around us, impact so much of what we do, that we need* *to "talk" about them, to examine our implication in them (part of which is why we don't feel we need to talk about them)?*]

What messages might have been conveyed by the lack of explicit engagement with issues of gender and multiculturalism in the methods course? How did those operate in conjunction with messages conveyed by the teacher education program as a whole and particularly with the messages coming from the other methods course—the one that *did* address the place for gender and multiculturalism in social studies? It is the particular combination of what the latter offered and the former did not, I propose, that shaped prospective teachers' understandings of how one does (and should) engage difference in social studies education both as students, then as teachers.

By relegating discussions about gender and multiculturalism to a second social studies methods course required only of students for whom social studies was the only teaching focus (hence excluding, for example, Jocelyn, Charles, and Ron) and not making them part of the "basic" social studies methods course, two important messages were simultaneously conveyed. First, that gender and multiculturalism are not part of, or not relevant to, basic social studies instruction. They can therefore be considered an afterthought, an aspect social studies teachers might add to the existing curriculum if and when time permits, if and when materials are available, if and when the student body necessitates it; they are not issues fundamentally embedded in and always relevant to everything social studies teachers already do, regardless. Second, by addressing gender and multiculturalism in the other social studies methods course as content and not infusing them into the explicit discussion about pedagogy in either of those courses, students could be left with the impression that while it might be important to include those issues in *what* social studies teachers teach, they are not as pertinent to how they teach any content, whether or not it includes Other texts.

Elements of both messages come through as Jack and Ron speak about their practicum.

Jack: In the grade nine classes, we briefly discussed the lack of women in history and that everything is about men, studying men. I tried to get a few women in the biographies we did, but not many. I'm trying to think if I talked about it with other classes. [Pause]. Not a lot. Not enough. I would like to do it more.

Avner: So why don't you?

Jack: It's difficult to find opportunities. Again, I'm teaching the curriculum. And [when you do so] you try whenever possible to talk about women's issues or issues with women or you can briefly talk about their omission. . . . But I think it would take a lot of work to put together any sort of unit or even a few lessons on women and their role; it's just hard. The sources aren't out there and I didn't have a ton of time on my hands.

Ron: I did a bit [of incorporating multiculturalism] in the grade eleven, but not much. I could have talked a lot about the Asian Exclusionary Act or the Head Tax [but I didn't]. I did, however, bring in a little bit about some of the battalions in the First World War being made up, for example, of Japanese Canadians or Chinese Canadians. . . . When I gave that class an assignment to write a letter to Prime Minister Borden either supporting or criticizing the Conscription Act, I gave them a list of possible perspectives from which to write. On the board, I gave examples of a farmer, a loyalist, a woman. But afterwards I thought: "What about a Chinese immigrant? What about a Native Canadian or a Japanese Canadian? What would their thoughts be about the conscription issue?" But because I only thought of it much later, after they had all started doing their writing, nobody took up that thread. Other than that, I haven't done anything explicitly multicultural.

Avner: How about gender?

Ron: With grade elevens, again, talking about women getting the right to vote. I managed to get in a couple of readings on that issue. But the majority of what I've been doing is very curriculum-based, very close to the textbook. So that, of course, restricts, in a way, how much I'm getting into issues of race and gender in class. . . . I mean it is quite a risk to stop the class and say, "Take a look at all the names I've just listed," in my grade nine socials class and ask, "How many women do you see?" "None." "Why is that?" and start thinking about that. Although I might very well do that now that I think about it. It might be an interesting point of discussion. But somehow that feels like I'm getting off topic, off track somehow. There's still a sense that by the end of my practicum, and I only have two weeks, I have to be at the end of Chapter 19. And if I go off on this tangent, I'm going to lose time.

Although Jack and Ron both included aspects regarding gender and multiculturalism in a variety of instances elsewhere in their practicum (and I will provide examples to that effect further on), the notion that those are somewhat external to the curriculum nevertheless persisted throughout. "It's difficult to find opportunities. I'm teaching the curriculum," claimed Jack. "What I've been doing," Ron added, "is very curriculum-based. . . . So that, of course, restricts, in a way, how much I'm getting into issues of race and gender in class." Why "of course"? Is the social studies curriculum inherently antithetical to issues of difference? Or is it merely Jack and Ron's conception of that curriculum? And if it is, as I believe, the latter, what positioned them to conceive of the curriculum that way? Moreover, what did Ron mean by "in a way" when speaking about the degree to which he was "able to get into issues of race and gender in class"? How and what did "that way" restrict? That is, what was it that the curriculum restricted and in what way did it do so?

Answers to these questions begin to emerge when one examines the different approaches for engaging issues of difference embedded in the responses Jack and Ron provide. Broadly, they speak of three different approaches. The first strives to teach students about women and Other by including information about their past contributions. This, from the examples Jack and Ron provide, is where much of their energy was directed (and if they only had more time and resources, would have gone even further). The second approach, perhaps compensating for the lack of resources necessary for the first, is to "briefly speak about their omission." The third approach, while beginning with inclusion (the essence of approach #1), not only highlights the omission of subjugated groups from the curriculum and moves on (as does approach #2) but, rather, by asking the "why" and "how" questions about their exclusion, engages the politics of representation. Contrary to the first two approaches, the third is overtly political in nature. Questioning how, in spite of its acts of exclusion, history, as a school subject, manages the illusion of a narrative that speaks equally to and for all, this third approach examines how (and whose) knowledge is positioned to tell and how it positions audiences to listen. It moves from the transmission of content to a discussion about the politics of annunciation and the relationship between power, politics, and knowledge.

The restricting elements of the curriculum come to light, in a self-regulating process more than as an imposition, through the degree of appropriateness Jack and Ron ascribe to each of the three approaches. Both believe the first two are permissible, perhaps desirable within current practices of social studies education ("I would like to do it more," Jack stated). The third, on the other hand, claims Ron, is a "risky" endeavor—"a tangent," "getting off topic," "a diversion" from the *real* business of social studies education.

The Politics and Poetics of Representation

In *A Philosophy of History in Fragments,* Heller (1993) claims that people "are thrown into a World, but only by having been thrown into History do they have a world" (p. 33). The question facing social studies educators, then, is not only how one "gets thrown" into history to claim a world, but, as Yerushalmi (1982) puts it, "what kind of past shall we have" (p. 99) in order to do the "claiming"?

Influenced by new understandings within academe as well as by grass-roots movements and curricula guidelines sensitive to community voices, her-story and Others'-stories are increasingly finding their way into the mainstream—his-story—of the history curriculum. Though often still relegated peripheral status through their marginalization as add-ons in particular highlighted and/or segregated sections of the text, women, Native Americans, and other un- and under represented groups nevertheless increasingly find their place in the history textbook, often not only as objects but as subjects of their own stories. Utilizing what already existed in their textbook and often supplementing it with other—more inclusive—textbooks and curricular materials, the student teachers participating in this study did their best to insert traditionally unrepresented groups into the curriculum. As Mary, for one, explained, she supplemented the existing textbook with another "because I wanted to focus on groups the school textbook doesn't cover, like women and native history and immigrant history."

Including those and other perspectives in the history classroom allows all—majority and minority—students an opportunity to learn about the contribution of many rather than only a few groups to our collective past. Exploring history beyond the limited lenses provided by the mostly white-, Eurocentric-, middle-class-dominated texts currently used in the classroom, however, might be most significant for students whose experiences have been excluded from the curriculum. For it is through the curriculum that students receive a sense of what culture and whose history are considered worthy of valorization, and what forms of culture and history are considered invalid and unworthy of public esteem (Giroux, 1995, pp. 109–110). An inclusive curriculum, claims Cummins (1986), reduces the dissonance and alienation characterizing current minority experience in schools (p. 24; cf. McCarthy, 1993, p. 292). Seeing their own cultures reflected in the official rendition of history gives marginalized students a sense of recognition, empowerment, and agency. When they are no longer silent in the past, the argument goes, they will be less inclined to be silent in the present of our (thus far) mostly silencing classrooms. But while "covering" previously excluded history is, no doubt, important, simply incorporating their experiences guarantees little beyond incorporation itself.

In his statement opening this chapter, Charles was passionate about the need to engage issues of gender in education because "gender equity is always an issue . . . [hence] you have to discuss it at some point." As a social studies teacher, he added, "you can decide whether you want to cover women in [history] or not." Charles himself said he would choose the former—to talk about women in history. "It's important," he added, because it's part of history and it doesn't get talked about much. It's important for me to know that my students are seeing some of it."

Visiting Charles during his practicum, it was apparent that he had made good on his initial decision. When asked about a lesson or unit he was especially proud of, Charles told me of a two-lesson mini-unit about the "King's daughters," one he received from his sponsor teacher who, in turn, had borrowed it a few years earlier from the school's vice principal (both males). These two lessons, Charles explained, were part of a grade nine unit about Canada in the 1600s, specifically about New France (Quebec).

> The king of France wanted to populate the colony but there were no women in New France [no white women, that is]. So he recruited interested orphans and young women in France, paid them, and sent them over to marry the men who were already here to start making families. My purpose was to have students understand that this is what happened and this is how it worked and this is how women came over and what marriage was actually like at the beginning.

After discussing "how things were in Europe at the time, who these girls were, and why they might have chosen to come over instead of living in France," and in preparation for the re-enactment of the selection process following the arrival of the King's daughters in New France, Charles had students create their own imaginary biographies—the boys of the white settlers, the girls of the King's daughters. "Each student could choose the character they wanted to be and their own name." In their biographies, "the King's daughters had to answer the following questions: Who are you, where are you from? What do you expect life to be like in New France? What are your expectations in marriage? And what qualities do you think you could offer your new husband?" The boys, too, had to write their biographies, responding to the following: "Who are you? What was your past job? Where did you come from? What are your expectation of marriage? And what kinds of things are you looking for in a wife?"

Using these biographies, Charles hoped to simulate the initial selection process experience

> whereby the girls [the King's daughters] didn't have much of a choice at all, where the women would get herded into a room and one at a time the guys would go, "That one," and that would be it. And they'd get married. . . . So I had the girls [in my class] come into the room and put the biographies they had written on the wall (no pictures!) and then leave the room. Then the guys came in and had 30 seconds to pick the one they wanted. . . . So now they are paired off and tomorrow they will actually get married in a ceremony."

Avner: Why are you particularly proud of this unit?

Charles: Because they were all right into it. It was fun. They were either pretty excited or not too thrilled when they found out who they were matched with. It's totally different from anything they've already done. It's a fun activity. I mean there are a couple of little paragraph assignments that they have to do. It's not worth a lot of marks. It's just something fun. I mean they're still learning but they're not taking notes and stuff.

Avner: What are they learning?

Charles: They're learning the whole process [of selection] without them even thinking about it. They know who these women were and they know why they came. And they're going to write about how life was back then on their own. [So] they're going to learn for themselves a little bit. Tomorrow they're going to get together [in their pairs] and create a little one- or two-minute dialogue of what kinds of things they would say to each other. And then for homework, they're going to write [about] how they feel the day after: Are they happy with their wife so far or their husband? What are they looking forward to? I mean it's not a lot of factual information. But it's getting them role-playing, getting them to kind of pretend they were in the time.

Avner: Will students continue exploring Canadian history for the rest of the year from the perspective of those couples and how those couples experienced life in Canada at the time?

Charles: No. They'll only be married for a total of four days, until the end of this unit.

Tempting as it is to unpack all there is to unpack in this excerpt, I will restrict my analysis to one aspect, with the intention of illustrating that in the strive for authenticity, empathy, and immediacy of experience, teachers eager to "include" may risk replicating, perhaps entrenching, oppressive systems rather than challenging them. Simply adding experiences of women in the history/social studies curriculum provides little more than what Scott (1996) defines as "a rediscovery of ourselves in the past." Experience itself, Scott (1991) argues, is "always already an interpretation and in need of interpretation" (p. 779; cf. Olesen, 1994, p. 167). Experience is experienced the way it is because the one experiencing has been positioned—through language, power, culture, and previous experiences—to experience certain things in particular ways. Thus "merely taking experience into account," claims Olesen (1994), "does not reflect on how that experience came to be. [Hence,] oppressive systems are replicated rather than criticized in the unquestioning reliance on 'experience'" (p. 167).

Not only did Charles refrain from having students explore the dynamics of how and why the King's Daughters or the colonial men in New France were positioned to experience what they did, the mini-unit he taught worked to reinforce the subjugation of women in the past as well as in the very present of his classroom. What, for example, do the different questions Charles posed to male and female students in his class as they were preparing for the marriage contract tell them about the nature of relationships between the two genders both in the past and in the present? And how does the entire experience inform students about the need to question rather than replicate relations of power and subjugation? How are students in Charles's class better able to address issues of power and privilege in the past, present, or future following this activity? Indeed, does such an activity reinforce power relations through an unproblematized reenactment, in effect making it more difficult for students to question them? Without inquiring into the pedagogical nature of the content, the inclusion of Other histories—in the case of Charles' class or the one presented below from Casey's class—will not necessarily translate into advancing the inclusion of Others in education.

Speaking to the importance of engaging multiculturalism in the social studies classroom in her statement opening this chapter, Casey mentioned that one of her goals as a teacher would be to encourage students to get to know each other's culture by having students share their experiences and culture with others.

> I would want students to look at what's around them too, you know, in their own lives with multiculturalism, getting to know the different students in their classroom—their backgrounds, their culture, where they came from, what they consider important, what holidays they celebrate, and to respect that and also be proud of their own culture.

Devoting a substantial effort to incorporate perspectives not normally included in the textbook, Casey encouraged her students to adapt class assignments to their own interests by choosing topics that spoke to their experiences, culture, and history, and share those with their peers.

The day I visited Casey's practicum classroom, she and her grade eleven students began a post–World War II history unit. Casey opened the unit by asking students to brainstorm, collectively, the most significant world events since the end of the Second World War. Having given students some time to think about their answers, Casey began putting their responses on the board. Fifteen minutes later, the following list emerged (in order of appearance): the Gulf War; the election of Nelson Mandela as president of South Africa; the breakup of the Soviet Union; the fall of communism; the Oklahoma City bombing; the Quebec referendum; the Meech Lake and Charlottetown Accords; the O.J. Simpson trial; the TWA air crash; the development of technology; the Rodney King beating and the Los Angeles riots; genetic engineering; the 1973 oil embargo; the Exxon Valdez oil spill; Chernobyl; Tienenman Square (Casey's contribution); famine in Somalia; the breakdown of Yugoslavia; AIDS; the war in the Falklands Islands.

Sitting at the back of the room, behind the teacher's desk, I observed the process with fascination. In spite of the fact that more than half of Casey's students were Asian, the majority of them Chinese (from Hong Kong, Taiwan, and Singapore), only one event on the board—Tienanmen Square—was directly reflective of their history. But what was even more striking, perhaps, was that although Asian students in Casey's class participated as equally as any others in the construction of the class list, the only event reflective of their history was put up on the board by Casey, not by one of her students—Asian or other.

Following an explanation by students as to why they thought those particular events were significant, Casey asked each student to construct his/her own top ten list of events. Students were informed that they could use five events already mentioned on the board but had to come up with another five on their own. As I walked around the room, I noticed that of the Asian students, at least those who were willing to share their lists with me, all elected to add five events from Chinese history to the five they chose from the board. Interestingly, none chose to make up an entirely new list, comprising events only from Chinese history. Rather, in a somewhat schizophrenic manner, the top half of their list included five events from Western history (taken from the board), the bottom part, five events from Chinese (or Chinese-related) history.

How does this example inform us about the politics of inclusion? A few issues spring to mind. First, the class list. Whichever way one analyzes the list, what becomes immediately apparent is that, in spite of Casey's ongoing efforts to include Other histories, most of the events that seemed significant to this group of students derived from or took place within Western history. (And even though some of those events include non-Western parties, events are nevertheless considered from a Western perspective—i.e., the Falklands rather than the Malvinas, the Gulf War, Famine in Somalia, etc.). Second, and more important, especially when one compares the class list to students' private lists, there was a disjuncture between the public and the private spheres regarding inclusion in this classroom; one emanating not because some students were excluded from the public sphere, but rather, because what was considered public, official history actively worked to exclude them. In a self-monitoring process, then, some students regulated what they chose to say in public and what they believed should remain private. Those students had apparently already learned the unwritten rules of the game: to give publicly what is expected in the public domain, and keep the Other in the private domain.

But what did and did not take place in Casey's classroom obviously exceeded the boundaries of her classroom and points to the idea that more than a validation is necessary to fully include the Other in the (dominant) educative process. This raises questions about how to use validation as a beginning, not an end; creating a pedagogy that allows all to contribute equally *within* difference while still speaking differently. **[ST¶**
Ron: *I think that this may point to some of the problems in ESL teaching; i.e., overcoming the "affective barrier." Chinese students, it seems to me, use Chinese language as a site of resistance—very few of us speak Chinese, after all. At the school I was teaching last year, myself, another teacher, and the librarian had students do a research project on the "outstanding events of the millennium." I adapted the list of 20-odd events that the other teacher and the librarian came up with, but I couldn't help noticing that all the events occurred after about 1860, most occurred in North America and Western Europe, and many were accidents such as the Titanic or Mt. St. Helens! I pointed this out to the students, who agreed with my observation but then generally chose to write about the Titanic, etc. One item, the return of Hong Kong to China, was initially seen as important by many Hong Kong–born students. But by the time they were writing their papers, none (maybe one) had followed through and written about it. I think the reason for this was that they couldn't find any sources in the school library about this event. The structure of the library collection itself may have sent a message about "public" and "private" knowledge.]*

The examples from Casey's and Charles's classrooms illustrate that simply adding or integrating content about ethnicity, women, or other marginalized groups to existing curriculum is insufficient (Spina, 1997, p. 32). Rather, and with the understanding that difference is organized within relations of power, the point becomes more than validating minority cultures or positioning the mere establishment of diversity as a final goal (Kincheloe & Steinberg, 1997, p. 26). Rather, the goal should be to "provide a sustained critique of institutional practices that position and/ or exclude them" (Aronowitz & Giroux, 1991, p. 102).

As important as inclusion may be, as Ron poignantly pointed out elsewhere,

> this whole thing of inclusion we are now all getting into is still an Othering be-
> cause we're still saying, "Oh, now we have to include aboriginal issues in educa-
> tion, now we have to include women, now we have to include this or another."
> And maybe now we're getting better at it and it can be a chapter rather than a
> few paragraphs in the textbook but it's still, "Here is history, here is women's
> history." How well would it go down to teach a course primarily based on women's
> history and say, "OK, now we have a section on men's history?"

What Ron brings up is the need to examine the relationship between center and margins, an issue inclusion in and of itself fails to address. By pointing to that relationship, Ron enters the pedagogical. Knowledge is no longer examined for itself, abstracted from the powers who put it there, but rather, in relation to other knowledge that makes it possible and the kind of knowledge it makes possible in return.

Engaging history with a critical eye, according to Willinsky (1998a), is not only about adding those who have gone missing in the story of the past, but about a way of interrogating their exclusion when (and even as) they are included. "When the world-history textbook terminates the timeline of Chinese history in the sixteenth century," what becomes necessary, according to Willinsky, is not simply an incorporation of the missed real-ity or truth about China since that time but "an explanation of the textbook's suspension of Chinese history that would increase the intelligi-bility of the West's project with history and its teaching." Good teachers, Willinsky adds,

> have long found supplementary works on China to cover what's missing from the
> traditional program. But it also needs to be made apparent to students that such
> exclusion is not simply an oversight but a feature of how the disciplines of geog-
> raphy, history, science, language, and literature (as well as the arts and math-
> ematics) have gone about dividing the world after the Age of Empire. (p. 250)

An explanation of this sort obviously requires more than "briefly speak-ing about their omission," as Jack suggested earlier. The exclusion of women, minority groups, and indigenous peoples from the curriculum, Giroux (1988a) points out, "is not politically innocent when we consider how existing social arrangements are partly constitutive of and depen-dent on the subjugation and elimination of the histories and voices of those groups marginalized and disempowered by the dominant culture" (p. 192). Without making these connections explicit, Mascia-Lees, Sharpe, and Cohen (1989) point out, the historical links between cultures and the hierarchies of discourses within them can be ignored. Consequently, the history of the colonial or the colonized in the case of Charles's King's Daughters "can be read as independent of that of the colonizer" (p. 29). The assumption, to borrow from Goodson's (1995) discussion of voicing in research, "is that by empowering new voices and discourses, by telling stories, we will rewrite and reinscribe the old white male bourgeois rhetoric." But "new stories do not by themselves," Goodson adds, "analyze or address the structures of power." Thus, he asks, is it not worthy to set the newly incorporated voices against the center's continuing power? Otherwise, he asks, "is it not more likely then that new discourses and voices that empower the periphery at one and the same time fortify, enhance, and solidify the old centres of power?"[3] (pp. 97–98; see also McCarthy, 1993, p. 294). What is needed, Spina (1997) suggests, is a shift "from superficial nods to subordinate groups which often celebrate deficits and disguise the legacy of colonialism, to a pedagogy of critical analysis of the inequities inherent in such a system" (p. 27).

Such a pedagogy, claims Bhabha (1994), "demands an encounter with 'newness' that is not part of the continuum of past and present" but rather "innovates and interrupts the performance of the present" (p. 7; cf. Benhabib, 1996, p. 16). Too often, however, marginalized histories are simply incorporated into the unproblematic, unquestioned discourse already established within the existing culture of the classroom and the appropriated/marginalized spaces within the pages of the textbook. Rather than make the Grand Narrative strange (Aronowitz & Giroux, 1991, p. 188), such a process co-opts the "strange" into the familiar and limits its ability to question the given, the taken-for-granted, to critically examine representation, the voicing of Other, and contribute to coherence *within* difference while speaking differently.

The very act of inclusion always already legitimizes the includer—its language, its codes and conventions, its methods of exclusion—and thus limits the ability (of the includer as well as the included) to question the presuppositions that allow the Grand Narrative to continue to exclude and at the same time be presented as "objective," as "real," as "true," as one narrative that speaks equally for all. What is abandoned in that process is the ability of subjugated voices—the voice of the minor—to call into question the conditions of history's own making (Jenkins, 1991) and explore the historicities that constitute the relationship between "majority" and "minority" voices. By exposing the relationship between 'major' and 'minor' texts, inclusion seeks "to destabilize the very majoritarianism that underlies disciplinary authority" to designate one as one and the other as the Other (Appadurai, 1996, p. 34; see also Giroux, 1990; LaCapra,

1994; Mehan, Okamoto, Lints, & Wills, 1995). What is called for, then, is not simply a new narrative—as inclusive and multiple as it may be—but a new understanding of narrativity itself—what the power to narrate entails, who maintains that power, and at what (and whose) expense (Allsup, 1995; Banks, 1993; hooks, 1990).[4]

Although a majority of participants in this study followed a mostly unproblematized method of inclusion, at times with a brief nod at, rather than an analysis of, exclusion, there were several instances to the contrary. Jocelyn, for one, consistently moved beyond the incorporation of content to the exploration of how content itself is positioned and positions students to know. Speaking, for example, about gender, Jocelyn explained that her goal was never to simply teach about women but to connect what was being taught about women to the politics of representation, connecting past and present, women and men.[5]

> It was never: "We're going to be dealing with women" or "This is a gender issue." [Rather], in my grade nine class, for example, we talked about "Why aren't there any women mentioned when we're dealing with the French Revolution? Women did an incredible amount, why aren't they in the textbook? Does that mean that they didn't contribute at all?" No, it doesn't. It just means that somebody figured it isn't important enough to put in the text. So I had students work with some primary documents and on another textbook which did highlight the role women played in the French Revolution and afterwards, I had them go through their own text[book] and analyze it to see if it actually has a fair representation of women's role in the French Revolution or not. In my grade ten class we looked at it more for current events: "How come most of the world news and the events we're looking at, it's all about men—male prime ministers and male leaders? Why? What's happening that keeps women out of those positions and out of the "news"?"

While Jocelyn, as did others, focused on the role of women in the French Revolution, by examining the politics of representation, she did more than have students simply rediscover women in the past. Instead, she had students engage history as a construction from a particular present that determines the kind of past they are able to find.

In another example, Jocelyn spoke of a unit she constructed about the history of the province for her grade 10 students.

> Jocelyn: We looked first of all at minorities and we looked at the whites as a minority group and how their experience, although they were really a minority group, dictated a majority mentality, a conquest mentality where the natives, although they were a majority, were treated like a minority and like an uncivilized group of people that we couldn't really understand.
>
> Avner: Why were they treated that way?

Jocelyn: I think it's part ignorance and part an imperialistic attitude that came along with the fur traders: divide and conquer. So we started from that and then looked at how that attitude affected other groups. We looked at the Chinese working on the CPR: "How did the railroad and the Gold Rush impact [our province]? How did that meeting of people with all their cultural baggage and philosophies and perspective affect [it]? How did each group respond to the geography, to the culture, to the history?" We also looked at why blacks were brought in to Canada. We looked at a couple of primary sources and how we come to a historical interpretation out of a photograph and we looked at literature and we ended on: "Is it the same now, is it different, and if so, why and what connections can you make between the history of the province and the present?" I think that by taking the issues up to the present, it put things a little more into perspective as opposed to studying the past and the present as disparate, as separate entities.

Ron, too, provided an example of how the perspective of Other can be used to question the dominant center, usually taken for granted as neutral.

At one point in my grade nine class we were discussing French and English rivalries in the Ohio River Valley and I had them debate as to whose claim was most justified and I made sure to include one perspective from the Natives themselves because the text, I noticed, was talking about French and English claims about something that wasn't even theirs. I think it was kind of valuable. It made the students recognize that: "Wait a minute! These are two foreign colonial powers going after somebody else's land."

What Ron's disrupting "Wait a minute!" allowed is an opportunity to teach students that nation-building in North America came at the expense of nations already inhabiting that land; that it was not the story of an empty land heroically discovered and cultivated by white settlers. That disruption also provides students a possibility to consider why and how this land came to be considered "empty" in the first place and what underlies the imperialistic notion of "emptiness" (emptiness of what?). But as Ron mentioned earlier, this critical attempt was an isolated endeavor. Often, Ron forgot to include Others at all. When he did, Ron admitted it rarely took the critical direction mentioned above. For, to repeat Ron's words, and those of others who might have been less articulate in that respect, it is quite a risk to stop the class and say, "'Take a look at all the names I've just listed' and ask, 'How many women [etc.] do you see?' 'None.' 'Why is that?' and start thinking about that. . . . [S]omehow that feels like I'm getting off topic, off track. . . . And if I go off on this tangent, I'm going to lose time." **[ST¶ Jack**: *I disagree with Ron. It is not risky, a tangent, or off topic. Perhaps he is referring to teaching this within the constraints of a practicum. These are in fact very much opportunities that engage students. My sentiment remains that I would*

*like to do it more—that is, discussing gender from a more critical/
postmodern perspective.*]

The Pedagogical in Learning to Teach

Part of one's understanding of difference as a teacher—and thus the possibility to address difference with students—derives from one's experiences as a student. How, then, and where did prospective teachers locate
themselves in relation to difference in their own education of, and experiences in, learning to teach? To what degree did they consider the relevance of difference (or the lack thereof) in their own education? How, if
at all, were those understandings translated into pedagogical opportunities for learning about teaching others? To discuss these questions, I
present two cases. The first pertains to a history of education course
three of the participants took during their final semester at UWC. The
second focuses around an event that took place during the last class of the
social studies methods course.

One of the four elective courses taken by Jack, Mary, and Jocelyn
during their final (Summer) semester of their teacher education program
was *History of Education.* The course, according to Jack, was "about
how the system of education in [our province] has, through the years,
marginalized minorities, mainly First Nations, Japanese, and, to some
degree, women." Having learned that much of the course focused on
students examining curricula, textbooks, and personal accounts of how
women and minorities were marginalized within [this province's] schools
for more than a century, I was interested in exploring the degree to which
participants were able to take that "content" and transform it into pedagogical understanding for the overwhelmingly multicultural classrooms they
were to occupy as teachers. "How, if at all, might what you learned in this
course," I asked students, "inform you as a teacher about your own future
classroom?" "Not too much," said Jack. "It informed me as a person. It
was great to just learn for myself rather than learning to become a teacher.
It was exactly the kind of history course I like." I paused and waited for
him to add something. After some hesitation, and realizing I expected
more, he added:

> Perhaps it did inform me as a teacher to some degree. I mean, all the stuff we did
> on residential schools, I could teach that in my classroom and the same with the
> Japanese Internment.

> Avner: Other than content—that is, teaching about this or that, is what you learned
> relevant in any other way to your teaching? To how and who you might teach?

Jack: I'm pretty sure it is.

Avner: In what way?

Jack: I don't know. . . .

What did Jack learn from this course about the marginalization of minority and female students in schools? As a teacher, "not too much." That is not surprising, considering his statement, "It was great to just learn for myself rather than learning to become a teacher." Pushed further, Jack realized that he did, after all, learn something as a teacher—the ability to incorporate content about residential schools and the Japanese Internment into the social studies curriculum. And while Jack was certain there was more to be learned from that course, he had no inkling of what that might be.

Mary responded similarly: "Ummm . . . I guess so," was how she chose to answer whether the course had informed her as a teacher.

> Mary: It taught us about the history of our province and about social history and those are the sort of things we need to convey to our students in social studies.
>
> Avner: Like what?
>
> Mary: Certain things that occurred in history that would translate straight from history of education to social studies, like residential schools.

Jocelyn, too, found the historical dimension of the course most significant.

> Jocelyn: It was fascinating to chart the general changes going on in Canada and how specifically they played out in [this province] and how that coincides with different historical events in [the province]. It also showed us how you can take the history of any one event or aspect, and by focusing on that, you can glean principles of historical interpretation of how history is created, how history is taught, how history is understood, all of which can be applied in a social studies classroom.
>
> Avner: If I understand you correctly, then what you learned about how First Nations students were put in residential schools and the treatment of minorities becomes content that you can teach in your social studies classroom?
>
> Jocelyn: Not content. I don't think I would teach that kind of content in my social studies classroom. But by looking at that you can apply skills and concepts of historical interpretation and development to your social studies classroom.
>
> Avner: How does learning about the maltreatment of women and minorities in schools actually inform you as a social studies *teacher*, in your own classroom? Or does it?

Jocelyn: Directly it didn't because much of the content, much of the historical facts and figures and information I learned as a result of the course won't be relevant to my classroom. Perhaps grade 10 in a unit on [the province], maybe some of it will come to play.

Apparently, this group of prospective teachers learned about the systemic marginalization of women and Other in the very system of education they were soon to be part of just as they would about Mesopotamia, the Crimean War, or plate tectonics. This new knowledge appears to have informed them about what teachers did in the past, not about what teachers must do in the present—a present that is, by and large, very much continuous with that past. It pertained to other women, other Other, not those in today's classrooms being subjected to similar, though often more subtle, forms of subjugation and discrimination. Further, student teachers' roles as students appeared to be separated from what might be expected of them as teachers. What they learned as students (and learning, as Jack put it, *as* a student), while impacting *what* they might teach students, had little relevancy for *how* or *who* they might be teaching.

Ignoring the implications of difference as teachers was, however, not the only aspect left unexamined by this group of participants. They also chose not to consider whether and how difference was inscribed in the pedagogies embedded in their own education as students. The first example of that tendency was provided in the passages opening this chapter. Asking participants how well issues of gender and multiculturalism were addressed in the methods course was not intended to learn whether or not those issues were actually addressed (after all, I was there to observe that myself). Rather, my question was directed to find out whether student teachers themselves, having been immersed in a program that encouraged them to incorporate issues of gender and multiculturalism in their own teaching, gave any consideration to whether such issues were incorporated into their own learning as student teachers. The responses participants provided at the outset of this chapter illustrated that they had not. Most were surprised by my question; it had not been a question they thought worthy of consideration up to that moment. Similar responses were provided when I asked participants whether any of the readings in the methods course were written by women or people of color. Here too participants' responses indicate a disconnection between their thinking about the value of that incorporation in their own teaching and the teaching they were provided with while learning to teach.

The Christmas Episode

When prospective teachers tend not to think that difference matters in the content of their courses, it is only a short distance for them not to consider it in the context of their learning in those courses. To make that point, I turn to an excerpt from my research journal that recounts an event (or, as you will soon see, a non-event) that took place during the final class of the social studies methods course.

> November, 29, 1996—the last day of classes. Winter Break (or Christmas Break, as it is referred to at UWC) and the ensuing practicum are just around the corner; their anticipation, felt everywhere. As class begins, I sit in my "usual" place under the wall-to-wall window, right behind the U-shaped formation of 37 student teachers' desks in this always overly air-conditioned classroom. Pen in hand, a notebook on my lap, and a mini–tape recorder already rolling at the center of the classroom, I am ready for my ethnographic endeavor. Two boxes of tangerines Simon had purchased with money left over from photocopying fees collected during the first week of classes are distributed among the students. A thank-you card for Simon is "secretly" exchanging hands as each student teacher writes something to be remembered by.
>
> The focus of today's class is interviewing techniques. While the ultimate purpose is to illustrate a way to elicit community members' recollections of the past, thus moving beyond the dry and decontextualized renditions of textbooks, Simon uses this activity to have students interview each other about their experiences in learning to teach. The resulting comments, Simon claims, will be most welcome by a college undergoing a restructuring of its teacher education program. As students pair up, I leave my tape recorder with one group and move to sit with another. Twenty minutes go by. Students are well into sharing their critiques of the program thus far. Some seem especially excited as this is one of the only opportunities afforded them to incorporate their privately held critiques of the program in a more formal, semipublic manner. Suddenly, the classroom door bursts opens and a dozen festively dressed student teachers with music sheets and a variety of small musical instruments in hand barge into the classroom, headed by one of the program's music education professors. Stunned, Simon and students remain silent as the "intruders" quickly align themselves at the front of the room and, to the "visiting" professor's signal, begin singing "Silent night," the first in a medley of three Christmas carols they share with us, their captive audience. Then, as quickly as they entered, and to the sound of a healthy round of applause, they leave the room to conduct their festive duties in yet another of the teacher education classrooms nearby.
>
> In the aftermath of their departure, Simon makes a variety of attempts to "regroup" the students and restart the interrupted interviewing activity. But the social studies student teachers are no longer interested in pursuing this or any other activity; their minds and interests are well beyond the confines of this activity, of this classroom. They have been transported to a "netherland" of holiday spirit, celebration, and festivities. No time for analysis in this mainly white, predominantly Christian classroom. With all indeed lost, Simon suggests they

adjourn. Following a few closing comments, Simon wishes students well in the practicum and bids them farewell. They'll be back at [the university] in the summer.

As students were saying their good-byes and leaving the classroom, I remember sitting in my chair overcome by a sense of disbelief. How can what just happened, I thought, go unexamined in a teacher education program that has so enthusiastically promoted (and promoted itself as subscribing to the ideas of) multiculturalism? How does that which took (and did not take) place in class relate to the three ornately decorated Christmas trees recently erected in the entrance to the library of the College of Education, in the Teacher Education Office, and outside the dean's office—the three most representative locations of knowledge, power, and authority? What does the lack of such an examination say about student teachers' own positionality and their understanding of that positionality? What does it hold for prospective social studies teachers who will not only be teaching a grade eight unit about world religions but who, more importantly, are expected to treat all religions and those who subscribe to them in their own classrooms fairly and equally? While a little, thankful researcher-voice inside of me was already planning where to position what would definitely become a section somewhere in this book, the educator in me was devastated; the Jew, offended. Could one have orchestrated a better opportunity to compare the verbal declarations of this program about multiculturalism and its practices of monoculturalism? What better opportunity to examine and disrupt the ways in which Christianity, to borrow from Nakayama and Krizek (1995) "makes itself visible and invisible, eluding analysis yet exerting influence over everyday life"? (cf. Giroux, 1997a, p. 292). What could be more pertinent for this reluctant group of prospective teachers than to explore how this unquestioned manifestation of Christianity, this "nothingness, this taken for granted entity," to use Kincheloe and Steinberg's (1997) discussion of whiteness, "assumes a superior shadow that transforms it into . . . a 'transcendental consciousness'" (p. 30)? Can we, as teacher educators in this day and age, allow Christianity to continue to maintain a positionality beyond history and culture? Is it not our role to explore the manifestation of that unquestioned positionality in our educative minds, in what we take as natural and neutral, in what we take for granted, in what we don't even consider problematic enough to textualize and discuss?

Dismayed by the lack of responsiveness to any of the above questions by the abrupt conclusion of class, and hoping participants might have considered similar questions but chose not to raise them in the rush to begin their vacation, I returned to what I now call the "Christmas episode" in my third set of interviews. Asked about the events of that last class, most claimed they were thrilled, enchanted by its message of celebration. "I thought it was great," said Mary, speaking for most. "I was in a really bad mood before that, so I thought it was fabulous." Some critical reflection, however, did come from Ron's direction.

> I wasn't thrilled. I felt very ambivalent about it. On the one hand I felt "OK, it's Christmas, it's the last class, we should lighten up and have some fun." But at the same time I was really enjoying the interviews we were doing and . . . didn't really like that interruption. And even though I was nominally brought up in a Christian background, . . . it felt imposed somehow. I kind of wondered how appropriate is it to march into a classroom and start doing that, especially in a classroom where not everybody necessarily celebrates Christmas.

Ron chose to raise two troubling aspects regarding that intrusion: the disruption of the interviewing activity and the imposition of Christmas. But when I asked him which of the two was more problematic, he said, "The marching into the class and interrupting the activity." **[ST¶ Ron:** *At the time, I resented the interruption of the activity, of the discussion. Why? Because I was enjoying the discussion. But now the question arises, why did I object to the interruption of an abstract, intellectual discussion of issues of Othering in education more so than to a real-life, concrete example of it? Was it because I, too, privilege the realm of the intellectual over the emotional? That I preferred to be "ignorant" of my own experience of being recolonized? Intellectual abstraction can also be a form of Othering. It's safe for me to read about Black slaves being recaptured in the American South, as long as I don't have the fear of that ever happening to me. But what happens when your own Christian past literally comes knocking at the door?*]

Finding it difficult to understand how prospective teachers could be blind to the educative possibilities embedded in the deconstruction of this "Christmas episode," and thinking that my particular questions might not have allowed them to articulate its importance, I chose another route. "Suppose you are the social studies teacher educator and this was your own classroom," I said. "Would you have done anything differently after the carolers left the room? Or would you have ended class on the same note as Simon had?" "I think I might have ended the class too," Casey responded. "I think Simon probably realized he didn't have our attention and if he did keep us there he wasn't going to accomplish a hell of a lot anyway." "What else could Simon have done?" Jack asked. After all, he tried for about 30 seconds to get us back on task and realized that it was absolutely hopeless; it wasn't going to happen. It was the last class so he let us go. I mean, what else could he do? Turn on the lights a few times and yell at everybody?

Avner: Is there anything else you feel *could* have been done?

Jack: We could have eaten the rest of the oranges or chatted. **[ST¶ Jack**: *It is very interesting to read the comments I made at that time. I am amazed that I was apparently unaware of the significance of the "Christmas episode." After my conversation with Avner on this I became very aware of the significance of this event. Since that conversation, I have become much more aware of similar incidents of "dominance," especially with regards to culture, gender, and sexual orientation. As a teacher, I am often puzzled at why other teachers in my own school don't seem to see the importance of "analyzing" those forms of dominance in the daily events and structures in our school.***]**

What do Jack's response and those of other participants point to? Are they a reflection of what is not apparent to this group of prospective teachers or a way of avoiding what is? Do these responses simply illustrate an absence of a pedagogical imagination or should this form of "not seeing" be considered an act of deliberate—even if unconscious—negation? And if it is, as I tend to believe, the latter, how does this form of creative absence actively participate in legitimating the practices that currently govern, regulate, and rule one's understandings of the social relations in which we live, those with which we are educated, and those with which we educate others? (I continue addressing the notion of "not seeing," albeit from another perspective, in the next chapter.)

PART III

POSTSCRIPT

Chapter Seven

Revisiting the Study

Let everybody tell me, in his own way . . . [h]ow, for him, is opened up—or closed—or how already he resists, the question as I pose it . . . (Lacan, 1978, p. 242; cf. Felman, 1982, p. 30).

This chapter addresses three questions pertaining to the study reported in this book and to its textualization: When is consent consent (and why is it given in the first place)? To what degree and in what ways did this study prove beneficial to its participants? And what does the Second Text, as a method of inquiry, offer the research act? Combined, these questions address the ability of research to examine what (and how) it made possible for participants to gain from their participation in the study and how it used that participation to reflect back on the study by creating a space for participants to comment about and question it.

When is Consent Consent (and Why is it Given in the First Place)?

Much of what we do as researchers remains unquestioned, taken as given. Introducing my research to students in the first class of the methods course and asking permission to observe classes and audio tape its sessions seemed one of those natural, unproblematic processes researchers go through in order to get to the "real" stuff—the data—they will then use to tell their research tales.

Accordingly, I walked into the methods course on the first day of classes and, with the blessing of the instructor, requested students' consent to allow me to research their course. But reflecting on it, after the fact, I realize that there was more to it than initially met my eye. While making every attempt to ensure that students understood I was requesting their permission for a study rather than imposing one on them, my request, I have come to learn, was something students, particularly at that time, had little ability to refuse.

After all, what response other than agreement could I have expected from a group of eager student teachers on the first day of their teacher education program? How feasible was it to expect anything else of students who had only moments ago walked into a classroom, who had barely introduced themselves to each other, and who had yet to forge alliances with any of their colleagues or establish themselves as members of a community? Could they have responded otherwise to a request that was allowed for, introduced, and backed by their instructor—the person who, in many ways, represented the power of the institution, of the discipline, of the profession they were soon to be part of? Was there really, I began to question, a way for students, in those particular circumstances, to honestly exercise their prerogative and actually say "no"?

The fact that none of the 37 students in the methods course refused consent (or even asked any question that would indicate a level of discomfort with anyone recording their actions and using that for their own purposes) might indicate that saying "no" was not a real, viable option, at least not for those students in that particular classroom at that time. Not realizing any of that at the time, I naturally proceeded without hesitation.[1]

While my request to the entire class was, in a sense, for passive consent (that is, to allow me to observe and record their actions), recruiting the six students whose stories have informed my study in a more substantial way required active consent. In other words, they were required to "volunteer" to be part of the in-depth part of this study, one that was to be held outside of, and in addition to, the research conducted in the methods course. Partaking in this part of this study required students to agree to six interviews throughout the year in addition to visits to their practicum classrooms and access to the assignments they produced for the methods course.

The question of consent in the case of this group was therefore not as much students' ability to say "no" (they were, after all, not *required* to volunteer for the in-depth part of the study), but rather, what their "yes" meant and why it was given. Why did the six student teachers whose stories you have read thus far agree to be part of this study? What, if anything, were they hoping to get in return for that participation?

When I asked Jack why he volunteered to be part of this study, he said,

> I thought it might be interesting and that it would help me learn more about the program, about the class. But to tell you the truth, I thought there was a good chance I wouldn't be selected. Yeah, I wanted to be a sport and I didn't want to

not agree to be in it. I mean, if I'm going to be a teacher I should volunteer for these things and be agreeable. But I guess that in the back of my mind I was hoping I wouldn't be selected. And then I did get selected and I thought, "Well, hopefully, I will learn something."

Charles, too, volunteered with the expectation that he would not be selected. He chose to put his name forward because

I thought everyone would and I thought I'd be the last person to be chosen. . . . You obviously have something that you think is important and if I can help, I mean, if I have an hour to kill, I don't mind helping. You obviously feel strongly that you want to take your time and come to every class and sit through all these laboring discussions we are having and tape-record everything and go home and listen to it again and again and type it all out. So why not help you out?

Beyond Mary's general belief in the importance of studies—"Everybody benefits sooner or later. You learn from the actions of the study participants and then you write about it and everybody who reads it learns as well"—her decision to join the study, very much like Charles's, was based on the idea of being a good citizen who helps others (me) in need. "I figured it was no skin off my nose," she said. "I'm not one of those people who don't get involved. If I see an accident I call the police and don't run in the opposite direction."

Casey's decision to take part in the study was based on her desire to be helped by helping me out:

I thought I would probably benefit from it and, at the same time, I thought that I would be helping you out. I also thought it would be interesting to see what kinds of questions you would be asking. . . . It didn't seem like a lot of time to me so I thought, "What the heck! I'll put my name in and if I get chosen, so be it."

Jocelyn's reasons for joining the group pertain to issues of voice as well as to her understanding of her own learning processes.

I thought it would be a neat way to talk about and to voice some of the things that were going on in the classroom. And if you were going to include students' voices, I wanted to be one of those voices. The way you described your research, I thought it would give me a good forum; if I was having problems or if there were things I wanted to discuss, it would be good to have somebody to discuss them with. That, I thought, would be a benefit for me.

Ron was somewhat brief about his decision: "If someone is interested in me and in my opinions," he said, "sure! I'll join. I like talking about myself."

These responses reveal as much about participants' conceptions of teachers and citizenship (as well as teachers as citizens) as they do about the study and their expectations of it. Beyond the idea of helping them learn more about the program and the class, or about themselves as teachers and learners (issues I address in the next section), we see a host of other reasons this group of participants gave for putting their names forward for the in-depth part of this study. For Jocelyn it was the desire to represent students and voice their concerns in an environment of learning to teach that she expected would otherwise be speaking mostly *to* students. For others it was primarily about exhibiting good citizenship, helping others in their hour of need. But what pervades most of the responses is the sense of ambivalent consent—consenting almost reluctantly, hoping not to be selected; displaying good citizenship through agreement but not wanting to act on that agreement beyond its declarative statement.

That said, and although some of the participants were initially not enthusiastic about becoming part of this study, in the final analysis, as the next section will show, none regretted participating.[2] Some were even able to have their initial expectations of the study fulfilled.

How (If at All) Did This Study Benefit Its Participants?

The purpose of critical research is not only to produce critical knowledge but also (and in the process) to have participants critically examine their own situation in the context of the research and in the process of its production. **[ST¶ Jocelyn**: *I think this, in particular, has been a strong point in your approach. As a participant, I have not only had a forum to unravel, expose, and question my learning, I have been able to revisit it in text and with a different perspective. Each encounter—a journey—has been fascinating and educative for me. Thanks.]* The fundamental question facing critical researchers is thus not only whether their study proved to be beneficial for the researcher or the research community as a whole but also whether it benefited the researched. This is primarily an ethical issue of reciprocity (Sparks, 1998). How, then, and to what degree, this section inquires, was this research beneficial to prospective teachers as participants, as students learning to teach? In what ways did it enable them to do what they would not have been able to do otherwise, in what ways did it disable them? Or, as Lacan asks in the quote opening this chapter, what has it opened up—or closed—for them?

When I asked Mary whether she found the study of any benefit, she said that it "definitely helped to clarify some of my own thoughts . . . to solidify stuff in my own mind." For Casey the study was "quite helpful," mostly, perhaps, as she thought forward to her role as a teacher:

Having you ask me questions makes me articulate a response in a way I would not have done otherwise and I think that's good. Because when I think in my own mind, I don't, in a way, ask myself those kind of questions. . . . So it helps me articulate my own goals and why I'm teaching what I'm teaching. It allows me to really think about what learning is, what I want the students to actually get out of my standing up in front of them for an hour or however long it is.

"I know that when I ramble on during interviews it doesn't sound like the study has helped," said Charles, "but I think it has. Some of the questions made me think more than I probably wanted to. And that was probably good for me. They raised things that I probably never thought about but that I maybe should have."

Asked whether she had found the interviews in this study helpful in any way, Jocelyn responded:

Oh, very helpful. Having to formulate answers to your questions helps clarify in my mind what is exactly going on; things that you know subconsciously or unconsciously or things that you really don't think about or you think about but you don't really articulate. If I don't actually articulate a lot of the things that are going on in my head, they stay that mess of ambiguities and asteroids whirling around in my head and I never really get a grasp on them. So that has really helped. . . . Also, I find that our conversations and clarifying things in my own head, as a result, affects the way I look at the next class or what's gone on in other classes too.

Responding to the same question in a later interview, Jocelyn added,

Your questions, like the one about gender and multiculturalism (which I just didn't even really think about as an issue before that), are such that they force me to actually look at things and say, "What is it that I actually feel? Hang on a second here! OK. Yeah. OK. This is what I feel" or "I don't really know what I feel about that, do I?" Often we don't do enough analyzing of what it is that we think and why it is that we think the way that we think. . . . Studies like this are important because it's important to wrestle with all of those things because you learn more about knowledge, you learn more about learning and even more about the situation and more about yourself in doing that.

Although Jack found himself in this study somewhat reluctantly—"I wanted to be a sport . . . [but] in the back of my mind I was hoping I wouldn't be selected"—he didn't regret having participated.

I am really glad that I did it because I did learn. I think I've learned a lot and I've actually told other people that I thought it's really given me an edge on learning and in terms of questioning. I mean, most of the time when we're talking I begin seeing things in a way that I hadn't thought of. So I'm less coasting through the course, simply learning everything and passing the exam, which I think is just what most people in the class are doing.

Considering himself initially "more inclined than most people to question things on [his] own" and ask, "Why has this happened? Should this happen?" Jack believed the study encouraged him to do even more of that. The interviews, he explained,

> make me reflect on what I've learned and how I'm going to apply it to my teaching so I don't just go in and learn without thinking about it. It's forcing me to think about what I'm learning and why I'm learning. So I think I'm probably getting twice as much from my methods class because of these interviews. It's given me an opportunity to critically assess the course more thoroughly. I mean you need to *talk* about ideas to get through them.
>
> Avner: Do you feel our interviews have allowed you to act, not only to think and reflect, differently in the methods course itself?
>
> Jack: I think so. I think my question in class roughly a week ago when Simon showed us a unit he used with his students about the Maritimes—about the poverty of the region—is a good example. I raised my hand and asked what sort of view that unit would leave the students with. I was afraid it might lead students to resent the Maritimes because the rest of Canada needs to subsidize the region through transfer payments. So I guess these interviews have led me to more critically think of things like that. I mean your questions involve values and critically looking at everything. They have led me to more critically think about the course in general: How would I improve it? I mean I'm constantly thinking about it after every class.

For Ron, who opened our first conversation with a discussion on Hegel and Foucault, this study was often the only place he could actually articulate the kind of understandings with which he came into the program, a place to move outside the immediacy and utility of practice and think about education and his own process of education in broader, more critical terms. Above all, this study was a learning experience for Ron: "It made me really think. I mean I have to do a lot of thinking back to answer your questions . . . and they also serve as a model in some way for some of the questions I'd like to be using in my classroom. . . . I learn from the questions you are asking and it gives me a chance to reflect on what I've been learning. . . . I often wonder," he added, "how much you're questioning me and how much you're actually teaching me something through those questions."

What this study offered Ron most, however, was an opportunity to become both an insider and an outsider, a participant in and a critic of his own education. "It sort of temporarily allows me to remove myself from [the situation] in order to stand outside of it and look back at it. It's kind of strange because at the same time I'm definitely part of it and participating in it."

Most of our cultural knowledge, writes Erickson (1991) "is implicit, consisting of overlearned ways of thinking and acting that, once mastered, are held outside conscious awareness." As a result, he adds, "we are too close to our own cultural patterns to see them without making a deliberate attempt to break our learning set—to introduce a bit of distance between ourselves and our taken-for-granted 'reality'" (p. 4). This study allowed Ron exactly that.

> Ron: By interacting with somebody who is observing the course, in a sense, from the outside, it allows me to do the same thing. I can step into your shoes for a moment and think about the same questions you're asking. And that's interesting and important too because, you know, even today we talked about some things that were reneging in the back of my mind but I hadn't quite figured out what it was about it. For example, when you raised the idea that the Christmas caroling thing could have been a perfect lesson in colonialism, [I thought:] "Yeah!" And then that makes me ask, "Well, why didn't I take up that thread at the time?"
>
> Avner: Why didn't you?
>
> Ron: Well, it didn't occur to me.
>
> Avner: Why do you think it didn't?
>
> Ron: I guess I had accepted it as a way of being, something to expect: "It's Christmas. It's really out there." And when that happens, and there's that cue to respond appropriately, which is to drop what I'm doing and to join in that definition of fun, it's hard to question it. So, in a way, I guess, I too have been colonized.

Although Ron was one to always appreciate the "difficult," unsettling questions posed during this study, even at difficult, unsettled times, such was not the case with all. One reason for that is provided by Ron. Within "this factory model [of teacher education] of which we're all products in one way or another," Ron suggested, "all most people seem to be concerned about is just getting this piece of paper and getting out and making money. They say: 'I don't have time.' 'Don't ask me these questions.' 'I don't want to deal with them right now.' 'I can't, they're too dangerous.' 'Don't upset me right now, I just want to get this over with.'"

These responses, as you will see, were indeed the case in some instances. But as a critical ethnographer, positioned to point out to participants what they could not see and encourage them to say what they would not or could not say otherwise (Britzman, 1995, p. 233), one necessarily puts forth questions, interpretations, and "provocations that disturb the impulse to settle meanings" (p. 236). Some participants appreciated throughout the study the opportunity to engage questions that raised what they, for various reasons, chose to ignore or repress. Others found such questions disturbing, especially during the practicum—a time to settle meanings, they claimed, rather than unsettle them, to gain competence, not to question one's confidence in one's competence.

This point came across clearly during an interview with Jack conducted at the end of the teacher education program. Asked to reflect on the study, Jack discussed the difficulties he had dealing with unsettling interview questions during the practicum:

> Jack: Sometimes your questions made me think more than I wanted to during the practicum because I didn't have time to sort them out. I mean, I had taken Simon's class and had thought about it in one mind-set and then sort of put everything together. But when I then talked about it with you and you'd make comments and bring different perspectives about it, I'd realize that maybe I wasn't thinking about it the way I wanted to and had taken things at face value and accepted things. So it would make me think about things at a time in my practicum when I didn't want to be thinking about them because I didn't have time to think them through and I was just confused as to what I really wanted to do. So at times it did cause problems for me, just within myself because I didn't want to think about them.
>
> Avner: That's fascinating. I mean, for me, the purpose of education is to unsettle things.
>
> Jack: Oh yeah. Absolutely. And I completely believe it. And I think the worst thing someone can do, and a lot of teachers do, and I see it, is that they become set in their ways and don't want to hear new ideas because they think the way things are is just fine. . . . And what I did like about these [our] talks is that as soon as I would sort of become accepting and set in what I wanted to think, I'd talk to you and get different ideas and realize that I wasn't really that comfortable and it forced me to re-analyze things. But sometimes it just confused me at a time when I didn't want to be confused because I was under too much pressure that the last thing I needed was to be confused and begin the process of self-doubt. I mean you just don't have time for self-doubt in your practicum. I think self-doubt is critical to someone's growth, [but] not during the practicum.

Jack's critique proves that he was in fact able to assume the "distance" Ron spoke of—the ability to take oneself out of one's own situation and reflect back on it—with regard to the study and how it positioned him to know (or, as he put it, to know what he preferred not to know). What it also illustrates, however, is that such a stance was not assumed with regard to his experiences *in* this study. Although Jack believed questioning is the basis of education and that self-doubt is critical to self-growth, those seemed luxuries one did not need to apply in the "survival mode" of the practicum—a time for doing, performing, not questioning.

Jocelyn, too, explained the problematics of posing questions to participants that might promote self-doubt during the practicum.

> I now think it's wonderful to have those interviews while you're in [the practicum] because it reflects back to you the state of mind that you were in. But I think that when I was in it I knew what I had to do: "Well, this is what I've got to do. This is the way it is and I can't change it." So I wasn't in the mind frame of asking those questions. It's not that there weren't things I wanted to change in my classroom. And I did have criticism about the way some classes were run and the ways that certain teachers did certain things. But it's like you almost don't want to hear those questions because in a sense you know the answer. Why acknowledge the fact that you are playing the game when in essence you don't want to play the game. So if I don't even ask the question, then maybe [I can pretend] I'm not doing it. It's a coping mechanism!

What we find, then, in Jack's and Jocelyn's desire to leave the "real" of the practicum unquestioned is, to quote from Zizek's (1989) discussion of ideology, "the paradox of a being which can reproduce itself only in so far as it is misrecognized and overlooked" (p. 28). Putting forward the thesis that ideology's dominant mode of functioning is cynical, Zizek (1989, using Sloterdijk, 1983) points out, renders impossible—or, as he puts it, vain—the classic Marxist ideology that states: "'They do not know it, but they are doing it.'" That concept of ideology, Zizek claims, "implies a kind of basic, constitutive *naïveté*: the misrecognition of its own presuppositions, of its own effective conditions, a distance, a divergence between so-called social reality and our . . . false consciousness of it" (p. 28). The cynical subject, however, as Sloterdijk proposes, and as Jack's and Jocelyn's comments illustrate,

> is quite aware of the distance between the ideological mask and the social reality, but he nonetheless still insists upon the mask. The formula, as proposed by Sloterdijk, would then be: 'They know very well what they are doing, but still, they are doing it.' Cynical reason is no longer naive, but is a paradox of an enlightened false consciousness: one knows the falsehood very well, one is well aware of a particular interest hidden behind . . . [it], but still one does not renounce it. (p. 29)

The desire not to renounce, to ignore, is thus not passive but active. As Felman (1982) explains, ignorance is not simply a lack of knowledge but an active refusal of knowledge. Ignorance, according to Felman,

> is tied up with repression, with the imperative to forget—the imperative to exclude from consciousness, to not admit to knowledge. Ignorance, in other words, is not a passive state of absence—a simple lack of information: it is an active dynamic of negation, an active refusal of information. . . . the incapacity—or the refusal—to acknowledge *one's own implication* in the information. (pp. 25–26)

With ignorance constituting not simply a lack of knowledge but the active negation of it, my role, as a critical researcher, was never only to have students examine the "real" of their practicum or any other experience of learning to teach but, rather, and as irritating as it might have been for some, to better understand their own implication in maintaining that real through ignorance. Thus, turning this ignorance—the seductive, soothing tendency to "not see"—into what Felman calls "an instrument of teaching" (p. 27). This becomes possible only when participants' own education is actively questioned, when their own implication in knowledge and its negation are interrelated, when the process of learning, as Felman suggests, "does not just reflect itself, but turns back on itself so as to *subvert itself* and truly *teaches* only insofar as it subverts itself" (p. 35).

Just as psychoanalysis refuses to simply accept self-explanation but uses it against itself to show what it conceals in its unsuspected mechanism (Ankersmit, 1994, p. 129), so my research attempted to show participants what lay behind the apparently open self-presentation of the knowledge offered by them and how they themselves, while struggling to change their situation, often became part of the "problem" by refusing to implicate themselves in their situation. **[ST¶ Simon**: *I don't think you have taken seriously what students say about the challenges of the practicum.* **Avner**: *I recognize those challenges, but that does not mean one should become paralyzed in their midst, unable to critically engage them. A critical engagement does not entail refusing those challenges; it means that one recognizes and explores their potentialities and problematics as one often has to go along with them. Doing what one must do in one's practicum in order to "pass" does not mean one must believe—even temporarily—that the practices one does not believe in should be endorsed because one is asked to perform them by one's supervisor. Learning, I believe, occurs through continuously questioning that which we do (or are asked to do) rather than letting "action" eradicate thought about action.*]

The Second Text As a Method of Inquiry, a Reflective Conversation About Practice

The Second Text **[ST¶]**—the combination of participants' comments appearing in italics throughout the book—was born out of my desire to create a polemic, text that invigorates discussion about preservice education rather than stifles it through the (misleading) appearance of consensus. Following Lather and Smithies's *Troubling Angels*[3] (1995), the Second Text attempts to reflect the impossibility of mapping an "untidy" world into a "tidy" text (Lather, 1996, p. 529) and the problematics inherent in the interpretation of (someone else's) lived experience.

This messy, polyvocal, interrogative function is not intended to imply that the voices of participants are equal to that of the researcher nor to allow the researcher to retreat from all that ethnographic authorship and authority imply. On the contrary, its purpose is to bring those issues to the surface, to question and engage the problematics of textuality, voice, authorship, and ethnographic authority.

Inviting participants to comment on the final draft of this book was therefore not designed to simply provide an additional (and currently fashionable) textual layer to this book but was methodologically and epistemologically in tune with the study underlying it. Having asked prospective teachers to critically examine their teacher education program and how it positioned them to know, inviting critique about my own work—which became part of their experiences and positioned them to think about those experiences in particular ways—was therefore integral to the process. As such, participants' comments in the Second Text should not be confused with member-checking. Member-checking (which was incorporated as part of this study's methodology at an earlier stage) tends to be used to "correct" initial drafts so as to make the final report more accurate and representative of participants' experiences. The purpose of the Second Text is different. Rather than devour participants' comments into my text (as is often done with the results of member-checking)—thereby leaving no traces of their objections, additions, or comments—the Second Text invited participants to speak in their own words about the work; words that are presented unedited and in full whereever participants chose to place them within this book.

Constructed in that fashion, the Second Text opened several possibilities for participants in this study. At one level, it invited them to revisit their situation as students learning to teach. Using this opportunity to "see their situation again," after the fact, a sense of reflexivity that did not exist during the research process was able to emerge. Having worked as teachers for almost a year when given the opportunity to revisit this study, participants could examine their experiences as student teachers from a space removed from the power relations inherent in the student-teacher/ sponsor-teacher nexus that often allowed or mandated them to "not see" particular things in particular ways. But the Second Text allowed participants to do more than talk back to their experiences of learning to teach. It also made it possible for them to converse with—agree, debate, dispute—the experiences of other participants (a conversation not possible when participants, as was the case in this study, are interviewed individually).

More than enabling participants to comment again on the culture of learning to teach under investigation, the Second Text also gave them an opportunity to comment on the process and product of that investigation, a space to voice their rejections and evaluate my own actions with them, my own words about them. In doing so, the Second Text both opened my text to interrogation and made that interrogation visible to its readers.

Though the Second Text, as I have explained, was intended as a means for doing and viewing research in which "the process of investigation is part of the object of knowledge and itself becomes an object" (Aronowitz & Giroux, 1991, p. 143), the degree to which it was successful in generating those results (and my claims that it has) can, of course, be judged only by you, the reader.

Chapter Eight

Theorizing Practice/Practicing Theory in the Preservice Classroom[1]

Why does student teaching assume such importance in the perceptions of preservice teachers? Are university courses so theoretical as to be bereft of practice? (Kersh, 1995, p. 103)

Underlying all previous chapters of this book, regardless of their topic, was a focus on the relationship between theory and practice in preservice teacher education. Addressing the connection between the knowledge prospective teachers were given and the knowledge they themselves produced, the relationship between theory and practice has been examined at two levels. First, between the theory prospective teachers were provided at the university and the pedagogies they then developed as teachers. Second, between the content (theory) prospective teachers were provided at the university and the strategies they developed to examine the pedagogical practices provided them as students learning to teach. The first level addressed the relationship between theory in one location and its potential transference to practices in another; the second the degree to which theory was used, reflexively, to interrogate the pedagogical practices of the very location within which it was promoted.

As I have tried to show in previous chapters, there is a close—some might argue eerie—connection between how prospective teachers learn and how they teach. Consequently, I propose, one cannot separate the ways in which prospective teachers relate theory to practice as students with the ways they relate the two as teachers. Indeed, and as this study has shown, by not theorizing their own experiences as students, prospective teachers are less likely not only to theorize their practices as teachers but also to infuse theory, pedagogically, in those practices. For theory to become a material force, as I argue, it has to be engaged pedagogically.

That is, theory must be used to learn from one's learning about teaching for it to be both meaningful and generative in one's teaching.

Teacher Education and the
Separation Between Theory and Practice

How is theory perceived in preservice education? What role does it play in relation to practice? Asked about their university-based teacher education courses, most students, claims Fullan (1991) "will say that they get too much theory, that it is irrelevant and a waste of time. Many professors of education, on the other hand," Fullan adds, "will argue that students get too little theory, that they are uninterested in developing a solid grounding in theories of education and teaching." In spite of that disagreement, Fullan concludes, "[m]ost seem to agree that the integration of theory and practice is a desirable, if elusive, goal" (p. 293).

This apparent disagreement between those who teach and those taught in preservice teacher education is perhaps illustrative that both the role and degree that theory and practice ought to play in teacher education classrooms as well as the relationship between them continue to be contested, unresolved issues in preservice education: What constitutes theory and how is the "practical" defined? Are the two inherently connected or do they constitute separate and separable aspects of learning to teach? How, if at all, should theory and practice be brought to operate with/on/against the other in order to make practice more theoretical and theory more practical?

With those questions in mind, it becomes clear that beyond the ostensible dispute as to whether student teachers get too much theory or too little of it in university-based courses lie much broader pedagogical questions. Why is it that prospective teachers believe they get too much theory in teacher preparation courses? Indeed, what in its treatment results in prospective teachers believing that theory in preservice education courses "is irrelevant and a waste of time"? And further, if, as Fullan (1991) suggests, the integration of theory and practice is an agreed-on, desirable goal, what conditions, structures, and practices make that integration so elusive?

Asked about their own teacher education program at the University of Western Canada, the six student teachers participating in this study generated answers very similar to those given by the student teachers Fullan (1991) had in mind. "It's all theory!" claimed Mary, as she spoke about her university-based teacher education courses.

It's all academic until you come back to the university after the short [two-week, mostly observational] practicum. . . . We learned so much more in the short practicum than we did in the whole semester at [the university]. . . . The first semester of this program is just all theory and we need to get more practical. Until we get more practical in the program, the theory will still just be a washout.

Jack responded similarly. What you learn during the fall semester at the university, he said,

helps you along and gives you some ideas but no real learning, I think, takes place until you get into your practicum . . . . [Instead of] just getting bombarded with all this theory [at the university], I think we should spend more time in the schools so we can apply that theory and so it can become more relevant. . . . I mean, you need to learn by experience.

This depiction of the relationship between the university and the practicum and, as a result, between theory and practice in preservice education is by no means unique to Mary and Jack. A disdain for theory among prospective teachers and a desire for the "practical" that can readily be implemented in the classroom is well documented (i.e., Britzman, 1991; Ginsburg, 1988; Sarason et al., 1986). But Mary's and Jack's statements provide more than the typical student teacher response. What they point to is not only the irrelevancy of theory in relation to practice (in a manner to which Fullan referred at the beginning of this chapter) but to a separation between theory and practice within teacher education itself. At the most apparent level, theory, according to Mary and Jack, is the domain of one part of learning to teach, practice the domain of the other. Theory— seen as useless and irrelevant—is what prospective teachers receive at the university, practice and relevant "doing" is what takes place in the practicum. As such, while generated in university-based courses, theory, it seems, is not pertinent to those courses; its application, if at all, is elsewhere—in schools.

What Mary and Jack offer can, however, also be read on a different level, one that points to a separation between theory and practice not only by locale but also within one locale—the university teacher education classroom itself. As Mary stated, university courses are "all academic until you come back from the . . . practicum." The significant words here are *until you come back from the practicum.* What those words imply is that university courses are not necessarily, by definition, "academic" (since after coming back from the practicum they are no longer defined as such) but only as long as they are devoid of the practical. It is the infusion of the practical with the theoretical, according to Mary, that allows university courses to no longer be considered merely "academic."

How is the "practical"—that which should infuse theory and in the process make it worthwhile—defined according to Mary? Is it only that which unfolds in the educative process taking place in schools? Or does her explanation about the relationship between theory and practice in teacher education also invite another—less traditionally student-teacher-like—interpretation? After all, Mary did not choose to conclude by saying that teacher education needs to become more practical by extending the practicum or by reshaping teacher education to better respond to and accommodate prospective teachers' experiences and needs in schools. Instead, she said, "Until we get more practical *in* the program, the theory [not simply theory but *the* theory of teacher education] will still just be a washout."

With Mary's particular emphasis on "*in* this program" and "*the* theory of teacher education" in that concluding sentence, a different picture emerges. It is one that, in corroboration with what other participants have offered throughout this book,[2] portrays the inefficacy of theory in teacher education not only as a reflection of how well it measures against what goes on in the practicum but of how well it measures against itself, against the practices of teacher education classrooms in which such theory is advocated.

Jack's words cannot be as easily reread the same way. Yet his final statement—"you need to learn by experience"—does make this second reading possible. While Jack's notion of the "practical" is more directly tied to life in schools, he nevertheless stated that wherever one learns—whether in schools or at the university—learning must be experienced. And learning by experience, as Jack explains further down, is equated with learning from one's experience, having one's experience in university-based courses theorized.

The fact that Mary's and Jack's words point (explicitly and/or implicitly) to these two particular levels of separation between theory and practice in teacher education is, as I have shown elsewhere, not coincidental. Rather, it can be considered a reflection, perhaps the result, of a separation between theory and practice permeating much of their teacher education program; a separation whereby theory learned at the university, while intended to infuse future practice in that "elsewhere" of the practicum, was not used to examine (and thus learn from) the here-and-now practices of university-based teacher education itself. As a result, learning to teach was, for the most part, not a process prospective teachers were encouraged to learn from, only an avenue to learn *about* something to be practiced with some other bodies some place else in the future.

Highlighting the problematics of having student teachers learn about education rather than learn from their own education does not mean to imply that the primary purpose of preservice teacher education should be to focus inward, on its own teaching, instead of preparing prospective teachers for that elsewhere of schools. What it does mean, however, is that for teacher preparation to be considered an education rather than training, it cannot avoid exploring how the elimination of the former operates to perpetuate the existing regularities of the latter.

When theory and pedagogy are not made to speak to each other in a dialectical fashion, theory becomes no more than a body of (someone else's) knowledge students are required to learn—what Giroux (1994b) terms a "pedagogy of theory." For theory to become more than that, it must be practiced, explored as a form of cultural production, examined for what it yields and for what it conceals. It is in that latter process that a "pedagogy of theory" can be transformed into what Giroux calls a "pedagogy of theorizing." What differentiates a pedagogy of theory from a pedagogy of theorizing, according to Giroux (1996) is that the latter is an activity to be practiced in the lived world of the educational experience (p. 50). It is an activity in which the practices of learning to teach are investigated in and of themselves, used as the material with which to learn about teaching and learning, about the relationship between them, and about their relations to broader societal contexts. From this perspective, and to use Barthes, theory does not mean abstract. Instead, "it means *reflexive,* something which turns back on itself: a discourse [or practice] which turns back on itself is by virtue of this very fact theoretical" (cf. Young, 1981, p. 1).

Using a pedagogy of theory rather than a pedagogy of theorizing, the university portion of teacher education, as examples from the teacher education at UWC have shown, not only separates theory from practice but also makes the relevancy of its own practice of educating prospective teachers in its own classrooms questionable. Without interrogating the relationship between what prospective teachers learn and how they come to learn it, indeed, without implicating the two, teacher education has little transformative impact on student teachers' existing understandings of teaching and learning. In other words, the university-based portion of teacher education, as indicated by Mary, Jack, or the student teachers Fullan described, becomes "irrelevant." It simply perpetuates and certifies student teachers' existing understandings rather than challenging them, and in so doing does not invite prospective teachers to imagine alternatives.

When teacher education elects not to challenge prospective teachers' previous understandings or allow them to challenge the practices enacted with them as students, it is not surprising to find students claim that preservice education has had little impact on their understandings of the educative process (see, among others, Bennett, 1996; Britzman, 1991; Goodman, 1988; Richardson, 1996; Tabachnick & Zeichner, 1984).

Students at the University of Western Canada were no exception to that rule. I don't think that taking this teacher education program, said Charles,

> has changed much of anything I was doing [in] my undergraduate [program] or anything I learned then. I don't want to say it had no effect . . . but off the top of my head I can't give you an example of something I do differently now than I would have done before I went into the program. . . . It's not that I regret going through the program, because it gave me a sense that I got through it and now I have confidence—not necessarily that I have learned anything but that I have done it and I can go into the schools now and be confident that I will be able to do what I want.

Charles's perceptions that his teacher education program had little transformative influence on his educational imagination were not unique. Other participants in this study shared similar opinions about the impact (or the lack thereof) of their teacher education program. According to Ron, student teachers coming out of this program would not be very different than what's out there now in the schools." They may be

> less likely to use a textbook, more likely to use a variety of materials. But really, the objectives will be the same; the topics of discussion will largely be the same. I think we'll be teaching the way we were taught.

Suggesting that his statement implied that the first semester of the program had little impact on student teachers' understandings about teaching, Ron responded:

> Exactly! And that's why we, as students, get so worked up about wanting lesson plans and wanting techniques and strategies and stuff. We've seen what teaching is like. We've had 16 years of it, at least, up to this point. Now we want to know how to do it. [We say to ourselves,] "How am I going to control a class of 32 kids and make them learn what I'm asked to make them learn?" So I think we are working with the model of teaching that, at some level, we're not really actively thinking about. We're working with this model of teachers that we have had in the past [and say:] "I'm going to do what they did. All I need to know are the tools they used to do that."

Although the desire for lesson plans and teaching techniques was very much an outcome of feeling unprepared to engage the demands of a looming practicum, Ron's words suggest an additional reason for students' desire for the "practical." It pertains to the fact that teacher education did not destabilize the images of teaching with which student teachers came into the program. When what one already knows gets validated, is taken as given, all that remains, according to Ron, is to learn how to "do" it, how to do what our teachers did to us. What Ron illustrates, then, is that although a pedagogy of theory might supply prospective teachers with new models of teaching, only a pedagogy of theorizing can get them to actively think about models of teaching—those presented to them and those they themselves will present to others.

Most courses in colleges of education, however, writes McLaren (1988), "rarely provide students with an opportunity to analyze the ideological assumptions and underlying interests that structure the way teaching is taught" (p. 42). Consequently, students in colleges of education, as do teachers and students in school, according to McLaren (1991), "come to believe and accept that the rules, regulations . . . and social practices that undergird and inform everyday life in schools [or in schools of education] are necessary if learning is to be successfully accomplished" (p. 237).

Because prospective teachers are not invited to critically examine the underlying assumptions in educational conventions and practices (Kincheloe, 1993), they tend to ignore not only how those aspects impact their own education as students but also how they will structure their own classrooms in the future. As a result, and as Ron stated earlier, student teachers become more interested in learning how to perform expected actions than in analyzing those actions or the expectations that generate such actions.

Revealing the (Already Present) Theories in/of Practice

While classroom discussions in colleges other than education tend to focus on content more than they do on the role of pedagogy in mediating (and thus determining) that content to students, such practices become problematic in a college of education, especially in teacher education courses. There, the process of teaching and learning itself—that which remains hidden in those "other" courses—must not only come to light but become the substance of the educative endeavor. That is, teaching in teacher education should include more than teaching *about* teaching as content, as an abstract entity, separate and separated from prospective teachers' own learning experiences as students preparing to teach.

It is the focus on that "hidden" aspect that invites a conversation about the relationship between theory and practice and points to the interconnectedness between them. I say hidden rather than absent because theory is always already present in practice. To make that presence more transparent, according to Willinsky (1998b), the relationship between theory and practice needs to be explored in a more "open, 'let's-talk-about-it' way." Our goal, Willinsky suggests, is "to practice a more explicit treatment of how we have theorized the world, and of how we live by those theories. We need to move practice into (a consideration of its underlying) theory" (p. 245). It is this kind of movement that might allow prospective teachers to better understand not only that *some* theory is always embedded in practice but to also question: Why these theories rather than others? Whose theories are they? What kind of practices do such theories generate? How do they invite students to learn about, be in, and act in the world (what and whose world is it?)? Who benefits from such theories and their resulting practices, who does not?

Ginsburg (1988) advocates a similar approach by calling for a process that would encourage students to identify and discuss the messages embedded in the explicit, implicit, and null curricula both in and of learning to teach. Such a process, however, Ginsburg warns, is not likely to be comfortable for either instructors or students. Instructors will be asked to subject their practice to critical examination. Students will be placed in the position of publicly questioning the practices of instructors who may hold the keys for their projected careers as well as discussing their own actions and statements and those of their peers. Indeed, asking a teacher education program to promote critical and public reflection on its own practices necessitates a level of educational courage not often evident in current conceptualizations of the teaching/learning environment. But recognizing the degree of courage it might take to overcome the difficulties in having those involved in preservice education read their learning environment critically, is not a reason to abandon the project. For it is precisely that kind of courage that would result in student teachers becoming students not only of education but of their *own* education.

Prospective Teachers as Students of Their Own Education[3]

A substantial part of what prospective teachers are asked to read and discuss in teacher preparation courses engages education as a contested terrain, a site of struggle over the organization, circulation, and legitimation of knowledge, meaning, and experience. In particular, the critical literature prospective teachers encounter in teacher education emphasizes the need to analyze the interests and power relations that structure teaching and learning by bringing instruction and the classroom setting to the fore to be critically analyzed (Yonemura, 1986). But while such an approach is often encouraged in teacher education classrooms as a general goal, the ways in which knowledge, meaning, and experience are organized, circulated, and legitimated in teacher education classrooms are too often given extraterritorial status, a form of immunity from such investigation. Critical analysis in teacher education classrooms is mostly directed elsewhere, toward other structures, other institutions, other educators, not toward the learning environments in which student teachers learn to generate such forms of critical analysis.

Indeed, although much of the readings prospective teachers discuss in teacher education courses depict a world in which the nature of knowledge and knowing are becoming increasingly contested, teacher education courses in which those readings are engaged tend to be characterized by orderliness, consensus, and compliance, where questioning is discouraged and contestation eliminated. While prospective teachers may be encouraged to ask questions about content or pedagogy *in* their teacher education courses they are much less frequently (rarely?) encouraged to ask similar questions *of* those teacher education courses.

Education that is premised upon, embedded in, and promotes the mechanisms of a priori agreement, Tyler (1991) explains, "teaches—indirectly, accidentally, and unbeknown to itself—the terror of consensus" (p. 82). The primary effect of what Tyler calls CON-sensus is the elimination of discourse. It brings discussion to an end "in the silence of agreement, in the elimination of difference, and the reduction of all opposing voices to a single, disembodied voice that having spoken in the authority of the all falls silent" (p. 82). Anesthetizing the urge to challenge the given, this culture of agreement, of silence eradicates both the desire and need to question consequences, to confront assumptions, to implicate learning.

Although this culture of consensus may be accepted as part of the "real" of teacher education in some (too many?) quartets, the question remains whether, as teacher educators, we can afford to continue ignoring its consequences, especially in light of the kind of education we hope our graduates would generate in schools. Does this culture of silence, we must continuously ask ourselves, embody our vision for preparing empowered educators who can question rather than celebrate the status quo? Does it encourage prospective teachers to become challengers, to take initiatives, to imagine alternatives? If, as I expect, the answer to these questions is in the negative, how then can we begin to transform teacher education into "places fundamentally committed to asking questions" (Greene, 1986b, p. 73)? Further, how can we encourage prospective teachers not only to ask questions about education but to question education and their own education in particular? How do we afford them opportunities to examine why education is the way it is, how it got to be that way, and what could be done to make it otherwise—that is, more reflective of the kind of education we hope it can and should be?

Transforming colleges of education into places where students become committed to asking questions that implicate learning requires more than simply alerting teacher education students of the need to critically read, write, and act in the world. We must also allow them to act *on* and *with* that knowledge in order to publicly reflect on, converse with, and problematize their own lived world of learning to teach. If, as hooks (1989) suggests, we need teachers who can talk back to their situation by talking to their experience, is preservice education not the appropriate place to begin? Where better to initiate what Schon (1983) calls a reflective conversation with the situation; an "on-the-spot surfacing, criticizing, restructuring, and testing of intuitive understandings of experienced phenomena" (p. 42)?

The need to legitimate such a process in learning to teach did not escape Jack. A teacher education program, Jack suggested, "should establish procedures for students to question what they [teacher educators] are doing. I think it happens informally a lot [through students' conversations] in the hallways," he added, "but it gets left out there, it gets forgotten when students go back into the classroom." Forgotten? Probably not. Excluded from classroom dynamics? Most often. And yet what becomes pedagogical by opening the kind of spaces advocated by Jack, according to Britzman and Pitt (1996), "is the possibility of learners [and teachers] implicating themselves in their learning" (p. 117). Through such a provision, claim Britzman and Pitt, "one makes a finer distinction in learning. This concerns the difference between learning about [education as] an experience . . . and learning from one's own reading of one's own [educational] experience" (p. 119). Having become aware "of one's implication, one begins to examine what prior knowledge or understanding one brings into [and those that are already inscribed in] the educative process and what knowledge and understandings are affirmed or made strange in the process" (pp. 119–120).

By bringing the teacher, the organization of knowledge, and the classroom setting to center stage as legitimate "content" to be examined, both instructors and students can begin to break with and disrupt the taken-for-granted. Resulting, different questions emerge; questions that explore the dominant concepts of knowledge and power, teaching and learning, and community; questions students can use to make connections between the overt, the hidden, and the null curriculum, not only in education but in their *own* education, through their own learning.

Though we often tend to regard the course timetable, the allocation of students' "airtime," the choice of readings, or the particular course assignments and their grading as a necessary yet transparent, unproblematic grid on which students' learning can then be maintained, such procedures, structures, and processes are not simply what enables learning to take place thereafter or an infrastructure that is provided before "real" learning occurs. Directing students to engage knowledge and knowing in particular ways, procedures, processes, and structures determine the kind of learning that can and cannot take place. As such, their examination draws attention to the process through which knowledge, knowing, and experience are produced. Addressing the "how" and "why" questions of their production makes it possible for student teachers to gain better understanding of how the ways one is invited to learn determine not only how one learns but also what one learns.

The Teacher Education Classroom As an "Oppositional" Space

To afford prospective teachers the opportunity to become students of their own education requires more than a cosmetic reshaping of preservice education in which courses are simply reorganized or amalgamated, names changed to reflect "current" educational thinking, and the practicum portion extended/reduced. While providing an aura of reform, they do little to meaningfully alter the purpose, nature, culture, or process of preservice teacher education. To initiate reform that allows both student teachers and teacher educators to conceive of education otherwise, teacher education must work to abandon practices that maintain "politics of the usual" and establish itself as an "oppositional space" (Alvarado, 1992). In contrast to the traditional teacher education classroom, an oppositional space would encourage students to question how teaching is taught rather than simply explore techniques to impart what is (already) taught.

Conceiving of teacher education as an oppositional space does not mean that teacher preparation should relinquish its responsibility to teach prospective teachers how to plan for instruction, design assessment and evaluation that reflect instruction, or acquire technical skills and competence in general and subject area methodology. What it does mean, however, and this is where the oppositional classroom parts ways with more traditional approaches to teacher education, is that it attempts to make those issues and the theories and practices that traditionally go along them problematic even as those issues are the focus of instruction. In other words, a critical examination of the theories underlying current practices of planning, assessment, evaluation, and subject area methodology is considered not only as a preface for (future) practice but in order to help prospective teachers critically examine the origins, purposes, and consequences of educative actions—in teacher education classrooms and in schools—and the political, economic, and social contexts that give rise and meaning to them.

By challenging educational practices as inescapable reality, and in making a pedagogical shift from the expected to the unexpected (Britzman & Pitt, 1996), teacher education as an oppositional space strives to avoid that which, to borrow from Lather (1996), maps easily onto student teachers' taken-for-granted regimes of meaning. Rather than simply teach unproblematized meanings—in a sense endorsing, legitimating, and reenforcing them—an oppositional teacher education strives to undo existing meanings by undermining students' confidence in the obvious and the given.

Making itself strange, different from students' prior classroom experiences, this oppositional—what Zavarzadeh and Morton (1994) call the "defamiliarizing"—classroom helps problematize itself as a cultural and political situation. In such a context, Zavarzadeh and Morton suggest, students can begin to read experience differently by becoming *theorists*. Theory, the authors propose, is not "an abstract apparatus of mastery, but an inquiry into the grids of social intelligibilities produced by the discursive activities of a culture. Theory is a critique of intelligibility" (p. 53).

Attempting to challenge rather than affirm, the defamiliarizing classroom works to estrange the habitual by provoking learners and challenging their expectations, inviting them to wonder about practice—what it is, how it can be otherwise. Rather than fitting onto the structures for making meaning of educational experience that student teachers already know well and therefore no longer question, this latter approach opens deliberate gaps between students and their expected environment (Daloz, 1986). It is in the recognition of those gaps and in the attempt at closing them that student teachers become more critically aware of their experiences as learners; an awareness they can then utilize to further understand their own teaching in its relation to the learning of others.

Applying a pedagogy that invites prospective teachers to read and write against the grain of unquestioned tradition, the defamiliarizing classroom encourages students to examine their own environment critically, to make connections between how they learn and what they learn, between the overt, the hidden, and the null curriculum of their own experiences of learning to teach. Education, teaching, and learning in that case are no longer studied for "their own sake," as ends in and of themselves, but for the kinds of cultural forms, subjectivities, and social and power relations they make possible and intelligible. Asking students to critically read their own education allows them not only to rethink the nature of educational theory and practice but also to realize how the two shape, and are shaped by, each other.

What then might preservice teacher education be like if it thought of its work primarily as producing creative dialogues on practice through "debate, multiple perspectives on events, practices, and effects" (Britzman et al., 1997, p. 20)? And how would the experience of learning to teach, and the experiences those learning to teach might provide others in the future, be different if instead of allowing current practice to reproduce itself, teacher education moved toward a theoretical dialogue on practice that offers opportunities to rethink the nature of (and the relationship between) educational theory and practice?

Comprising only a brief phase in prospective teachers' accumulative educative experience, it is no doubt difficult for preservice teacher education to undo understandings built in and on close to two decades of schooling. Difficult but not impossible; difficult yet worth the effort. For it is the kind of educative process provided in teacher education that will determine whether the understandings student teachers arrive with are also those with which they depart. If, as teacher educators, we believe that education could be more than it currently is, do more than it does, teacher preparation cannot assume that either will materialize by providing preservice students educative experiences that reproduce what most teacher education programs believe must be changed in public education.

Rather than perpetuate those regularities and the understandings they produce by granting them legitimation through pedagogies of the obvious, preservice teacher education ought to provide those learning to teach qualitatively different experiences; experiences that interrogate and defamiliarize the given; experiences that allow students to understand not only *that* education is never neutral but also to explore *why*, and to recognize how *every* action (and in-action) inside (or outside) the classroom positions learners to know and experience the world in particular ways. To become more reflexive both about "the pedagogies argued for and the pedagogies of arguments made" (Gore, 1993, p. 127) while learning to teach, preservice courses need to enable students experiences that better allow them to examine how teaching is taught rather than simply explore techniques to impart what is (already) taught. That means experiences that engage teacher education courses not only as preparation for a future practicum but as practicum environments in and of themselves. Environments where practice as-it-is-practiced gets theorized, where theory is considered not only *for* practice but is indeed practiced, and where practice is interrogated for the kinds of theories and practices it produces and for those it does (and does not) make possible.

Chapter Nine

Conclusion

Teacher education matters. Its utterances and silences, its actions, nonactions, and interactions, all combine to play a significant role in shaping prospective teachers' understandings of education, teaching, and learning by establishing the parameters of the actual, the possible, and the imaginable. If, however, we want teacher education not only to matter but to matter in the direction we desire, desire itself is insufficient. Instead, the impact of teacher education's explicit, implicit, and null curriculum (and how the three come together to educate) must be critically examined. Are those curricula sending the messages we, as teacher educators, hope to convey to student teachers? If not, in what ways are they obstructing the intended messages and at what cost?

Change will not materialize either in teacher education or for student teachers' future practice in schools if innovative theories of change in teacher education are simply preached to, or adopted uncritically by, student teachers. For such theories to become a real, viable option they have to be experienced and their experience theorized. If we believe in teachers who are thoughtful, critical, and reflective, we ought to provide them meaningful opportunities to be so as learners. In other words, teacher education should be a place where student teachers don't only learn *about* education but where they actively and publicly engage their own education as students learning to teach. Often, this book has illustrated, it is not student teachers' inability to imagine otherwise that restricts the possibility of educational change but teacher education's inability to provide them "otherwise" experiences that break with the traditional, the expected, the obvious, and the taken-for-granted. And if that is the education prospective teachers are provided in preservice education, is it feasible to expect them to be critical teachers who provide critical education in our schools?

By asking what kind of future teacher education's politics of the present make possible, this book has sought to highlight and publicly engage such politics and their consequences in order to bring more of what we do (and how what we do, by definition, creates the "what we don't do") in teacher education into the fold of the discussion and, in the process, to see again what many have come to take for granted about the nature and activities (and the nature of activities) in our teacher education classrooms, to reflect anew on practice and the meanings and actions emanating from it.

Exploring the production of knowledge and knowing in preservice education in this fashion helps refocus some of the debate in teacher education. Much of the discourse in research on teacher education has focused on whether teacher education does or does not change student teachers' beliefs and understandings. This book has illustrated that that is perhaps the wrong question (or at least one that doesn't take us further in meaningful directions). It is not *whether* or not teacher education changes prospective views about teaching and learning, but rather, how and in what ways it does so. For whether teacher education affirms or challenges the understandings student teachers come with, it nevertheless always impacts them, often affirming those we most hope to challenge (and vice versa).

To be sure, not all will agree with my reading of this teacher education program. "Critical inquiry into a particular practice or practices of teacher education," states Adler (1993), "can inform an audience and spark debate. Indeed, debate and dialogue are crucial to critical inquiry" (p. 44). As I have demonstrated throughout this book (i.e., in the form of the Second Text), I value and encourage such a debate. Keeping the playing field of signifiers open, it helps to sustain a critical conversation about the signified—teacher education—to rediscover what we, as teacher educators and educational researchers, believe we have already discovered, to unlearn what we feel we know so well and, thus, learn further by learning again.

While some may reject my interpretations and analyses on a variety of grounds—experiential, methodological, ideological, or political—I hope they are nevertheless able to see what has led me to my specific claims to knowledge as well as recognize the validity of such a study in learning to teach. Whether one views the issues I have raised about the teacher education program at the University of Western Canada or the conception of an oppositional, critical teacher education I have proposed in the previous chapter as a crisis or an opportunity will ultimately depend on the experiences with, and the visions of, teacher education readers bring to their reading of this study.

What I do hope readers take away from this book are not only my theories about the practice of a particular teacher education but my practice of theorizing teacher education. For most of the current, pressing issues facing teacher education will hardly be addressed meaningfully by importing theories—mine or anyone else's. What is required, instead, is a process of theorizing that takes place within the practice of learning to teach, creating a form of critique that works to highlight the problematics embedded in current manifestations of, and the relationship among, theory, policy, and practice in teacher education, to publicly engage them in order to bring more of what is and is not done in teacher education into the fold of the discussion not only *about* but also *in* teacher education.

That said, I believe an examination of the relationship between this study and the conversations about teacher education it makes possible can say something about the limits and possibilities of critical pedagogy as an epistemological and methodological stance to generate and maintain such conversations. As I mentioned at the outset of this book, critical pedagogy—particularly as it combines with cultural studies—creates the conditions for such a conversation by posing a series of questions that inquire into how current structured utterances, absences, and silences work to "deny the link between knowledge and power, reduce [teaching] to an unquestioned object of mastery, and refuse to acknowledge the particular ways of knowing and being they produce and legitimate (Giroux et al., 1996). Such questions, which strike at the essence of preservice education as a cultural and pedagogical practice, invite new ways to analyze teacher education; the answers they generate are opportunities for teacher educators to rethink the impact their pedagogies and the knowledge legitimized by them on those learning to teach. But to engage such a conversation not only *about* teacher education but also *in* it, critical pedagogy ought to further connect (or, in returning to its original roots, to reconnect) the academy and the field.

Although critical pedagogy has, in the last two decades, provided incisive critiques *of* preservice teacher education, the language of possibility it generates through that critique seems to be directed primarily toward the education student teachers will find and provide in schools, not the one they themselves receive in colleges of education. These powerful critiques prospective teachers encounter in preservice education no doubt empower them to think otherwise about education—its purposes, processes, and outcomes. Yet they often do little to position prospective teachers to act otherwise as students learning to teach when rethinking the essence of their own teacher education is precluded from the discourse of critique they encounter in it, if opportunities to act on those critiques are not part of the experience of learning to teach.

To trouble not only the silence about the culture of teacher education but also the culture of silence within it, critical pedagogy must incorporate more critical research conducted *in* preservice teacher education. The benefits of such research are twofold. First, it will generate much-needed data about actual practices in teacher education classrooms to go along with and substantiate the existing, more "theoretical" literature in critical pedagogy. Second, such research will provide an environment in which the researched—teacher educators and prospective teachers—are invited to critically reexamine the predominantly technical and otherwise mostly unquestioned culture of teacher preparation. Using the questions posed by critical pedagogy to encourage prospective teachers to critically read preservice teacher education as a text will highlight the ideologies underlying the practices of teacher education as well as allow them to distance themselves from the immediacy of experience "in order to uncover the layers of meanings, contradictions, and differences inscribed in the form and content of classroom materials," thus opening that "text to deconstruction, interrogating it as part of a wider process of cultural production" (Giroux, 1997b, p. 137). All are immensely important dispositions to help guide them as educators of others in the future.

But if the purpose of critical pedagogy research is indeed, as Giroux suggests, to uncover the layers of meanings, contradictions, and differences in texts and to open them to deconstruction and interrogating, such an approach cannot be directed only to teacher education as a text while excluding the research text produced as a result of that reading. In other words, if, as critical pedagogy advocates, knowledge is socially constructed, contested, and thus open to multiple interpretations, the form and content of the research texts critical pedagogues produce ought to reflect those understandings. To better align the epistemologies advocated by critical pedagogy with its methodologies, research labeled as critical pedagogy needs to produce critical knowledge that opens up its own knowledge (and its production) to similar modes of critique. This would mean a movement from more traditional monovocal critiques of teacher education toward "messy," polyphonic, or "acoustic texts, with fractured, overlaid, multiple soundtracks" (Denzin, 1995a, p. 17). Providing openness rather than closure, messy texts signal "uncertainty about how to draw text/analysis to a close" (Marcus, 1994, p. 567). Making visible the complexity of narrating an "untidy" world (Lather, 1997), messy texts invite the much-needed conversation in and about preservice education by unsettling both the researcher's and readers' tendency to cohere and conclude.

Finally, a few words about critical pedagogy as a possible form of empowerment for the researched. The previous chapter focused on the benefits (and problematics) of critical research in preservice education for those learning to teach. Not mentioned there was how this study was perceived by Simon, whose preservice course served as the main venue for data collection for this study. I raise that issue since the limited number of critical studies in preservice education may result not only from the reluctance of critical researchers to enter teacher education classrooms but from the reluctance of teacher educators, fearing the consequences of such studies, to invite them into their classrooms. After all, and regardless of how committed teacher educators might be to the general idea of critical pedagogy, not everyone would relish the idea of having their practice open to external, critical scrutiny.

Critical research can be thought of as a double-edged sword—a weapon or a tool (or a combination of both). One of the most important issues determining whether critical research is considered a weapon or a tool depends on the ability and inclination—of those involved in the research process as well as of those reading it—to distinguish and value the difference between criticism (a weapon) and critique (a tool). Criticism, as I discussed in more detail at the outset of this book, seeks to uncover the "real" meaning of a text (in its broad sense) and, in the process, tends to end the conversation by handing down a verdict about qualities or lack thereof pertaining to that text. Critique, on the other hand, attempts to advance the discussion by keeping the field of signifiers open. Contrary to criticism, critique is not intended to devalue or destroy that which has been read. Rather, critique strives to highlight the politics of knowledge and knowing by re-articulating "the tensions between and within words and practices, or constraints and possibilities, as it questions the consequences of the taken-for-granted knowledge shaping responses to everyday life and the meanings fashioned from them" (Britzman, 1991, p. 13).

The distinction between criticism and critique, however, is not always as clearly defined during research or in the reception of its findings by the researched as critical researchers hope it might be. What may appear to the researcher as critique may be viewed as criticism by the teacher educator (or any other person) being researched, turning critique from an intended tool into what could be perceived as a rather lethal weapon. While Simon and I had numerous discussions about the benefits of this study for his own understanding of practice and its relation to theory, to the analysis of the messages conveyed by and through them, I was never quite able to pin Simon down to articulate, specifically, what this study opened or closed for him. What I do know, however, from those conversations is that by believing that the purpose and process of this study was critique rather than criticism, Simon was further able to distance himself from the immediacy of his teaching situation, to think again about the explicit, implicit, and null messages (often unknowingly) conveyed to prospective teachers, and to explore the relationship between his teaching and their learning in new ways. Perhaps Simon's most telling comment in that regard came following the conclusion of this study. Addressing a group of participants and colleagues gathered to mark the end of the study, Simon posed a question that speaks to the tensions—potential and real—in the work of critical pedagogy; a question that might also begin to engage readers in the kind of conversation this book has been advocating. Pointing to an early draft of this book, and playing on the title of Elizabeth Ellsworth's (1989) in/famous critique of critical pedagogy, Simon asked, somewhat rhetorically: "If this is critical pedagogy, why then does it feel so empowering?"

Notes

Chapter One

1. All names of people and places mentioned in this book are pseudonyms.

2. Eisner (1985) defines the null curriculum as the nonrandom, structured absences and silences within a curriculum.

3. For a more comprehensive account of cultural studies see, for example, Blundell, Shepherd, & Taylor, 1993; Giroux & McLaren, 1994; Grossberg, Nelson, & Treichler, 1996; Hall, 1996; Storey, 1996.

4. The terms *pedagogy* or *the pedagogical* are often used in this book in their broad sense. That is, to include any message—action, structure, or text—that organizes someone's experience as well as someone to experience by positioning those it engages to know of, and be in, the world in particular ways. As a form of cultural production (Bernstein, 1996), pedagogy should not be reduced to nor equated with methods of teaching. While not diminishing pedagogy's concern with "what's to be done?" in the realities of classrooms, Giroux and Simon (1988) explain, pedagogy is more than "the integration of curriculum content, classroom strategies and techniques, a time and space for the practice of those strategies and techniques, and evaluation purposes and methods." Rather, they stress, pedagogy "organizes a view of, and specifies particular versions of, what knowledge is of most worth, in what direction we should desire, what it means to know something, and how we might construct representations of ourselves, others, and the world" (p. 12).

5. While all six participants responded to a draft of the first chapters of this book (chapters two, four, and five), only three—Jack, Jocelyn, and Ron—responded to the entire text. Mary, Charles, and Casey found their teaching commitments too burdensome to allow them to respond to the last several chapters. Though I would have liked all of the participants to comment on the entire book, I was quite surprised at the extent to which participants *did* respond to this text, especially considering that it was made available to them more than a year following the conclusion of their teacher education program, while they were all engaged in full-time teaching in some way or another.

Chapter Two

1.   The year this study was conducted, 405 student teachers were enrolled in the
     secondary teacher education program at UWC. Two other programs exist within
     the UWC Teacher Education Program: an elementary and a middle-school teacher
     education program (with enrollments of 386 and 33 respectively, that year). While
     the elementary program, at that time, was completely separate from the second-
     ary program, students in the middle-school program often shared courses with
     their secondary counterparts.

2.   When visiting student teachers' classrooms during the practicum I made it very
     clear, both before and during the discussions that followed, that I was not there to
     evaluate their teaching (too many others—a sponsor teacher, a faculty advisor—
     were already involved in that process). What I was interested in, and what we
     discussed during the interviews, was their thinking about their teaching and how
     they felt they were positioned (by Simon's course, by their sponsor teachers,
     faculty advisors, culture of schooling, etc.) to teach in particular ways.

3   Two sponsor teachers, both sponsoring the same student teacher, while permit-
     ting access to their classrooms to conduct this study, declined to be inter-
     viewed.

4.   While the last set of interviews with participants was not specified in the study's
     original design, as the focus of my research evolved toward a larger emphasis on
     the teacher education program itself and less on the practicum, and with the
     approval of all six participants, this last interview substituted for the third origi-
     nally scheduled interview during the practicum.

5.   I use the term "post"-fieldwork analysis to highlight the notion that there are also
     pre- and in-fieldwork analyses; that analysis does not begin when fieldwork is over
     but rather is embedded in every aspect of research. As Hammersley and Atkinson
     (1983) point out, "data analysis is not a distinct stage of the research. It begins in
     the pre-field work phase, in the formulation and clarification of research prob-
     lems, and continues into the process of writing up" (p. 174).

6.   Referring to the collection of data and its interpretation as distinct and separate
     phases of research—whereby one precedes the other—is obviously problematic
     and obscures the complexity of the research process as a multidirectional rather
     than a unidirectional process with data collection its beginning and interpretation
     of data its end. Interpretation is not a veneer added to data after its collection; it
     is embedded in the already theoretically driven interpretive process of collecting
     (What counts as data? How does data count? What does it account for? Which
     data should I record, which should I ignore?). As researchers, we do not enter the
     "field" as *tabula rasa*. Our research (data collection and/as interpretation) is
     created, informed, and continuously mediated by our theories of and in the world.
     Indeed, we read and write our ethnographic world with them, against them, and
     through them (see Fiske, 1991).
       Interpretation not only influences the kind of data we choose to collect in the
     field; interpretation creates data even when (what we traditionally call) "fieldwork"
     is over. That is, interpretation not only infiltrates and directs the collection of data

"There"; it generates new data "Here." In other words, data generation does not end when ethnographers return from the field to do their writing in the academy (see Denzin, 1995a; Scheurich, 1995). Choices ethnographers make pertaining to the editing of, sprucing up of, and other forms of manipulating data; decisions they make regarding where to include such data, how to include it, or how to frame it; are all decisions that give data a different life, a new meaning. And as they give new meaning to each chunk of data they include, they give the data they do include new meaning by the data they exclude. In the process "new" data is born. Data, therefore, is continuously generated until the last letter describing the research and its findings has been typed (see Smyth & Shacklock, 1998).

But the complexities of data creation go even further. If we subscribe to the idea that meaning resides not in a text but rather in the negotiation between reader and text, and if we believe that different readers make different meanings of the very same text—in fact, as Birch (1989) points out, that "each time a [new] reader reads the text, a new text is created" (p. 21), then the creation of "data" continues long after one's research is signed and bound; it continues as long as someone is willing to actively read it.

7. Meaning making—reading or writing—is always a political and ideological act. And yet, exploring a text's silences, gaps, and absences seems to make the ideological and the political ever more apparent. Omissions in a text are made to be so only through their commission by a particular reader; they need to be identified—in a sense, created—and activated in order to make them speak, a prerogative already provided that which is made available there for discovery by its author. In other words, while a critical reading of what is present in a text requires its deconstruction, engaging what is absent in that text requires construction. And although all meaning making is inherently creative, the former works with or against that which is offered, the other invents that which is withheld. It is this creative act of invention and construction that brings the ideological and the political(both in the text and its reading—to the surface.

8. "Clearly, the traditional model of the one-way passage of knowledge from interviewee to interviewer did not fit with these experiences" (Limerick, Burgess-Lomerick, & Grace, 1996, p. 456). In fact, "the very terms interviewer and interviewee are problematic [in describing the interviewing process] in that they embody an assumed passive role of the subjects of the research" (p. 449). Rather, as much as participants shared their views with me, they often inquired as to my thoughts about issues and events under consideration. In addition, questions about my research, education in general, the practicum, future career possibilities (theirs and mine), the process of doing a Ph.D. and graduate studies in general, as well as about my background and life experiences, were all raised by the interviewees and woven into equal parts of the conversation. Further, each interview ended by asking participants what they thought I had neglected to ask, what else they wished to discuss, and inviting them to critically reflect on the interview and the degree to which it and the process itself was beneficial to them.

9. Since I had often taught all of the above-mentioned students as a substitute ESL and Resource teacher, I could fully appreciate the difficulties facing Charles as he attempted to create a learning environment that was equally shared by all.

Chapter Four

1. See Chapter Two for more details about that course.

2. While all six students participating in this study began designing a unit specific for the methods course along with another two units they were required to design for *POT* and a second methods course, they all ended up submitting the same unit in all three courses. Despite their initial inclination to be "creative" and design three different units, they soon "read" the program well enough to realize that creativity and working through one's ideas would probably not be as rewarded as conformity with an "exact science of planning." As a result, they all abandoned their initial plans and settled on their first unit (the one for the social studies methods course) which, having been evaluated by Simon and corrected by students, was then a sure success in their other two courses.

3. I did not have the opportunity to discuss the SCETs with Charles, since our interview was interrupted and cut short by a group of students entering class early that day.

Chapter Five

1. For a critical exploration of critical thinking see, for example, McLaren, 1994; Phelan & Garrison, 1994; Walters, 1994; Warren, 1994.

Chapter Six

1. My use of the terms *gender* and *multiculturalism* and the separation between them are obviously problematic. They should not be seen as an endorsement of either but, rather, a reflection of an already existing use and separation taking place within the discourse about diversity in the teacher education program at UWC. Consequently, and since such a use and separation were already part of how participants thought about difference, I found it necessary to incorporate them in my discussions with students. Using the term *Other* is equally unsettling. As Madrid (1993) points out, Other means "someone of different gender, race, class, national origin; somebody at a greater or lesser distance from the norm; someone outside the set" (p. 385; cf. Zinn, 1995, p. 10). With that in mind, my use of Other is not intended to render the other as Other. On the contrary, it is meant to point to (and problematize) a process by which the other is Othered by those considering themselves the norm against which all else must be measured. For a lack of a more appropriate term I also use the words "people of color." This term is also questionable since, as I discuss later, it designates non-whites as having color while rendering whites colorless.

2. For a further discussion about the consequences of such a separation, see Zeichner et al., 1998.

3. The degree to which it is appropriate for women's issues to "dominate" the curriculum and, specifically, how women's issues ought to be presented, was demonstrated when I asked Jack whether he had found any role models in the school. After naming his two male sponsor teachers, Jack mentioned a female social

studies teacher who teaches "the women's studies course—the women's perspective on social studies." When I questioned why he found her a good role model, Jack said: "I respect the principle of what she's trying to do. I mean social studies is traditionally pretty male-dominated and she's attempting to bring a woman's perspective to it, which I really think is worth doing. But she doesn't rant and rave, you know. She's not a man-hater. And I like that; it's a nice combination."

4. Among the "modes of masculine, phallocentric writing, history is particularly indicted," according to Kellner (1989), "not only because it is the substance of a story that has, to a large extent, excluded women from its scope, but, far more important from a post-structuralist perspective, because its alliance with narrative has indentured it to hidden forms of authority that are far more repressive to *woman* than being nameless in histories." The problem confronting women is "how to speak, to find a voice within a discourse of reason and representation that has not only failed generally to speak of woman, but has more generally repressed the possibility of speaking as a woman from [their] very imaginations" (p. 302).

5. Interestingly, in spite of Jocelyn taking the teaching about women to a level other participants did not, she was the one student teacher most regularly criticized by her supervisors for allowing boys in her class more airtime than girls. [¶**ST Jocelyn**: *Of all the criticisms during my practicum, this one hurt me the most. I believe in incorporating gender issues—I think as a woman, I embody many of these issues. For my supervisors, gender issues ended with "you asked four more males than you did females." How could I ever respond to that criticism when for me gender was so much more problematic and incorporated so much more than that?]*

Chapter Seven

1. There is little a researcher can do to alter the situation, especially if one needs unanimous consent for a study in a three-month course and not lose precious time to allow students a position from which they could say "no." What must be asked, however, is whether (and to what degree) researchers, whose research is dependent on such consent, use that as a strategy to ensure that participants in fact don't have the opportunity to actually say that "no"?
Another related issue about consent is raised by Street (1998), who asks: "How informed is informed consent?" (p. 150). When we invite participants to take part in a study, claims Street, "we are ethically bound to acquaint them with all the potential issues that their involvement might entail. This assumes in [researchers] a capacity of foresight which requires a reliable crystal ball" (ibid.). But, as Street explains, in critical research "the outcome is never predictable. The outcome will be redefined as the emergent issues are addressed. If we are unsure of where our research activities will take us how can we provide *informed* consent to those we travel the research journey with?" (ibid.).

2. While asking participants this question at the beginning of the study might have provided answers reflective of "real time" reasons, I chose to leave it for mid-study interviews. I believed that having established a relationship with them over the

first three months of the study might provide answers that go beyond what they thought might be appropriate to say in a first interview. Such a question can obviously be asked only once during a study. In hindsight, the data provided in this chapter, at least from my perspective as a researcher, justified that decision.

3.   *Troubling Angels: Women Living with HIV/AIDS* is organized "as a hypertextual, multilayered weaving of data, method, analysis, and the politics of interpretation" (Lather, 1997, p. 1), where Lather and her co-researcher, as authors, continuously both get out of the way and get in the way (p. 2). Splitting the page, the words of the participants are on the top and the researchers' narrative is on the bottom. "Interspersed among the interviews, are inter-texts which serve as 'breathers' between the themes and emotions of the women's stories; a running subtext where the authors spin out their tales of doing the research; factoid boxes on various aspects of the disease; and a scattering of the women's writing in the form of poems, letters, speeches, and e-mails" (p. 1).

Chapter Eight

1.   An earlier, extended version of this chapter, entitled "Re-thinking theory and practice in the preservice teacher education classroom: Teaching to learn from learning to teach," first appeared in *Teaching Education 12* (2), pp. 225–242, 2001.

2.   I am referring here in particular to Ron's comments regarding his discomfort about the degree to which theory promoted in his *Principles of Teaching* course was not used to inform its own pedagogy and his inability to raise those issues in that course. I am also referring to broader aspects presented in all chapters in Part II that worked to separate the theory of teacher education from the practices that engaged student teachers in it.

3.   I borrow the term "students of their own education" from John Willinsky. The need to make students aware of what and how their own education has positioned them to know (and not know) has been an important theme throughout Willinsky's work (see, for example, Willinsky, 2001).

References

Adler, S. (1991). The education of social studies teachers. In J. P. Shaver (Ed.), *Handbook of research in social studies teaching and learning* (pp. 210–221). New York: Macmillan.

Adler, S. (1993). The social studies methods course instructor: Practitioner researcher. *The International Journal of Social Education 7* (3), 39–47.

Ahlquist, R. (1991). Position and imposition: Power relations in a multicultural foundations class. *Journal of Negro Education 60* (2), 158–169.

Allsup, C. (1995). What's all this white male bashing? In R. J. Martin (Ed.), *Practicing what we teach: Confronting diversity in teacher education* (pp. 79–94). Albany: State University of New York Press.

Alvarado, M. (1992). The question of media studies. In M. Alvarado & O. Boyd-Barrett (Eds.), *Media education: An introduction* (pp. 94–96). London: The British Film Institute.

Ankersmit, F. R. (1994). *History and tropology: The rise and fall of metaphor*. Berkeley: University of California Press.

Appadurai, A. (1996). Diversity and disciplinarity as cultural artifacts. In C. Nelson & D. P. Gaonkar (Eds.), *Disciplinarity and dissent in cultural studies* (pp. 23–36). New York & London: Routledge.

Arends, R. I. (1991). Challenging the regularities of teaching through teacher education. In N. B. Wyner (Ed.), *Current perspectives on the culture of schools* (pp. 203–230). Brookline, MA: Brookline Books.

Armento, B. J. (1996). The professional development of social studies educators. In J. Sikula, T. J. Buttery, & E. Guyton (Eds.), *Handbook of research on teacher education* (2d ed., pp. 485–502). New York: Macmillan.

Aronowitz, S., & Giroux, H. A. (1985). *Education under siege: The conservative, liberal, and radical debate over schooling.* South Hadley, MA: Bergin & Garvey.

Aronowitz, S., & Giroux, H. A. (1991). *Postmodern education: Politics, culture and social criticism.* Minneapolis: University of Minnesota Press.

Bakhtin, M. M. (1981). Discourse in the novel. In M. Holquest (Ed.), *The dialogic imagination: Four essays by M. M. Bakhtin.* Austin: University of Texas Press. (Original work published 1935)

Banks, J. A. (1991, Spring). Multicultural literacy and curriculum reform. *Educational Horizons,* 135–140.

Banks, J. A. (1993). *Approaches to multicultural curriculum reform in multicultural education: Issues and perspectives.* Boston: Allyn & Bacon.

Banks, J. A. (1995). Transformative challenges to the social science disciplines: Implications for social studies teaching and learning. *Theory and Research in Social Education 23* (1), 2–20.

Banks, J. A. (1997). *Educating citizens in a multicultural society.* New York: Teachers College Press.

Banks, J. A., & Parker, W. C. (1990). Social studies teacher education. In W. R. Houston (Ed.), *Handbook of research on teacher education* (pp. 674–686). New York & London: Macmillan.

Barthes, R. (1972). *Critical essays* (R. Howard, Trans.). Evanston, IL: Northwestern University Press.

Barthes, R. (1981). Theory of the text. In R. Young (Ed.), *Untying the text: A post-structuralist reader* (pp. 31–47). London & New York: Routledge.

Benhabib, S. (1996). The intellectual challenge of multiculturalism and teaching the canon. In M. Garber, R. L. Walkowitz, & P. B. Franklin (Eds.), *Fieldwork: Sites in literary and cultural studies* (pp. 11–17). New York & London: Routledge.

Bennett, C. (1996). Teacher perspectives: Strengthening reflective teacher education. *Teaching Education 8* (1), 3–12.

Bernstein, B. (1996). *Pedagogy, symbolic control and identity: Theory, research, critique.* London: Taylor & Francis.

Beyer, L. E. (1987). What knowledge is of most worth in teacher education? In J. Smyth (Ed.), *Educating teachers: Changing the nature of pedagogical knowledge.* London: Falmer Press.

Bhabha, H. (1994). *The location of culture.* London & New York: Routledge.

Birch, D. (1989). *Language, literature and critical practice.* London: Routledge.

Blundell, V., Shepherd, J., & Taylor, I. (Eds.). (1993). *Relocating cultural studies: Developments in theory and research.* London & New York: Routledge.

Borko, H. (1989). Research on learning to teach: Implications for graduate teacher preparation. In A. E. Woolfolk (Ed.), *Research perspectives on the graduate preparation of teachers* (pp. 69–87). Englewood Cliffs, NJ: Prentice Hall.

Borko, H., & Niles, J. A. (1987). Descriptions of teacher planning: Ideas for teachers and researchers. In V. R. Koehler (Ed.), *Educators' handbook: A research perspective* (pp. 167–187). New York: Longman.

Boxer, M. (1982). For and about women: The theory and practice of women's studies in the United States. *Signs: Journal of Women in Culture and Society 7* (3), 661–695.

Britzman, D. (1986). Cultural myths in the making of a teacher: Biography and social construction in teacher education. *Harvard Educational Review 56* (4), 442–456.

Britzman, D. (1991). *Practice makes practice: A critical study of learning to teach.* Albany: State University of New York Press.

Britzman, D. P. (1995). "The question of belief": Writing poststructural ethnography. *Qualitative Studies in Education 8* (3), 229–238.

Britzman, D., Dippo, D., Searle, D., & Pitt, A. (1997). Toward an academic framework for thinking about teacher education. *Teaching Education 9* (7), 15–26.

Britzman, D. P., & Pitt, A. J. (1996). Pedagogy and transference: Casting the past of learning into the present of teaching. *Theory into Practice 35* (2), 117–123.

Brown, D., & Wendel, R. (1993). An examination of first-year teachers' beliefs about lesson planning. *Action in Teacher Education 15* (2), 63–71.

Bullough, R. (1989). *First year teacher: A case study.* New York: Teachers College Press.

Calderhead, J., & Robson, M. (1991). Images of teaching: Student teachers' early conceptions of classroom practice. *Teaching and Teacher Education 7* (1), 1–8.

Case, R., Daniels, L., & Schwartz, P. (1996). *Critical challenges in social studies for junior high students.* Unpublished paper.

Cherryholmes, C. H. (1988). *Power and criticism: Poststructural investigations in education.* New York: Teachers College Press.

Clark, C. M., & Peterson, P. L. (1986). Teachers' thought processes. In M. C. Wittrock (Ed.), *Handbook of research on teaching* (3rd ed., pp. 255–296). New York: Mcmillan

Clark, C. M, & Yinger, R. J. (1987). Teacher planning. In J. Calderhead (Ed.), *Exploring teachers' thinking* (pp. 84–103). London: Cassell.

Cochran-Smith, M. (1991). Learning to teach against the grain. *Harvard Educational Review 61* (3), 279–310.

Cole, A. L., & Knowles, J. G. (1993). *Shattered images: Understanding expectations and realities of field experiences.* Paper presented at the annual meeting of the American Educational Research Association, Atlanta.

Cronon, W. (1992). A place for stories: Nature, history, and narrative. *Journal of American History 78* (4), 1347–1376.

Cuban, L. (1984). *How teacher taught: Constancy and change in American classrooms: 1900-1980.* New York: Longman.

Cummins, J. (1986). Empowering minority students: A framework for intervention. *Harvard Educational Review 56* (1), 18–36.

Daloz, L. (1986). *Effective teaching and mentoring.* San Francisco: Jossey-Bass.

Denzin, N. K. (1995a). The experiential text and the limits of visual understanding. *Educational Theory 45* (1), 7–18.

Denzin, N. K. (1995b). On hearing the voices of educational research. *Curriculum Inquiry 25* (3), 313–329.

Derrida, J. (1976). *Of grammatology* (G. C. Spivak, Trans.). Baltimore, MD: John Hopkins University Press.

Derrida, J. (1978). Structure, sign, and play in the discourse of the human sciences. In A. Bass (Trans.)*Writing and difference* (pp. 278–294). Chicago: University of Chicago Press.

Doyle, W. (1986). Content representation in teachers' definitions of academic work. *Journal of Curriculum Studies 18*, 365–379.

Doyle, W. (1990). Themes in teacher education research. In W. R. Houston (Ed.), *Handbook of research on teacher education* (pp. 3–24). New York & London: Macmillan.

Eagleton, T. (1983). *Literary theory: An introduction.* Minneapolis: University of Minnesota Press.

Edgerton, S. H. (1996). *Translating the curriculum: Multiculturalism into cultural studies.* New York & London: Routledge.

Eisner, E. W. (1985). *The educational imagination: On the design and evaluation of school programs* (2d ed.). New York: Macmillan.

Ellsworth, E. (1989). Why doesn't this feel empowering? Working through the repressive myths of critical pedagogy. *Harvard Educational Review 59* (3), 297–324.

Erickson, F. (1991). Conceptions of school culture: An overview. In N. B. Wyner (Ed.), *Current perspectives on the culture of schools* (pp. 1–12). Boston: Brookline Books.

Feiman-Nemser, S. (1983). Learning to teach. In L. Shulman & G. Sykes (Eds.), *Handbook of teaching and policy* (pp. 150–170). New York: Longman.

Feiman-Nemser, S. (1990). Teacher preparation: Structural and conceptual alternatives. In W. R. Houston (Ed.), *Handbook of research on teacher education* (pp. 212–233). New York: Macmillan.

Feiman-Nemser, S., & Buchmann, M. (1986). The first year of teacher preparation: Transition to pedagogical thinking? *Journal of Curriculum Studies 18* (3), 239–256.

Felman, S. (1982). Psychoanalysis and education: Teaching terminable and interminable. *Yale French Studies 63*, 21–44.

Fish, S. (1980). *Is there a text in this class? The authority of interpretive communities.* Cambridge, MA: Harvard University Press.

Fiske, J. (1990). Ethnosemiotics: Some personal and theoretical reflection. *Cultural Studies 4* (1), 85–99.

Fiske, J. (1991). Writing ethnographies: Contribution to a dialogue. *Quarterly Journal of Speech 71*, 330–335.

Flinders, D. J., & Eisner, E. W. (1994). Educational criticism as a form of qualitative inquiry. *Research in the Teaching of English 28* (4), 341–357.

Foucault, M. (1977). *Language, counter-memory, practice.* (D. F. Bouchard & S. Simon, Eds. & Trans.). Ithaca, NY: Cornell University Press.

Foucault, M. (1979). *The history of sexuality* (R. Hurley, Trans.). London: Allen Lane.

Foucault, M. (1981). The order of discourse. In Robert Young (Ed.), *Untying the text: A post-structuralist reader* (pp. 48–78). London: Routledge & Kegan Paul. (Original work published 1972)

Fullan, M. G. (1991). *The new meaning of educational change.* London: Cassell.

Garibaldi, A. M. (1992). Preparing teachers for culturally diverse classrooms. In M. Dillworth (Ed.), *Diversity in teacher education* (pp. 23–39). San Francisco: Jossey-Bass.

Gay, G. (1986). Multicultural teacher education. In J. Banks & J. Lynch (Eds.), *Multicultural education in Western societies* (pp. 154–177). New York: Praeger.

Gee, J. P. (1987). What is literacy? *Teaching and Learning: The Journal of Natural Inquiry 2* (1), 3–11.

Gee, J. P. (1990). *Social linguistics and literacies.* London: Falmer Press.

Gee, J. P., & Green, J. L. (1998). Discourse analysis, learning, and social practice: A methodological study. In P. D. Pearson & A. Iran-Nejad (Eds.), *Review of research in education 23* (pp. 119–169). Washington, DC: American Educational Research Association.

Geertz, C. (1973). *The interpretation of cultures: Selected essays.* New York: Basic Books.

Geertz, C. (1983). Blurred genres: The refiguration of social thought. In C. Geertz (Ed.), *Local knowledge: Future essays in interpretive anthropology.* New York: Basic Books.

Ginsburg, M. B. (1988). *Contradictions in teacher education and society: A critical analysis.* London: Falmer Press.

Ginsburg, M. B., & Clift, R. T. (1990). The hidden curriculum of preservice teacher education. In W. R. Houston (Ed.), *Handbook of research on teacher education* (pp. 450–465). New York & London: Macmillan.

Giroux, H. A. (1988a). *Schooling and the struggle for public life: Critical pedagogy in the modern age.* Minneapolis: University of Minnesota Press.

Giroux, H. A. (1988b). *Teachers as intellectuals: Toward a critical pedagogy of learning.* Granby, MA: Bergin & Garvey Publishers.

Giroux, H. A. (1990). The politics of postmodernism: Rethinking the boundaries of race and ethnicity. *Journal of Urban and Cultural Studies 1* (1), 5–38.

Giroux, H. A. (1994a). Doing cultural studies: Youth and the challenge of pedagogy. *Harvard Educational Review 64* (3), 278–308.

Giroux, H. A. (1994b). *Disturbing pleasures: Learning popular culture.* New York: Routledge.

Giroux, H. A. (1995). The politics of insurgent multiculturalism in the era of the Los Angeles uprising. In B. Kanpol & P. McLaren (Eds.), *Critical multiculturalism: Uncommon voices in a common struggle* (pp. 107–124). Westport, CT: Bergin & Garvey.

Giroux, H. A. (1996). Is there a place for cultural studies in colleges of education? In H. A. Giroux, C. Lankshear, P. McLaren, & M. Peters (Eds.), *Counter narratives: Cultural studies and critical pedagogies in postmodern spaces* (pp. 41–58). New York: Routledge.

Giroux, H. A. (1997a). Rewriting the discourse of racial identity: Towards a pedagogy and politics of Whiteness. *Harvard Educational Review 67* (2), 285–320.

Giroux, H. A. (1997b). *Pedagogy and the politics of hope: Theory, culture, and schooling.* Boulder, CO: Westview Press.

Giroux, H. A., & McLaren, P. (1986). Teacher education and the politics of engagement: The case for democratic schooling. *Harvard Educational Review 56* (3), 213–238.

Giroux, H. A., & McLaren, P. (1987). Teacher education as a counter-public sphere: Notes towards a redefinition. In T. Popkewitz (Ed.), *Critical studies in teacher education: Its folklore, theory and practice* (pp. 266–297). London: The Falmer Press.

Giroux, H. A., & McLaren, P. (Eds.). (1994). *Between Borders: Pedagogy and the politics of cultural studies.* New York & London: Routledge

Giroux, H. A., Shumway, D., Smith, P., & Sosnoski, J. (1996). The need for cultural studies: Resisting intellectuals and oppositional public spheres. *http://eng.hss.cmu.edu/theory/need.html*

Giroux, H. A., & Simon, R. I. (1988). Schooling, popular culture, and a pedagogy of possibility. *Journal of Education 170* (1), 9–26.

Glatthorn, A. A., & Coble, C. R. (1995). Leadership for effective teaching. In G. Appelt Slick (Ed.), *The field experience: Creating successful programs for new teachers* (pp. 20–34). Thousand Oaks, CA: Corwin Press.

Gollnick, D. M. (1992). Understanding the dynamics of race, class, and gender. In M. E. Dillworth (Ed.), *Diversity in teacher education: New expectations* (pp. 63–78). San Francisco: Jossey-Bass.

Gomez, M. L. (1994). Teacher education reform and prospective teachers' perspectives on teaching other people's children. *Teaching and Teacher Education 19* (3), 319–334.

Goodlad, J. I. (1984). *A place called school: Prospects for the future.* New York: McGraw-Hill.

Goodman, J. (1988). Constructing a practical philosophy of teaching: A study of preservice teachers' professional perspectives. *Teaching and Teacher Education 4* (2), 121–137.

Goodman, J. (1992). *Elementary schooling for critical democracy.* Albany: State University of New York Press.

Goodson, I. F. (1995). The story so far: Personal knowledge and the political. *Qualitative Studies in Education 8* (1), 89–98.

Goodwin, A. L. (1994). Making the transition from self to other: What do preservice teachers really think about multicultural education? *Journal of Teacher Education 45* (2), 119–130.

Goodwin, A. L. (1997). Historical and contemporary perspectives on multicultural teacher education: Past lessons, new directions. In J. E. King, E. R. Hollins, & W. C. Hayman (Eds.), *Preparing teachers for cultural diversity* (pp. 5–22). New York & London: Teachers College Press.

Gore, J. M. (1993). *The struggle for pedagogies: Critical and feminist discourses as regimes of truth.* New York: Routledge.

Graddol, D. (1994). What is a text? In D. Graddol and O. Boyd-Barrett (Eds.), *Media texts: Authors and readers* (pp. 40–50). Clevedon, UK: The Open University.

Grant, C. A., & Sleeter, C. (1985). The literature on multicultural education: Review and analysis. *Harvard Educational Review 37* (2), 97–118.

Greene, M. (1986a). In search of critical pedagogy. *Harvard Educational Review 56* (4), 427–441.

Greene, M. (1986b). Reflection and passion in teaching. *Journal of Curriculum and Supervision 2* (9), 68-87.

Grimmett, P. P. (1991). Teacher planning, collegiality, and the education of teachers: A developmental integration of research-validated knowledge with practice. In L. G. Katz & J. D. Raths (Eds.), *Advances in teacher education* (vol. 4, pp. 50–81). Norwood, NJ: Ablex.

Grossberg, L., Nelson, C., & Treichler, P. A. (Eds.). (1996). *Cultural studies.* New York: Routledge.

Haberman, M. (1991). The rationale for training adults as teachers. In C. Sleeter (Ed.), *Empowerment through multicultural education* (pp. 275–286). Albany: State University of New York Press.

Hall, S. (Ed.). (1996). *Stuart Hall: Critical dialogues in cultural studies.* London: Comedia.

Hammersley, M. (1992). *What's wrong with ethnography: Methodological explorations.* London & New York: Routledge.

Hammersley, M., & Atkinson, P. (1983). *Ethnography: Principles in practice*. London & New York: Tavistock.

Heller, A. (1993). *A philosophy of history: In fragments*. Oxford, UK: Blackwell Publishers.

Helsel, A., & Krchniak, S. (1972). Socialization in a heteronomous profession: Public school teaching. *Journal of Educational Research 66* (2), 89–93.

Hicks, L. E. (1990). A feminist analysis of empowerment and community in art education. *Studies in Art Education 32* (1), 36–46.

Hidalgo, F., Chavez-Chavez, R., & Ramage, J. C. (1996). Multicultural education: Landscape for reform in the twenty-first century. In J. Sikula, T. J. Buttery, & E. Guyton (Eds.), *Handbook of research on teacher education* (pp. 761–778). New York: Macmillan.

Hollingsworth, S. (1989). Prior beliefs and cognitive change in learning to teach. *American Educational Research Journal 26* (2), 160–189.

Holstein, J. A., & Gubrium, J. F. (1995). *The active interview*. Thousand Oaks, CA: Sage Publications.

hooks, b. (1989). *Talking back: Thinking feminist, thinking black*. Boston: South End Press.

hooks, b. (1990). *Yearning: Race, gender, and cultural politics*. Boston: South End Press.

Jenkins, K. (1991). *Re-thinking history*. London: Routledge.

Johnson, R. (1996). What is cultural studies anyway? In J. Storey (Ed.), *What is cultural studies? A reader* (pp. 75–114). London: Arnold.

Kagan, D., & Tippins, D. (1992). The evolution of functional lesson plans among twelve elementary and secondary teachers. *Elementary School Journal, 92* (4), 477–489.

Kanpol, B. (1998). Where was I? Or was I? In G. Shacklock & J. Smyth (Eds.), *Being reflexive in critical educational and social research* (pp. 191–201). London & Bristol, PA: Falmer Press.

Kellner, H. (1989). *Language and historical representation: Getting the story crooked*. Madison: University of Wisconsin Press.

Kenway, J., & Modra, H. (1992). Feminist pedagogy and emancipatory possibilities. In C. Luke & J. Gore (Eds.), *Feminism and critical pedagogy* (pp. 138–166). New York & London: Routledge.

Kersh, M. E. (1995). Coordinating theory with practice: The department chair's perspective. In G. Appelt Slick (Ed.), *The field experience: Creating successful programs for new teachers* (pp. 99–110). Thousand Oaks, CA: Corwin Press.

Kickbusch, K. W. (1987). Civic education and preservice educators: extending the boundaries of discourse. *Theory and Research in Social Education 15*, 173–188.

Kincheloe, J. L. (1993). *Toward a critical politics of teacher thinking: Mapping the postmodern.* Westport, CT: Bergin & Garvey.

Kincheloe, J. L. (1998). Getting beyond the limits in social studies: Reconceptualizing the methods course. In S. R. Steinberg & J. L. Kincheloe (Eds.), *Students as researchers: Creating classrooms that matter* (pp. 188–198). London & Bristol, PA: Falmer Press.

Kincheloe, J. L., & Steinberg, S. R. (1996). A tentative description of post-formal thinking: The critical confrontation with cognitive theory. In P. Leistyna, A. Woodrum, & A. Sherblom (Eds.), *Breaking free: The transformative power of critical pedagogy* (pp. 167–195). Cambridge: Harvard Educational Review.

Kincheloe, J. L., & Steinberg, S. R. (1997). *Changing multiculturalism.* Buckingham, UK & Philadelphia: Open University Press.

Koeppen, K. E. (1998). The experiences of a secondary social studies student teacher: Seeking security by planning for self. *Teaching and Teacher Education, 14* (4), 401–411.

Kretovics, J. P. (1985). Critical literacy: Challenging the assumptions of mainstream educational theory. *Journal of Education 167* (2), 50–62.

Lacan, J. (1978). *Le Seminaire, livre II: Le Moi dans la theorie de Freud et dans la technique de la psychanalyse* [The seminar, book II: The ego in Freud's theory and in the techniques of psychoanalysis] Paris: Seuil.

LaCapra, D. (1994). Canons, texts, and contexts. In L. Kramer, D. Reid, & W. L. Barney (Eds.), *Learning history in America* (pp. 120–138). Minneapolis: University of Minnesota Press.

Ladson-Billings, G. (1995). Multicultural teacher education: Research, practice, and policy. In J. A. Banks & C. A. McGee (Eds.), *Handbook of research on multicultural education* (pp. 747–759). New York: Macmillan.

Lanier, J., & Little, J. (1986). Research on teacher education. In M. C. Wittrock (Ed.), *Handbook of research on teaching* (pp. 527–569). Oxford, UK: Pergamon.

Lather, P. (1986). Research as praxis. *Harvard Educational Review 56* (3), 257–277.

Lather, P. (1996). Troubling clarity: The politics of accessible language. *Harvard Educational Review 66* (3), 525–545.

Lather, P. (1997). *Postbook: Working the ruins of feminist ethnography toward economies of responsibility and possibility.* Paper presented at the annual meeting of the American Educational Research Association, Chicago.

Lather, P. (1999). *Hard questions about research on teaching.* Paper presented at the annual meeting of the American Educational Research Association, Montreal.

Lather, P., & Smithies, C. (1995). *Troubling angels: Women living with HIV/AIDS.* Columbus, OH: Greyden Press.

Lears, T. J. Jackson (1985). The concept of cultural hegemony: Problems and possibilities. *American Historical Review 90* (3), 567–593.

Lemke, J. L. (1995). *Textual politics: Discourse and social dynamics.* London and Bristol, PA: Taylor & Francis.

Lewis, M. (1993). *Without a word: Teaching beyond women's silence.* New York & London: Routledge.

Limerick, B., Burgess-Lomerick, T., & Grace, M. (1996). The politics of interviewing: Power relations and accepting the gift. *Qualitative Studies in Education 9* (4), 449–460.

Lincoln, Y. S., & Denzin, N. K. (1994). The fifth moment. In N. K. Denzin & Y. S. Lincoln (Eds.), *Handbook of qualitative research* (pp. 575–586). Thousand Oaks, CA: Sage Publications.

Liston, D. P., & Zeichner, K. M. (1991). *Teacher education and the social conditions of schooling.* New York: Routledge.

Luke, C., & Gore J. (1992). Introduction. In C. Luke & J. Gore (Eds.), *Feminism and critical pedagogy* (pp. 1–14). New York & London: Routledge.

Macherey, P. (1978). *A theory of literary production* (G. Wall, Trans.). London: Routledge & Kegan Paul.

Madrid, A. (1993). Diversity and its discontents. In V. Cyrus (Ed.), *Experiencing race, class, and gender in the United States* (pp. 381–386). Mountain View, CA: Mayfield Publishing.

Marcus, G. E. (1994). What comes (just) after "post"? The case of ethnography. In N. K. Denzin & Y. S. Lincoln (Eds.), *Handbook of qualitative research* (pp. 563–574). Thousand Oaks, CA: Sage Publications.

Martin, R. J. (1995). Introduction. In R. J. Martin (Ed.), *Practicing what we teach: Confronting diversity in teacher education* (pp. xi–xxii). Albany: State University of New York Press.

Mascia-Lees, F. E., Sharpe, P., & Cohen, C. B. (1989). The postmodernist turn in anthropology: Cautions from a feminist perspective. *Signs: Journal of Women in Culture and Society 15* (1), 7–33.

McCarthy, C. (1993). After the canon: Knowledge and ideological representation in the multicultural discourse on curriculum reform. In C. McCarthy & W. Crichlow (Eds.), *Race identity and representation in education* (pp. 289–305). New York & London: Routledge.

McDiarmid, G. W., Ball, D. W., & Anderson, C. W. (1989). Why staying one chapter ahead doesn't really work: Subject-specific pedagogy. In M. C. Reynolds (Ed.), *Knowledge base for the beginning teacher* (pp. 193–205). Oxford, UK: Pergamon Press.

McLaren, P. (1988). Broken dreams, false promises, and the decline of public schooling. *Journal of Education 170* (1), 41–65.

McLaren, P. (1991). Decentering cultures: Postmodernism, resistance, and critical pedagogy. In N. B. Wyner (Ed.), *Current perspectives on the culture of schools* (pp. 231–258). Boston: Brookline Books.

McLaren, P. (1994). Foreward: Critical thinking as a political project. In K. S. Walters (Ed.), *Re-thinking reason: New perspectives in critical thinking* (pp. x–xv). Albany: State University of New York Press.

McLaren, P. (1997). Critical pedagogy. *Teaching Education 9* (1), 1.

McLaren, P., & Giroux, H. A. (1995). Radical pedagogy as cultural poli-
    tics: Beyond the discourse of critique and anti-utopianism. In
    P. McLaren, *Critical pedagogy and predatory culture: Opposi-
    tional politics in a postmodern era* (pp. 29–57). London & New
    York: Routledge.

McLaren, P., & Lankshear, C. (1993). Critical literacy and the postmodern
    turn. In C. Lankshear and P. McLaren (Eds.), *Critical literacy: Poli-
    tics, praxis, and the postmodern* (pp. 379–419). Albany: State
    University of New York Press.

Mehan, H., Okamoto, D., Lints, A., & Wills, J. S. (1995). Ethnographic
    studies of multicultural education in classrooms and schools. In
    J. A. Banks & C. A. McGee (Eds.), *Handbook of research on
    multicultural education* (pp. 129–144). New York: Macmillan.

Melnick, S. L., & Zeichner, K. M. (1997). Enhancing the capacity of teacher
    education institutions to address diversity issues. In J. E. King, E. R.
    Hollins, & W. C. Hayman (Eds.), *Preparing teachers for cultural
    diversity* (pp. 23–39). New York & London: Teachers College Press.

Mohanty, S. P. (1986). Radical teaching, radical theory: The ambiguous
    politics of meaning. In C. Nelson (Ed.), *Theory in the classroom*
    (pp. 149–176). Urbana & Chicago: University of Illinois Press.

Nakayama, T. K., & Krizek, R. L. (1995). Whiteness: A strategic rhetoric.
    Quarterly Journal of Speech 81, 291–309.

Olesen, V. (1994). Feminism and models of qualitative research. In N. K.
    Denzin & Y. S. Lincoln (Eds.), *Handbook of qualitative research*
    (pp. 158–174). Thousand Oaks, CA: Sage Publications.

Paine, L. (1989*). Orientation towards diversity: What do prospective
    teachers bring?* Research report 89–9. East Lansing, MI: National
    Center for Research on Teacher Learning.

Phelan, A. M. (1994). Unmasking metaphors of management: A peda-
    gogy of collaborative deconstruction. *Teaching Education 6* (1),
    101–111.

Phelan, A. M., & Garrison, J. W. (1994). Toward a gender-sensitive ideal
    of critical thinking: A feminist poetic. In K. S. Walters (Ed.), *Re-
    thinking reason: New perspectives in critical thinking* (pp. 81–
    97). Albany: State University of New York Press.

Popkewitz, T. S. (1987). Knowledge and interest in curriculum studies. In T. S. Popkewitz (Ed.), *Critical studies in teacher education: Its folklore, theory, and practice* (pp. 335–354). London & New York: Falmer Press.

Postman, N., & Weingartner, C. (1969). *Teaching as a subversive activity.* New York: Delacorte Press.

Ramsey, P. G. (1987). *Teaching and learning in a diverse world.* New York: Teachers College Press.

Richardson, V. (1996). The role of attitudes and beliefs in learning to teach. In J. Sikula (Ed.), *Handbook of research on teacher education (second edition): A project of the Association of Teacher Educators* (pp. 102–119). New York: Simon and Schuster Macmillan.

Sarason, S., Davidson, K., & Blatt, B. (1986). *The preparation of teachers: An unstudied problem in education.* Cambridge, MA: Brookline Books.

Sardo-Brown, D. (1993a). A longitudinal study of novice secondary teachers' planning: Year two. *Teaching & Teacher Education, 12* (5), 519–530.

Sardo-Brown, D. (1993b). Descriptions of two novice secondary teachers' planning. *Curriculum Inquiry, 23* (1), 63–84.

Scheurich, J. J. (1995). A postmodernist critique of research interviewing. *Qualitative Studies in Education 8* (3), 239–252.

Schniedewind, N. (1987). Feminist values: Guidelines for teaching methodology in women's studies. In I. Shor (Ed.), *Freire for the classroom: A resourcebook for liberatory teaching* (pp. 170–179). Portsmouth, NH: Heinemann.

Scholes, R. (1985). *Textual power.* New Haven, CT: Yale University Press.

Schon, D. A. (1983). *The reflective practitioner: How professionals think in action.* New York: Basic Books.

Schumacher, S., & Macmillan, J. M. (1993). *Research in education: A conceptual introduction* (3rd ed.). New York: HarperCollins College Publishers.

Scott, J. W. (1991). The evidence of experience. *Critical Inquiry 17,* 773–779.

Scott, J. W. (1996). *After history?* Paper presented at the History and the Limits of Interpretation Symposium, Rice University, TX. March 15–17. http://www.ruf.rice.edu/culture/papers/Scott.html

Shor, I. (1986). Equality is excellence: Transforming teacher education and the learning process. *Harvard Educational Review 56* (4), 406–426.

Shrewsbury, C. M. (1987). What is feminist pedagogy? *Women's Studies Quarterly 15* (3 & 4), 6–13.

Sikes-Scering, G. E. (1997). Themes of a critical/feminist pedagogy: Teacher education for democracy. *Journal of Teacher Education 48* (1), 62–68.

Simon, R. I. (1992). *Teaching against the grain: Texts for a pedagogy of possibility.* New York: Bergin & Garvey.

Sleeter, C. E. (1993). How white teachers construct race. In C. McCarthy & W. Crichlow (Eds.), *Race, identity, and representation in education* (pp. 157–171). New York & London: Routledge.

Sloterdijk, P. (1983). *Kritik der zynischen vernunft* [Critique of cynical reason]. Frankfurt.

Smyth, J. (1989). A critical pedagogy of classroom practice. *Journal of Curriculum Studies 21* (6), 483–502.

Smyth, J., & Shacklock, G. (1998). Behind the "cleansing" of socially critical research accounts. In G. Shacklock & J. Smyth (Eds.), *Being reflexive in critical educational and social research* (pp. 1–12). London & Bristol, PA: Falmer Press.

Sparks, A. (1998). Reciprocity in critical research? Some unsettling thoughts. In G. Shacklock & J. Smyth (Eds.), *Being reflexive in critical educational and social research* (pp. 67–82). London & Bristol, PA: Falmer Press.

Sparks, C. (1996). The evolution of cultural studies. In J. Storey (Ed.), *What is cultural studies? A reader* (pp. 14–30). London: Arnold.

Spina, S. U. (1997). Demythifying multicultural education: Social semiotics as a tool of critical pedagogy. *Teaching Education 9* (1), 27–35.

Stables, A. (1996). Studying education as text: Parameters and implications. *Westminster Studies in Education 19*, 5–13.

Storey, J. (Ed.). (1996). *What is cultural studies: A reader*. London & New York: Arnold.

Street, A. (1998). In/forming inside nursing: Ethical dilemmas in critical research. In G. Shacklock & J. Smyth (Eds.), *Being reflexive in critical educational and social research* (pp. 146–158). London & Bristol, PA: Falmer Press.

Sultana, R. G. (1995). Ethnography and the politics of absence. In P. L. McLaren & J. M. Giarelli (Eds.), *Critical theory and educational research* (pp. 113–125). Albany: State University of New York Press.

Tabachnick, R., & Zeichner, K. (1984). The impact of the student teaching experience on the development of teacher perspectives. *Journal of Teacher Education 35* (6), 28–35.

Treichler, P. A. (1986). Teaching feminist theory. In C. Nelson (Ed.), *Theory in the classroom* (pp. 57–128). Urbana & Chicago: University of Illinois Press.

Tyler, S. A. (1991). A post-modern in-stance. In L. Nencel & P. Pels (Eds.), *Constructing knowledge: Authority and critique in social science* (pp. 78–94). Newbury Park, CA: Sage Publications.

Walters, K. S. (1994). Introduction: Beyond logicism in critical thinking. In K. S. Walters (Ed.), *Re-thinking reason: New perspectives in critical thinking* (pp. 1–22). Albany: State University of New York Press.

Warren, K. J. (1994). Critical thinking and feminism. In K. S. Walters (Ed.), *Re-thinking reason: New perspectives in critical thinking* (pp. 155–176). Albany: State University of New York Press.

Werner, W., & Nixon, K. (1990). *The media and public issues: A guide for teaching critical mindedness*. London, ON: University of Western Ontario Press.

Willinsky, J. (1998a). *Learning to divide the world: Education at empire's end*. Minneapolis & London: University of Minnesota Press.

Willinsky, J. (1998b). Teaching literature is teaching in theory. *Theory Into Practice 37* (3), 244–250.

Willinsky, J. (2001). *After literacy: Essays*. New York: Peter Lang.

Wineburg, S. S. (1991). On the reading of historical texts: Notes on the breach between school and academy. *American Educational Research Journal 28* (3), 495–519.

Yerushalmi, Y. H. (1982). *Zakhor: Jewish history and Jewish memory.* Seattle: University of Washington Press.

Yonemura, M. (1986). Reflections on teacher empowerment and teacher education. *Harvard Educational Review 56* (4), 473–480.

Young, R. (1981). Poststructuralism: An introduction. In R. Young (Ed.), *Untying the text: A post-structuralist reader* (pp. 1–28). London: Routledge.

Zavarzadeh, M., & Morton, D. (1994). *Theory as resistance: Politics and culture after (post) structuralism.* New York and London: Guilford Press.

Zeichner, K. M. (1983). Alternative paradigms of teacher education. *Journal of Teacher Education 34* (3), 3–9.

Zeichner, K. M. (1986). Content and contexts: Neglected elements in studies of student teaching as an occasion for learning to teach. *Journal of Education for Teaching 12* (1), 5–24.

Zeichner, K. M. (1992). Rethinking the practicum in the professional development school partnership. *Journal of Teacher Education 43* (4), 296–307.

Zeichner, K. M., Grant, C., Gay, G., Gillette, M., Valli, L., & Villegas, M. (1998). A research informed vision of good practice in multicultural teacher education: Design principles. *Theory Into Practice 37* (2), 163–171.

Zeichner, K. M., & Hoeft, K. (1996). Teacher socialization for cultural diversity. In J. Sikula, T. J. Buttery, & E. Guyton (Eds.), *Handbook of research on teacher education* (pp. 525–547). New York: Macmillan.

Zeichner, K. M., & Liston, D. P. (1987). Teaching student teachers to reflect. *Harvard Educational Review 57* (1), 23–48.

Zimpher, N. L., & Ashburn, E. A. (1992). Countering parochialism in teacher candidates. In M. E. Dilworth (Ed.), *Diversity in teacher education: New expectations* (pp. 40–62). San Francisco: Jossey-Bass.

Zinn, M. B. (1995). *Doing diversity: Dangers, deceptions, and debates.* Memphis, TN: Center for Research on Women.

Zizek, S. (1989). *The sublime object of ideology.* London & New York: Verso.

Index

Questions about the Purpose(s) of Colleges and Universities

Norm Denzin,

Josef Progler,

Joe L. Kincheloe,

Shirley R. Steinberg

General Editors

What are the purposes of higher education? When undergraduates "declare their majors," they agree to enter into a world defined by the parameters of a particular academic discourse—a discipline. But who decides those parameters? How do they come about? What are the discussions and proposed outcomes of disciplined inquiry? What should an undergraduate know to be considered educated in a discipline? How does the disciplinary knowledge base inform its pedagogy? Why are there different disciplines? When has a discipline "run its course"? Where do new disciplines come from? Where do old ones go? How does a discipline produce its knowledge? What are the meanings and purposes of disciplinary research and teaching? What are the key questions of disciplined inquiry? What questions are taboo within a discipline? What can the disciplines learn from one another? What might they not want to learn and why?

Once we begin asking these kinds of questions, positionality becomes a key issue. One reason why there aren't many books on the meaning and purpose of higher education is that once such questions are opened for discussion, one's subjectivity becomes an issue with respect to the presumed objective stances of Western higher education. Academics don't have positions because positions are "biased," "subjective," "slanted," and therefore somehow invalid. So the first thing to do is to provide a sense—however broad and general—of what kinds of positionalities will inform the books and chapters on the above questions. Certainly the questions themselves, and any others we might ask, are already suggesting a particular "bent," but as the series takes shape, the authors we engage will no doubt have positions on these questions.

From the stance of interdisciplinary, multidisciplinary, or transdisciplinary practitioners, will the chapters and books we solicit solidify disciplinary discourses, or liquefy them? Depending on who is asked, interdisciplinary inquiry is either a polite collaboration among scholars firmly situated in their own particular discourses, or it is a blurring of the restrictive parameters that define the very notion of disciplinary discourse. So will the series have a stance on the meaning and purpose of interdisciplinary inquiry and teaching? This can possibly be finessed by attracting thinkers from disciplines that are already multidisciplinary, for example, the various kinds of "studies" programs (women's, Islamic, American, cultural, etc.), or the hybrid disciplines like ethnomusicology (musicology, folklore, anthropology). But by including people from these fields (areas? disciplines?) in our series, we are already taking a stand on disciplined inquiry. A question on the comprehensive exam for the Columbia University Ethnomusicology Program was to defend ethnomusicology as a "field" or a "discipline." One's answer determined one's future, at least to the extent that the gatekeepers had a say in such matters. So, in the end, what we are proposing will no doubt involve political struggles.

For additional information about this series or for the submission of manuscripts, please contact Joe L. Kincheloe, 128 Chestnut Street, Lakewood, NJ 08701-5804. To order other books in this series, please contact our Customer Service Department at: (800) 770-LANG (within the U.S.), (212) 647-7706 (outside the U.S.), (212) 647-7707 FAX, or browse online by series at: www.peterlangusa.com.